DANCING TANGO

Dancing Tango

Passionate Encounters in a Globalizing World

Kathy Davis

NEW YORK UNIVERSITY PRESS
New York and London

NEW YORK UNIVERSITY PRESS
New York and London
www.nyupress.org

References to Internet websites (URLs) were accurate at the time of writing. Neither the author nor New York University Press is responsible for URLs that may have expired or changed since the manuscript was prepared.

LIBRARY OF CONGRESS CATALOGING-IN-PUBLICATION DATA
Davis, Kathy, 1949–
Dancing tango : passionate encounters in a globalizing world / Kathy Davis.
pages cm   Includes bibliographical references and index.
ISBN 978-0-8147-6029-1 (hardback) — ISBN 978-0-8147-6071-0 (pb)
1. Tango (Dance)—Social aspects. I. Title.
GV1796.T3D37   2014
793.3'3—dc23   2014028225

New York University Press books are printed on acid-free paper, and their binding materials are chosen for strength and durability. We strive to use environmentally responsible suppliers and materials to the greatest extent possible in publishing our books.

Manufactured in the United States of America

10 9 8 7 6 5 4 3 2 1

Also available as an ebook

For Guille, with love

CONTENTS

ACKNOWLEDGMENTS

My intellectual journey into the passionate encounters that emerge through dancing tango began with the uneasiness about my own personal passion for a dance that—when seen through the normative lens of contemporary critical feminist and postcolonial theories—appeared, at best, odd and, at worst, disreputable and even a bit shameful. I have used this disjuncture between the incorrect pleasures and complicated politics of dancing tango as a resource for exploring the workings of passion as experience, as performance, and as cultural discourse. In writing this book, I had to juggle my different positions: as tango *aficionada* who, when all is said and done, would rather dance tango than do just about anything else; as ethnographer who has spoken with tango dancers, observed their interactions on the dance floor, and struggled to understand the complexities and nuances of the dance subculture; and as critical feminist scholar with a penchant for postcolonial studies who has tried to engage constructively, but also critically, with the rapidly growing field of tango studies.

Books are collaborative endeavors, and I have many people to thank. I am grateful to the dancers in Amsterdam and Buenos Aires for agreeing to tell me their tango stories and help me figure out this strange passion that we share. An extra word of thanks goes to my informants in Buenos Aires who were so patient with my faulty Spanish during our interviews and untiring in their willingness to explain to me the workings of their salon culture.

Many thanks to the friends and colleagues who commented on earlier chapters, answered e-mail queries, provided a sounding board, and supplied me with scientific references, newspaper articles, novels and short stories, sites of interesting blogs, and even tapes of tango music that were the inspiring backdrop to my writing: Anna Aalten, Peter Arends, Rolf Butzmühlen, Yerpun Castro, Maria Teresa de Matos Matilde, Peter Esser, Corine Groenewegen, Sylvia Heijting, Lena Inowlocki, Janice Irvine, Charlie Kaplan, Rudi Leiprecht, Beate Littig, Helma Lutz, Lorraine Nencel, Gül Ozyegin, Andrea Pető, Jorge Luis Sánchez, Arjan Sikking, Marcel Toth, Marianne Van Berlo, Rob Van Marrewijk, and Dubravka Zarkov.

A special word of thanks to Marta Klopman for helping me get started in Buenos Aires and for introducing me to the joys of interviewing in Spanglish; to Anna Aalten for reminding me to write for my readers; and to Janice Irvine for her snarky humor and constructive editing.

I am grateful to the biographical research community of the International Sociological Association and the German Society for Sociology for inviting me to talk about my work on several occasions and especially to Roswitha Breckner for reassuring me that tango is a legitimate topic for a sociologist. The sociology department at the VU University in Amsterdam provided a congenial and stimulating context in which to finish the book.

I was lucky to be able to use photographs that capture so beautifully in pictures what I have tried to convey in words. An additional thanks to Mirjam van Niel for her enthusiasm and support. Tori Egherman provided invaluable and creative assistance in selecting photos and getting permissions.

I am grateful to the anonymous reviewers for their provocative and helpful comments. Ilene Kalish of NYU Press has been a supportive and enthusiastic presence throughout the writing of this book. Thanks to Caelyn Cobb, too, for cheerful and speedy practical support.

I hardly know where to begin in thanking Willem de Haan, my partner in love, life, and tango. Should I start with our endless conversations about tango or with his never-ending supply of quirky references and interesting articles, not to mention photographs, music, and translations of tango lyrics? Or should I first mention his willingness to read and re-read every single chapter, too many times to count, and usually at a moment's notice? Or maybe I should begin with his frequent reminder that I should not forget the rules of logic just because I am writing about passion. I'm afraid that thanking him enough is simply a mission impossible, so I'll leave it at an *abrazo enorme por todo* and please let's keep dancing!

Introduction

Dancing Argentinean tango[1] is a global phenomenon. Since its origin among immigrant workers living in the slums of Buenos Aires and Montevideo, it has crossed and re-crossed many borders. However, never before has tango been danced by so many people and in so many different places as it has today. In the wake of its latest revival, tango has become both a cultural symbol of Argentinean national identity and a transnational cultural space in which a modest yet growing number of dancers from different parts of the globe participate.

Dancing tango enables a passionate encounter, in which two individuals join each other on the dance floor. This passionate encounter embodies a mixture of tango music, a style of dancing, a community of dancers, and a shared imaginary. The music is characterized by its hybridity, nostalgic lyrics, and soulful chords that seem to express the loneliness and longing of those who are far from home. The dance form involves a couple, one leading and the other following, who enter into an intimate embrace, bodies touching and legs entangled, improvising steps in wordless communication with each other and the music. The tango community is composed of individuals of different genders, class and ethnic backgrounds, sexual orientation, and national belonging, who meet in dance venues across the globe, secure in the knowledge that they will not only be able to dance tango together, but will probably also share the same kinds of desires, hopes, and expectations about what makes dancing tango worthwhile. And, finally, tango is irrevocably entangled in cultural imaginaries that evoke intense passion, (hyper)heterosexuality, and dangerous exoticism. Dancing tango epitomizes desire and difference, sensuality and antagonism, connection and loss. It promises togetherness, and yet it is always a togetherness that requires a bridging of differences, through the dance and for as long as the dance lasts.

In this book, I explore Argentinean tango through the eyes of those who love to dance it—the *aficionados* and *aficionadas* for whom tango is more than a hobby and, at times, even a way of life. Their passion for tango raises several questions. For example, why does tango appeal to dancers in so many different locations? What are these individuals looking for when they dance tango, and what happens to them as they become embroiled in its culture? What do they gain, what do they give up, and when, if ever, do they reach that for which they are so passionately longing? And, last but not least, how do they negotiate the ambivalences, contradictions, and hierarchies of gender, sexuality, and global relations of power between North and South[2] in which Argentinean tango is—and has always been—embedded?

Before tackling these questions, let me begin my foray into the world of tango with three personal stories—stories that not only chart my own engagement with Argentinean tango but also provide the thematic and theoretical framework for the present inquiry.

Getting Started: Three Stories

My first encounter with Argentinean tango happened in the late 1980s as I was walking around Amsterdam with a friend on a Friday night. We stumbled across something called a "tango salon" that was being held in a cultural center called Roxy (since burned down and forgotten). I will never forget walking into this room with couples circling the dance floor to the scratchy strains of tango music from the 1930s and '40s. They were a motley crew—all sizes and shapes, different ages and from different walks of life, some elegantly dressed and others in jeans, although all the women seemed to be wearing high heels. I was particularly entranced by a young couple, both with Punk hair, she in a short black leather skirt and he with multiple earrings and tattoos. What were they doing in *this* place, dancing to *this* music? I would have expected them at a rave, pogo'ing to the tunes of Sid Vicious and the Sex Pistols. And yet as I watched them and the other couples, I was struck by how totally absorbed they were in the music, in the dancing, in one another. Even the ones who clearly were having trouble with the steps were engrossed in the encounter. Their feet were stumbling, but in their faces you could see the dream of better times. And then a couple sailed by who clearly knew what they were doing. In tune with each other, moving together in the music, they had become one body. I still remember the woman's face with her closed eyes and expression of pure and utter joy. It made me want to feel that way, too.

While it was many years before I actually decided to learn to dance tango myself, I never forgot that evening. I often wondered what it was about this dance that made such a diverse group of individuals want to get out on the floor and dance to such unfamiliar music from another era whose lyrics must have been incomprehensible to their Dutch ears. I asked myself what it was that they were dreaming about as they stumbled through dance steps that were clearly more challenging than the kind of dancing most of us were used to at the time. But, most of all, I kept thinking about that woman's face, trying to imagine how she must have felt. Ultimately, I discovered what dancing tango felt like, but only after many years of taking lessons, practicing steps in my living room, frequenting tango salons on a regular basis—first in Amsterdam, later in other parts of Europe and the United States, and, last but not least, in the birthplace of tango, Buenos Aires.

The second story involves an incident that took place several years after I had taken up tango. I was having dinner with some colleagues, following a conference. While we had attended many such conferences together in the past, this was one of the first times that we strayed from our shared academic interests and began talking about other aspects of our lives. Inspired by the relaxed atmosphere of the meal, I launched into an account of my passion for tango, describing my experiences on the dance floor and my frequent trips to Buenos Aires "just to dance." While most of my colleagues appeared to be mildly entertained by my story, one sociologist looked at me with undisguised dismay: "But, Kathy . . . tango? How can *you* possibly be involved in something like tango? You're a *feminist*."

My colleague's reaction confronted me with the fact that my passion for tango had taken me into a subculture that was incomprehensible to the non-initiated. At the same time, the question of whether a feminist should be dancing tango provided a glimpse of the cultural imaginary that automatically comes into play the moment one hears the words

"Argentinean tango": macho men in black shirts with chests thrust forward and their hair slicked back, and hyperfeminine women in revealing dresses with side splits and stiletto heels. Tango is the symbolic embodiment of traditional notions of gender—the man leads, the woman follows. He is active, calling the shots, moving purposively across the dance floor. She is passive, waiting for his signals, eyes closed. Tango is aggressively heterosexual, with its public display of eroticism and passion. No wonder my colleague was shocked that a longtime feminist like me could so eagerly throw herself into such a blatantly sexist dance.

It wasn't until many years later that tango became a potential research topic for me, and how this came about is my third story. During one of my annual trips to Buenos Aires, I stayed with a group of Dutch tango dancers in a shabby tango hotel in San Telmo.[3] One of the women in our group became romantically involved with an Argentinean man whom she had met in one of the *milongas* (venues where people get together to dance tango). Their affair started with an offer of private tango lessons and ended in bed. I watched with a certain amount of envy as she was whisked away on the dance floor in his capable arms and, later, commiserated with her despair when he turned out to be married with children. I found myself taking a closer look at the tourists in the *milongas*, in many cases "women of a certain age," white Europeans or North Americans, dressed in sexy clothes and expensive shoes, dancing with eyes closed and ecstatic expressions on their faces. Their partners were seasoned local tango dancers, clearly less affluent than the tourists. They appeared to be working very hard to maneuver their less adept partners around the floor. They did not look particularly happy, let alone ecstatic. Instead their expressions were deadpan, bordering on the pained, or even the outright bored.

These discrepancies were disturbing on several levels and added some uncomfortable dissonances to my experiences with tango. While tango brings strangers together in a seemingly intimate embrace, it does not necessarily have the same meanings for partners who are separated by gender, social class, age, ethnicity, and national belonging. What is the significance of these divisions to the image of tango as a dance of passion? How do differences between dancers get played out in their encounters on the dance floor? What kinds of excitements and tensions do they generate, and how are they negotiated?

These stories all raise issues that clearly require a more analytical and, at the same time, more critical approach to tango. However, tackling these issues is not an easy undertaking and, indeed, presents what at first glance seems like an intractable dilemma to the would-be tango researcher who also dances tango.

On the one hand, as a dancer, she may worry that a scholarly, analytical approach to tango will interfere with her passion for dancing. If she views tango as an important part of her life, even as something essential to her happiness and well-being, she may be concerned about spoiling her pleasure in dancing and becoming critical of her own undoubtedly complicated desires. She will probably wonder whether it is possible to be a participant observer in a tango salon and still experience the same excitement and sense of adventure she craves as a tango dancer.

On the other hand, as a researcher, she may be concerned that her passion for tango will cloud her vision and prevent her from producing the critical ethnography of Argentinean tango that she envisions. She may fear that she is too much of an "insider" to the tango scene to be able look at it with the proper analytic distance. Indeed, she may wonder whether it is even possible, let alone desirable, to do research on a subculture of which she is a member. An even thornier problem, long familiar to the feminist researcher, concerns the difficult enterprise of situating herself as a white European academic writing about the non-European "Other." How can she acknowledge her own complicities in the economic disparities and global imaginaries that shape relations between Argentineans and non-Argentineans and still engage in the passionate transnational encounters that dancing tango enables?

Between Passion and Critique

The dilemma between being personally involved (as insider, albeit slightly "off center" [Creef, 2000]) and being reflexively critical (as outsider with the necessary skills of self-critique) is familiar to ethnographers. Most ethnographers provide lengthy accounts of how they manage their identities as insider and outsider. For example, Eduardo Archetti (1999), writing about masculinity in Argentinean football, reflects on being an "insider" as an Argentinean-in-exile who has always been interested in football. When he started interviewing

Argentinean men of his own class, age, and education, he stressed being on home turf, with all the advantages of language, social contact, and knowledge of the cultural context. At the same time, his training as an anthropologist, not to mention his long-term residence in Europe, set him apart from his football buddies. Ultimately, he concludes—drawing on Strathern (1987) for help—what ultimately makes his ethnography acceptable is his ability to produce through football a sociologically informed account of masculinity that organizes his informants' stories in ways that correspond to and enhance or deepen their own points of view.

Not every ethnographer is as optimistic as Archetti, however. Feminist ethnographers have been considerably more wary of whether it is possible to do critical ethnography at all (Stacey, 1988; Abu-Lughod, 1990). Ethnographic encounters are so permeated with differences marked by conflict, domination, and objectification on the side of the researcher and her informants that it is hard to see how one's status as an insider (woman) or even well-intentioned critic (feminist) can make for accurate representations of the subject at hand. Kamala Visweswaran (1993) adopts a radically deconstructionist approach to ethnography that focuses on "betrayals, refusals, and impossibilities" as the only point of entry into the field, the only way to make dominant discourses and power inequalities visible. That this sometimes occurs to the detriment of thick descriptions[4] and ethnographic detail is just the price one must pay. However, despite these differences in approach, the conclusion seems to be that the combination of passion and critique is less a problem to be resolved than a set of issues to be discussed.

Ethnography, Carnal and Global

In this research, I have taken a different tack, drawing on two recent—and some might argue incommensurable—branches of ethnographic research.

The first is "carnal sociology,"[5] which addresses the way bodily practices (the work of the body as sentient and embodied praxis) constitute social formations (Crossley, 1995). I have drawn upon my embodied experiences as a dancer, my encounters on dance floors around the world, conversations with fellow *aficionados*, as well as my frequent trips between Europe and Argentina, to understand the contradictory meanings of tango, here and there, now and then. In this, I have been particularly inspired by Loïc Wacquant's (2004) study of the boxing world in which he himself was an active participant for many years. His ethnography is not a run-of-the-mill description of life in a Chicago gym catering primarily to lower-class African American men. By entering this scene with "body and soul," Wacquant provides a visceral account of what it actually feels like to fight (the "taste and the ache" of being in the ring). He allows the reader to enter the boxer's body, to understand the discipline and the training required in learning to master the "manly art." Based on this study, he makes an argument not for a sociology *of* the body but rather one *from* the body. In his view, sociologists have to immerse themselves as "deeply and as durably" as they can into the microcosm they are investigating if they want to convey to the reader what is at stake in social practices that are passionately pursued (Wacquant, 2005:468).

Wacquant's ethnography of boxing provides a useful model for investigating tango as a preeminently embodied practice, passionately pursued by a select group of enthusiasts. Like boxing, tango also requires a long and difficult apprenticeship, through which the practitioners learn the complex techniques of the dance. Like the gym, the social order of the *milonga* has its own rules and regulations that need to be learned and negotiated. While boxing produces a specific variant of masculinity—one that is inflected by race and class—tango also entails the ongoing performance of masculinity and femininity, a performance that is shaped by intersections of race, class, and age and that takes different forms depending upon the historical and social context in which it is enacted. From the perspective of carnal sociology, my own passion for tango is not only desirable; it is a requirement if I am to understand and consequently be able to describe what my informants tell me about their involvement. In the microcosm of the tango world, my position as insider lends me credibility. And, indeed, many of my informants noted that it was easy to talk to me because "of course, *you* know what I'm talking about." Being an insider also allowed me easy access to the field. I had no problems spending time in *milongas* and approaching potential informants about the subject we all most liked to talk about anyway. Even in Buenos Aires, where I am clearly an outsider, a visitor, albeit one who reappears regularly year after year, I had no difficulties finding fellow dancers who were more than willing to talk to me.

And yet, this is more than a carnal ethnography à la Wacquant, who has been criticized—and rightly so—for his lack of reflexivity about his own position as a white academic interacting with lower-class African American men. He can leave—and will—as soon as he finishes his book. His boxing informants, however, will have gone on to lives constrained by poverty, racism, and hardship. I would display a similar lack of reflexivity if I were simply to assume that I am an "insider" in my research on the tango. I also want to use tango as an opportunity to think analytically and critically about the politics of passion and about gender relations in all their complicated intersections—intersections that will, from time to time, also situate me as an "outsider" vis-à-vis my informants. Moreover, I want to explore the ways in which the North and the South have historically been and continue to be linked through the tango, the configurations of power that have emerged in these passionate encounters, and the ways its *aficionado/as* are differently embedded in global hierarchies of power.

In order to investigate these linkages, I draw upon *global ethnography*. This unconventional form of ethnography, inspired by the work of Michael Burawoy et al. (2000), extends the representation of a local setting, the bread and butter of ethnographical research, beyond national and cultural borders, grounding it both in local histories and in the changes that have been and continue to be wrought by processes of globalization. Global ethnographers employ three strategies for "extending out" their ethnographies into the world. They delve into the *external forces* that shape individuals' everyday lives. They explore existing *transnational connections* between different sites. They uncover shared *global imaginaries* that people employ in different ways to make sense of their worlds (Burawoy et al., 2000:25). One of the refreshing features of this approach to ethnographical research is the refusal to either idealize or demonize globalization. The authors assume that globalization is experienced differently in different contexts. Globalization may be perceived as an external force to be resisted or accommodated. People may participate in the creation and reproduction of connections stretching across the world in ways that are empowering or disempowering. Global imaginaries are often mobilized in ways that are beneficial, but they may also become objects of protest and contestation.

Global ethnography has enabled me to think about the history and practice of tango as a global phenomenon. I examine how external forces—for example, the growing global tourist industry—has allowed tango to become a commodity for relatively affluent and highly mobile individuals across the globe who are searching for a specific kind of "tourist experience" as part of their cosmopolitan lifestyles (Urry, 2005; Anzaldi, 2012b). Recurrent economic recessions in Argentina due to neo-liberal policies ("dollar democracy") as well as the desire for "innocent" symbols of Argentinean identity in the wake of the military regime of the 1970s have also attributed to the recent revival of tango as export item and tourist attraction. I investigate the transnational connections that have emerged through tango, as *milongas*[6] across the globe are transformed into transnational spaces. Tango produces encounters across national and cultural borders, between visitors who travel to Buenos Aires to learn to dance or simply to watch tango and Argentineans who open up their tango salons to them or, in some cases, travel to Europe to teach and perform tango. I explore how these differently located dancers think about their experiences and identities as dancers, as well as their encounters with one another on the dance floor. And, finally, I use the methodology of global ethnography to take a critical look at how global imaginaries produce a global tango dance culture and shared community while re-creating tango as a specifically Argentinean cultural product, a symbol of *argentinidad*.[7] I show how dancers from different national and cultural as well as gender and class locations negotiate in specific and contradictory ways the tensions between their cosmopolitan sensibilities and their desire for authenticity.

Tango as Global Dance

Tango is both the symbol of Argentinean national identity and a global dance (Pelinski, 2000). Argentinean tango (sometimes referred to as *Tango Argentino*) is different from the ballroom dance version of tango that has recently become popularized in the TV series *Dancing with the Stars*.[8] For more than two centuries, tango has been appropriated and reappropriated throughout the global North and South. Never the province of one culture or geographical region, it has made multiple crossings of class, racial, and national borders, becoming refined, "whitened," and desexualized or, alternatively, eroticized and exoticized (Desmond, 1997). These appropriations and reworkings continue to characterize the global tango culture today.

According to most histories,[9] tango has its roots in the rhythms and movements of the African *candombe*,[10] but its birth tends to be fixed at the turn of the twentieth century in the dockside neighborhoods of Buenos Aires, where it was the dance of migrant workers and prostitutes. Early tango was danced cheek-to-cheek, with partners glued together, rocking and zigzagging in dialogue with the music, and with lots of leg play, for example the man thrusting his leg between the woman's, and vice versa (Thompson, 2005:233). In the 1920s it traveled to the fashionable salons of Paris, London, Tokyo, and Istanbul, where it became popular in leisure class and bohemian circles. The dance was "smoothed out" ("Euro verticality with Afro bent knees and legs intermingled") and new steps were introduced (Thompson, 2005:243). It then returned to Argentina, where respectable and more affluent Argentineans, once skeptical of this "immoral" dance, proceeded to embrace it as part of the universalist conception of modernity to which they aspired. The "Golden Age" of tango (1935–52) marked a boom in the dance in Argentina with the emergence of new tango orchestras, composers and songwriters, and dance venues. Tango was becoming a popular dance for urban elites throughout the metropolises of Europe and North America. While tango had previously appealed to members of "high society" interested in some "spicy entertainment" under President Juan Perón, it was reappropriated as the very cornerstone of Argentinean working-class culture, allowing it to become a symbol of the national identity, the essence of *argentinidad* (Anzaldi, 2012a).[11] However, in the 1960s and early '70s when rock 'n' roll was imported from the United States, becoming a popular dance for Argentinean youth, tango once again fell out of fashion. Following the defeat in 1976 of Perón's second wife, Isabela, who had assumed the presidency after his death in 1974, and the installment of a military dictatorship under General Jorge Rafael Videla with its repressive "Dirty War,"[12] dancing tango became even less popular as a terrified populace fearfully avoided any social gathering in a public place. Following the demise

Figure I.1. Benito Bianquet "El Cachafaz" and Carmencita Calderón, a well-known Argentinean tango couple at the turn of the twentieth century. They taught tango in Paris and are credited with shaping the "look" of the dance to make it more refined.

of the military regime in 1983, a battered nation emerged from the reign of terror and a renaissance in the arts marked a national effort to retrieve unsullied Argentinean traditions. Tango made its appearance, once again, when a group of Argentinean dancers and musicians put together a dance and music show, *Tango Argentino*, that toured Europe and North America. Political refugees had already begun to introduce tango (as popular music and dance) in many European cities as part of their survival strategy in conditions of exile. Recurrent economic crises compelled their compatriots to follow suit, and they, too, began to look to Europe and North America as places to teach and perform the tango. Tango has, once again, become a global dance, with a growing subculture of fervent fans willing to devote a considerable part of their everyday lives to dancing, listening to tango music, traveling to salons, and, of course, ultimately making their way to the mecca of tango: Buenos Aires.

Given the history of tango and its travels, appropriations, and reappropriations, it is clear that tango cannot be pinned down to one time or place. It would, therefore, be impossible to understand the most recent tango revival in Europe without understanding tango in Argentina, and vice versa. More generally, the premise of the present inquiry is that the transnational encounters that tango engenders provide insights into the ways cultural practices travel, the processes by which they are rearticulated and transformed, and the implications this has for how we think about the relation between the global and the local.

From the Politics of Passion to Passion across Borders

It would be impossible to write about tango as a transnational phenomenon without taking into account Marta Savigliano's seminal book *Tango and the Political Economy of Passion*. Her book, which appeared in 1995, has been the undisputed touchstone for recent tango scholarship. Moreover, it is the obvious starting point for any critical investigation of tango as a global dance. Savigliano provides a critical reading of tango that draws upon feminist theory, on the one hand, and postcolonial theory, on the other. She explores the history of tango during the first half of the twentieth century, drawing upon the lyrics of the music and the representations of tango in literature and popular culture. In her analysis, the culture of machismo is central, whereby the figure of the knife-wielding *compadrito*[13] who competes with other men for the affections of women is replaced by the more acceptable but still macho "whiny ruffian" who merely laments his betrayal by duplicitous females (Savigliano, 1995:40–72). The female counterpart was the "rebellious broad," a working-class woman who had left home (maybe just to dance) in search of autonomy, adventure, and the chance for social mobility. For Savigliano, tango reflected the gender and class tensions at a particular moment of Argentinean history when industrialization and women's entrance into the public sphere had made gender relations precarious and even antagonistic. These representations of macho men and victimized yet recalcitrant women were recycled as tango moved to other places and became entangled in the global legacies of imperialism and colonialism. The crux of Savigliano's argument is that tango's popularity outside Argentina was just one more case of cultural imperialism—an unequal encounter whereby the political, historic, and economic asymmetries between the North and the South were played out on the dance floor (Savigliano, 1995:73–106). In her view, tango generates a political economy of passion that draws upon the same rules of exoticism which are part of any colonial and imperial project (Young, 1990). It feeds the fantasies and desires of the white European or American colonizer for the exotic/erotic Latin "other."

Savigliano's reading has much to recommend it, both as an account of tango's early history and as a critical perspective. However, it also leaves some pieces missing. For example, she focuses on the *politics* of passion while leaving the *experience* of passion unexplored. This leaves one wondering how it might actually feel to be passionate about tango and what this passion means for the *aficionados* who love to dance tango and take every opportunity to do so. Moreover, gender relations take shape under very different conditions now from what was the case during the early days of tango in Buenos Aires. While there are still tensions in relations between the sexes in late modernity, they are configured differently than they were at the turn of the twentieth century, both inside and outside Argentina. Because Savigliano is predominantly concerned with the way tango has historically been represented and performed, she does not do justice to the recent global revival of tango that has, as Deleuze and Guattari (1972) would put it, so thoroughly "deterrioralized" tango that it can no longer be neatly encompassed by North–South divisions. The globalization of tango requires an approach to tango that connects the personal to the political, the experiential to the performative, and the local to the global.

The present inquiry focuses on two tango "centers." The first is Buenos Aires, the historical and symbolic "home" of tango; the second is Amsterdam, which is a typical European tango center. While Amsterdam has its own local specificities as a tango scene, it is similar to many urban centers across the globe where flourishing tango communities exist, replete with professional dancers and teachers, multiple dance venues and *milongas*, and a sizeable and avid community of dancers. In this sense, Berlin, New York, San Francisco, Montreal, Sydney or, for that matter, Seoul, Tokyo, or Singapore would have been equally good sites for the kind of ethnography envisioned in this book. They all share an orientation toward Buenos Aires as the home of Argentinean tango and have a population of dancers with enough time and money to dance and the desire for the kind of social outlet that tango provides. The present inquiry uses ethnographies of two specific locations—Buenos Aires and Amsterdam—in order to explore the ways in which tango cultures in a globalizing world become connected and mutually interdependent in and through tango dancing. Thus, it is framed as a transnational encounter, a coming together of two places in a shared cultural space, a confrontation between "here" and "there" as well as "now" and "then" rather than a comparison between tango communities across the globe.[14]

While I begin the book with an ethnographic description of two tango cultures, those of Buenos Aires and Amsterdam (chapter 1), my treatment of these sites has not been symmetrical in the rest of the book. Depending on the focus or theme of the chapter, I have concentrated in some cases more on Amsterdam (chapters 2 and 4) and in others on Buenos Aires (chapters 5 and 6). Because the dancers are a highly mobile group (chapter 3), they do not permit themselves to be neatly pinned down to one place. Thus, while I have encountered them in one of these two sites, they have hailed from all over the world— from Morocco to Russia, from Japan to Canada. My research has been largely ethnographical, involving many hours of participant observation in *milongas* in Buenos Aires and Amsterdam and interviews with tango *aficionados* as well as some dancers who have made tango their profession.[15]

I have organized the book around three separate, but interrelated themes: passion, gender, and transnationality. Drawing upon Savigliano's work, I have treated these themes as essential for any analysis of the politics of tango. However, I have elaborated them in order to understand why people in different parts of the world are so enthusiastic about dancing tango.

Passion is what is performed when tango is danced. It is how dancers describe what they experience in one another's arms. It is the metaphor for tango in popular discourse, literature, and the media. Passion is central to the politics of gender and transnationality in which tango is embedded. Critical feminist and postcolonial scholars have devoted considerable attention to the problematic ways in which passion is mobilized as part of a binary with reason in constructing gender and race. Reason and rationality are linked to white, Anglo-European masculinity, while passion is the domain of women, people of color, and non-European "others." Situating herself in this tradition, Savigliano assumes that contemporary dancers simply cannot dance tango without drawing upon the exoticized/eroticized images that are part of tango's imbrications in the gendered, racialized legacies of colonialism. As she puts it, they "*cultivate* passion, passionately" (Savigliano, 2003).

This book takes a different tack. Beginning with the standard definition of "passion" as "a strong feeling or enthusiasm for something,"[16] I explore what a passion for dancing tango means for the people who are attracted to it. What are the ingredients of this passion, and how does the actual activity of dancing tango generate it? My approach is similar to the one taken by Claudio Benzecry (2011) in his ethnography of hardcore opera fans in Argentina. While he uses the term "love" rather than "passion" to explore his informants' strong attachments to opera, his insights have inspired me to take the passion of tango enthusiasts more seriously than I might otherwise have done. This has meant recognizing that being passionate about something means, first and foremost, loving to do it. Passion is not only an activity (something that is done with great enthusiasm) but also and, more important, a sensation (excitement, pleasure, joy) and an experience (as lived, subjective, embodied event). Passion may begin as a liking that gradually grows in intensity until it resembles an addiction or even an obsession, or it may emerge suddenly as a love at first sight, as the thing the person has been waiting for all her life. Either way, passion uproots a person from her ordinary life, dissolving the boundaries of her normal self-identity and taking her outside herself. In chapter 2, I put the embodied component of tango passion (i.e., how it feels to dance) under scrutiny along with the conditions that enable the production of the experience of passion. I show how a passion for tango can produce a liminal experience that allows the dancer to transcend the mundane, to go beyond the ordinary.[17] A passion for tango (as is the case with any strong feeling or enthusiasm) will affect dancers' identities, their relationships on and off the dance floor, sometimes spilling over into their everyday lives in unexpected ways. For many philosophers, passion is potentially disruptive, confusing, and overwhelming. It prevents people from acting rationally—that is, with moderation or in accordance with their ideals (Sabini and Silver, 1996). However, passion is also fabulous and sublime. It is what makes life worth living (Unger, 1984; Philippe et al., 2009). In chapter 3, I explore how dancers negotiate the paradox of passion (as unsettling and even a bit dangerous and yet essential for happiness and well-being) within the constraints of their everyday lives. In fact, dancing tango can become a trajectory that has dramatic consequences for their lives, their relationships, and their sense of self.

Tango seems to be the ultimate embodiment of (heterosexual) masculinity and femininity, shaping the ways dancers encounter one another on the dance floor as well as their interactions within the culture of the salon. It would be impossible to investigate tango without exploring the ways in which tango mobilizes cultural meanings associated with gender. In this sense, Savigliano's (1995) thesis that social tensions (around gender, class, race, and nationality) are played out in eroticized encounters on the dance floor continues to be salient for a critical analysis of the gendered underpinnings of tango. However, while her analysis of "whiny ruffians" and "rebellious broads" was emblematic for how gender manifested itself in tango in the first half of the twentieth century in Argentina, times have changed, as have contemporary configurations of masculinity and femininity, both in Argentina and abroad.

In this book, I show how tango dancers take up tango's iconic images of masculine machismo and feminine rebelliousness and give them a modern twist (chapter 4). I analyze how the dynamics and meanings of gender in tango have been transformed in accordance with the constraints and enablements of late modernity with its fluidity, individualism, and transformations in intimacy (Giddens, 1992; Bauman, 2000). As a case in point, I take a closer look at one of the more recent transformations of the performance of gender in tango—queer tango—which explicitly aims at sanitizing tango of its heteronormativity and gendered inequalities of power (chapter 5). In addition to being an interesting case for examining tango's multiple origins and trajectories (queer tango has its origins in Europe and subsequently traveled to and became popular in Buenos Aires), it provides a site for analyzing the ways tango can (or cannot) be subversive in the domain of transnational gender relations.

As a global dance, tango increasingly involves *transnational* encounters. It has always been a global dance, moving from Argentina (where it was also the dance of immigrants) to Europe and back again. However, international tourism and a growing contingent of relatively affluent individuals with a cosmopolitan lifestyle in search of a specific kind of touristic experience have made tango one of Argentina's most important export items as well as a significant source of revenue at home. A postcolonial reading à la Savigliano that frames tango as a relic of an imperialist and postcolonial past does not do justice to these more contemporary realities. For example, her emphasis on the problematic complicity of Argentineans in the colonializing practices of exoticization and "othering" does not take into consideration the active, eager, and creative participation of contemporary Argentineans in transnational encounters through tango. Nor does her analysis leave much space for the possibility that passionate encounters between Argentineans and tango *aficionados* from other parts of the world are not only asymmetrical in terms of power, but also mutually beneficial and—in some cases—conducive to new forms of community.

In this book, I explore tango as a transnational cultural space for passionate encounters (chapter 6). Drawing upon Burawoy (2000), I show

how tango enables transnational connections at different levels—economic and historical (through international tourism), interactional (through encounters between locals and visitors on the dance floor), and imaginary (in representations of tango as "authentic" expression of *argentinidad* or as cosmopolitan experience *par excellence*). These encounters are never free of power, and yet, as I will demonstrate, they also provide possibilities for excitement, interaction, and a shared sense of community across the very differences that divide the participants from one another.

I began this Introduction with a story about how I entered a *milonga* in Amsterdam by chance and was puzzled at what an antiquated dance from another continent could possibly have to offer the thoroughly modern residents of a metropolis like Amsterdam. In the pages that follow, I will be embarking on a journey—both personal and intellectual—that will allow me to reframe this puzzle, moving the story from what is so fascinating about tango, to what this fascination tells us about the transnational connections engendered by and reproduced in and through tango. To do this, I will use and, at the same time, critically interrogate my own passion for dancing tango—a passion that has both helped and hindered me in untangling the complexities and contradictions that emerge when differently located people from different parts of the world come together to dance tango.

1

Salon Cultures

Dancing tango is both a social and a cultural phenomenon. Nowhere is this more apparent than in the tango salon—the place where people meet in order to dance tango. My first encounter with the culture and social practices of the tango salon took place in a well-known tango academy in Amsterdam. I had roped my initially hesitant husband into learning tango by giving him ten tango lessons as a Christmas present, and this was our first lesson. The instructor explained to a motley group of would-be dancers that we would not be learning the tango that we probably all knew from films. Images of *Scent of a Woman*[1] and Al Pacino sweeping a beautiful young woman off her feet in a tango dramatically performed between the tables of a posh New York restaurant briefly floated through my head, only to be dispelled by the announcement that we would be learning tango "the way it is danced in the salons of Buenos Aires." Of course, we had no idea what a salon was, let alone how tango was danced in one, but it sounded intriguing, combining the association of a French literary gathering with Latin dance rhythms. After watching a demonstration by two clearly experienced dancers, locked in a close embrace and gracefully circling the dance floor to the melancholy chords of unfamiliar yet hypnotic music, we were hooked. We, too, wanted to be able to dance like that, "the way tango is danced in the salons of Buenos Aires."

Many lessons later, we embarked upon our first trip to Buenos Aires, determined to discover what dancing tango would be like in the city where it all began. Like many visitors, we began our quest in Confiteria Ideal, a salon in the center of Buenos Aires where many foreigners go to watch Argentineans dance tango. Not surprisingly, this is also the salon that Sally Potter chose for the dance scenes in her film *The Tango Lesson*, which will be described in more detail in chapter 6. Confiteria

Figure 1.1. Confiteria Ideal in Buenos Aires. (Photo: Layne Randolph.)

Ideal has, indeed, all the ingredients of what one imagines a tango salon to have: a battered marble floor with ornate pillars, a dark wooden bar in the back, mirrors on the walls, an old-fashioned fan, and small tables along the sides of the dance floor. Music of the 1940s and '50s (tango's Golden Age) emanates from a less-than-perfect sound system, while couples move slowly around the dance floor. There is a ubiquitous sense of past-ness here, of a bygone era that has been frozen in time (Coza-rinksy, 2007).

I remember the mixture of strangeness and familiarity that assailed me upon my first entering this salon. Single men and women were seated in separate corners of the room, facing each other, while the couples and tourists were shuffled toward the back, slightly removed from the action around the dance floor. This segregation by sex was the most immediately noticeable feature of the salon for me, as it is for many European visitors. I saw women sitting alone or in groups of two or three at tables, with their fans, breath mints, and shoe bags arranged neatly in front of them. While there was some conversation, they remained alert, eyes moving about the room, ready to accept or reject invitations to dance. The men were sitting together at tables drinking beer or champagne and watching the dancers on the floor intently, making comments to one another and laughing. Those who had the prime spots along the dance floor didn't seem to dance much and, indeed, appeared to be more interested in socializing with one another than in finding a dance partner.

The ages of the dancers varied, from teenagers in baggy jeans and sneakers to octogenarians in old-fashioned suits exuding a faint whiff of mothballs. But what I most remember about this first visit to a salon was that many women "of a certain age" (as it is euphemistically called in Europe and North America) were provocatively dressed, with lots of exposed cleavage, long flowing hair, and dramatic makeup. This was clearly a setting where women could engage in some sartorial transgression: Age-appropriate clothing could be abandoned for overtly sexualized attire which flaunts a body that is otherwise expected to be concealed in the gendered and ageist norms of feminine propriety (Savigliano, 2003). As I looked around, I discovered that the salon was, in fact, full of transgressions: svelte, perfumed, and expertly coiffed women dancing with men in synthetic pants with gold chains around their necks; elderly men with paunches and dyed hair dancing with slender young beauties who were rapturously smiling; young men leading women old enough to be their grandmothers with unmistakable tenderness and gallantry. And, of course, dancers from all parts of the world circling the floor, locked in a close embrace with local *milongueros* and *milongueras*.[2]

While the diversity of these couplings and the gendered transgressions of class, age, and ethnicity are interesting in and of themselves, the way in which the dancers connect with one another is the most puzzling feature of the salon for the uninitiated. For example, it is bewildering to observe couples who have been dancing together with apparent enjoyment suddenly returning to their tables as soon as the music stops. Once back in their seats, the tension in the air is electric, becoming increasingly palpable. Then, as if by magic, the men stand up and begin walking, each toward a particular woman, who then stands up and, without a word being said, accompanies the man onto the dance floor. Within seconds, the previously empty floor is once again filled with couples, and the next set begins.

The mechanics of this process—a process that takes, at the most, a minute or two—is nearly invisible to the newcomer, and, indeed, I remember turning to my husband during this first salon and saying, "Did you see that? How do they do that? How do they know that they are going to dance together?" We were intrigued and without a clue.

Since this initial experience, we have returned to Buenos Aires again and again, and it has taken many more visits to salons before we could begin to understand the nuances of these invitation rituals, let alone uncover the many layers of complexity inherent in the salon culture there. While these visits allowed me to better understand and participate in the salons of Buenos Aires, I continued to perceive them as specifically Argentinean, and, therefore, I expected them to remain mysterious to me as a European. It is only through the writing of this book that I have begun to critically interrogate this assumption of tango as a typical product of Argentinean culture as well as the underlying notion of authenticity that underpinned not only my own perceptions but also discussions within tango communities both in Buenos Aires as well as elsewhere in the world.

In this chapter, I critically reassess the question of authenticity—that is, what is the essence of tango and whose tango is it—as a necessary preamble to understanding the reception of tango across the globe as well as its development at home in Argentina. In other words, what happens to tango when it is exported from Buenos Aires to other parts of the world? In what ways does it retain its connection to the place and time of its origins, and how has it been transformed into something both exotic and yet reassuringly European? Using Buenos Aires and Amsterdam[3] as sites for an ethnographic investigation of tango, I show how these salon cultures are both specific and yet also interconnected. Rather than situate myself as neutral observer—if such a position were even possible—I adopt the stance of the insider-outsider (Wacquant, 2005), along with the dual strategy, long popular among anthropologists, of making a culture that is initially strange (that of Buenos Aires) familiar and a culture that is initially familiar (Amsterdam's) strange.

The Tango Scene in Buenos Aires

Tango salons began to crop up during the 1980s in the city of Buenos Aires and, along with them, a small but committed community of local dancers consisting of oldtimers who had been dancing tango before it fell out of fashion and newcomers who, while they had grown up listening to tango music, had only recently learned how to dance tango. As tango became increasingly popular abroad, the tango scene in Buenos Aires underwent a rapid and dramatic expansion. By the twenty-first century, tango tourism had become a booming industry with thousands of Europeans, North Americans, and Japanese and Koreans heading to Buenos Aires each year to dance tango. In addition to the numerous tango shows for tourists, tango cafés with dance demonstrations, dance performances in the streets, group lessons, and private workshops with private teachers, the tango scene within Buenos Aires now offers more than 300 *milongas* and *practicas* a week at which tango can be danced, and this does not include the myriad smaller clubs and cafés outside the city center where locals dance with one another. The salons in the city center are predictably diverse. Some hold *milongas* in the late afternoon or early evening, others at night, each catering to a different crowd. Many of the dancers attending afternoon *milongas* stop by for a dance after work and leave in time to get home for dinner with their families. In contrast, the nocturnal crowd is more likely to combine dancing with socializing, hanging out, or looking for an opportunity to "hook up" with someone after the *milonga*. Many women complain that in the nocturnal *milongas*, the men will spend more time drinking beer and talking with one another than dancing. As one of my informants put it, "Life is short and if you want to dance, you should go to an afternoon *milonga*."

The *milongas* are organized in different locations, ranging from beautiful colonial buildings, grungy backrooms that you have to ascend a narrow flight of steps in order to reach, community centers, and restaurants to—in one notable case—a gym. This particular *milonga*, called Club Sunderland, is one of the most famous in Buenos Aires and features regular performances by well-known dancers. Formerly the home of a local basketball team, it is now frequented by families (including grandparents and children) that have produced some of Argentina's most well-known tango dancers, many local dancers, and a large number of tourists who are familiar with Club Sunderland from having watched videos of the performances on YouTube. *Milongas* in Buenos Aires are hosted by different organizers with their own DJs, often taking

Figure 1.2. Club Sunderland in Buenos Aires. (Photo: Jorge Royan.)

place in the same location but on different days of the week. The public also changes, with some *milongas* catering to dancers with a predilection for dancing in a more open style (often called *tango nuevo*), while others are more traditional, playing music from the 1940s and '50s, with dancers who prefer a close embrace. The dancers vary in age, but the average age is probably in the fifties, with a fairly high percentage of older, retired men and younger, professional women. It is not always possible to judge the class background of the dancers, although women generally seem to be more educated and have a higher level of income than the men. As one of my Argentinean informants jokingly put it, a woman needs to be wary of any man who wants to know whether she has her own apartment or a car: "He's looking for a place to move in and a housewife who will cook his meals and iron his shirts."

In the wake of the latest economic recession and the increase in entrance fees, the crowds have diminished somewhat and are more solidly middle-class than before. Many older *milongueros* and *milongueras* of working-class origin have started dancing in their own neighborhoods, leaving the city salons to the more well-to-do Argentineans and the tourists. While nearly every *milonga* will have its share of tourists, numbers vary by season, with *milongas* drawing up to half of their clientele from tourists during the months of November through March.

There are many ways to find out about the *milongas*—the Internet, tango magazines, flyers, and, of course, word-of-mouth. Once you have entered the tango scene, you will meet other dancers who will gladly provide recommendations for places to dance. The world of tango is a subculture, but within this subculture are smaller groups that gravitate to particular salons, week after week.[4] Although tourists often visit as many different salons as they possibly can, with some even taking in two a day, locals are more likely to attend a smaller number of salons regularly.

Fees are paid at the door and, once you have entered the salon, a host or hostess or waiter will ask if you are "solo." Couples will be seated together, often in an out-of-the-way part of the salon. The unwritten rule is that local men do not dance with women who are sitting with men—out of respect for the man, to avoid possible confrontations, or simply because many men claim they cannot dance tango with a woman unless she is for him alone, at least in his fantasy and for the duration of their dance together.

Seating is important for other reasons than marking one's availability as a dancer. It is extremely rare to just walk into a *milonga* and take a seat, although this does happen in salons that cater to a younger crowd. Regulars tend to have their own seats at specific tables. While there is a strict pecking order in the assignment of tables, with the most valued seats usually being close to the dance floor, thereby providing the dancer with a good view of other dancers, this order is not the most important feature of the seating arrangements. Dancers are particularly interested in always having the same seat in a particular *milonga*. Even if they are located in a remote corner of the salon, their main concern is that other dancers—and, in particular, the dancer with whom they want to dance—will know where to find them.

Seating arrangements are also a source of ongoing power plays among dancers sitting at the same table, as I discovered once I started being seated "*sola*" in the *milongas*. For example, the women at my table would sometimes shift water glasses and fans from one side of the table to the other, or even take my seat while I was dancing, thereby forcing me to move to another seat. I was once offered a seat in a *milonga* at the back of a prime table spot by an Argentinean woman who had befriended me. However, she insisted that I not cut past her chair when I was invited to dance but instead take the long way around the back. "That's the way we do things here," she explained. For several dances, I took her at her word, making my laborious way along the back wall of the salon and up one of the free aisles until one of my dance partners, who also knew my table-mate well, stood in front of her, laughing: "Oh, come on! Just let her through." I soon learned that, while relations between women at the tables are often cordial and supportive, there is also plenty of competiveness. Many experienced *milongueras* are contemptuous of foreigners who—as they see it—"will dance with anyone just to be dancing." While there may well be some jealousy at play behind such remarks,[5] the issue of respect is also involved. Respect, however, is something that has to be earned. For example, I remember sitting at a table with a local woman who was quite unpleasant, moving my accessories around and positioning herself in such a way that my view was blocked. At one point, a man came up to the table and directly asked me to dance, something that is a clear transgression of the codes and rarely occurs except when local men ask foreign women to dance. I didn't want to dance with him and was insulted that he had put me on the spot in such a way, so I looked him squarely in the eye and refused. After several attempts to persuade me, he retreated. My table companion then turned to me, touching my arm and grimacing dramatically: "That *hombre*, he's horrible." She proceeded to offer me a glass of champagne and we chatted amiably together for the rest of the *milonga*.

The dancing itself is organized in sets (*tandas*) of three or four songs (*temas*), played by a particular orchestra.[6] After two sets of tangos, the DJ will play a set of either *milongas* or tango waltzes. The end of a set is marked by a change in music (*cortina*), a short musical intermezzo that can be anything from Latin music to classical music to rock. This interval allows couples to return to their tables and prepare for the next set. Once the couples move onto the dance floor, they immediately begin to dance, something that is done with concentration and without talking. However, in between the *temas* there is a brief interval for a conversation that may encompass up to sixteen bars of the next song. While this conversational space can be a bit daunting for the

foreigner with little proficiency in Spanish (involving endless renditions of "Where are you from?" and "How long are you staying?"), it
is important because it allows the music to sink in as preparation for
the next dance and gives partners an opportunity to get to know one
another. It also provides time for exuberant and exaggerated compliments. These *piropos* or, more negatively, *chamuyos*,[7] are quite specific
to the dance scene in Buenos Aires and belong to the ritual of the salon.
They open up a kind of game in which each partner tries to one-up the
other with an ever more lavish compliment, something that is called
in Spanish *se tiran flores* ("throwing flowers at one another"). While
some of the Argentinean women I spoke with distance themselves from
porteños[8] and their compliments, others insist that the compliments are
also what makes the *milonga* enjoyable ("It's a game, but I love it"). For
example, a *milonguero* may praise his partner's dancing by placing his
hand on his heart and turning his eyes toward the ceiling with a sigh,
dramatically exclaiming, "You are killing me," followed by a string of
poetic compliments. These intervals between dances can, however, also
become something of a minefield with queries about marital status and
attempts to discover whether one has come to the *milonga* alone, as well
as constant efforts to arrange assignations outside the salon (the ubiquitous code is: "Shall we go for a coffee later?"). Yet however amorous the
short intervals between dances may be, as soon as the music stops, the
woman will always be ushered safely to her seat, perhaps with a brief
glance full of unrequited longing from her partner. But, after all is said
and done, once the *cortina* comes to an end and the music of a new
tanda begins, the whole cycle starts all over again.

Seen through the eyes of a European visitor, the salon appears mysteriously orderly. Everyone seems to "know" what to do. However, the
more time the visitor spends in Buenos Aires, the more he or she will
discover that the salon culture is governed by a set of informal codes
(*codigos*) that are implicit yet also the subject of much discussion, both
locally and abroad.[9] These codes concern how to behave on the dance
floor, how to interact with other dancers, and how to ensure that the
dance does not get out of control. For example, dancers need to observe
certain conventions in order to avoid collisions on a crowded dance
floor. Couples are expected to move in a counterclockwise direction,
in a series of concentric rings. Leaders are supposed to respect one

another's space. A leader who engages in wild steps, moves unexpectedly backward (thereby disrupting a neighboring couple's dance), or has a partner who engages in high kicks may find himself "danced out" in a mysteriously concerted action by other dancers who have decided to deny him space on the floor. Or he may be elbowed, butted, or simply pushed to the center of the floor. On the other hand, dancers frequently display respect for one another. A case in point is a story told by Juan Carlos Pontorielo, a well-known *milonguero*, in a series of interviews with traditional tango dancers in Buenos Aires.[10] He recalled how, as a young dancer, he had once accidentally touched another man while he was dancing with his partner. Pontorielo was horrified, and although he apologized immediately, the other man refused to accept the apology, informing him that he just didn't "know how to dance." A week later in the same salon, this same man saw Pontorielo dancing well and came up to him, apologizing for having been mistaken about his lack of dancing skills. Thus, the dancers ensure that the order of the salon is maintained: Deference is provided, and each dancer is responsible for making things work.

The codes for inviting, accepting, and rejecting dances are often major hurdles for foreigners. In most salons in Buenos Aires, a dance must be initiated by a nod from the man—a *cabeceo*—and accepted by a return nod from the woman.[11] This is designed to avoid overt rejection and subtly negotiate an invitation. Sometimes an invitation will be set up in advance, through eye contact made from the floor, a brief smile, or an infinitesimal shrug as if to say, "Yes, now I am dancing with her, but it is you I would like to have in my arms." This process can be extended over many dances. Even after a dancer has lost all hope of an invitation's ever materializing, a long-awaited *cabeceo* may suddenly appear—mysteriously, unexpectedly, and yet also with a certain inevitability. It is a subtle form of seduction, often playful, sometimes frustrating, but invariably exciting. It allows dancers to avoid unwanted dances by pretending not to see an invitation, thereby protecting themselves and preventing the other person from losing face.

It is not easy for foreigners to "work the floor" in a salon, and there will inevitably be mistakes and misunderstandings. For example, for the person initiating the invitation, the codes require putting aside the more straightforward convention of walking up to someone and asking her to dance. Foreigners will have to attract the attention of locals who are hesitant to embark on a dance with someone whose level of dancing they don't know. The locals risk being ostracized by their regular dance partners if they are seen stumbling around the dance floor with a clumsy foreigner. For women, particularly if their first reflex is to look away when a stranger meets their eye, the *cabeceo* may seem to be a mission impossible (Taylor, 1998). Many of my female informants described having to force themselves to keep their heads up and look straight ahead in order to receive the looks of men wanting to dance with them. They have to learn to express just the right mixture of interest and availability without seeming pushy or desperate. This requires being alert to the tiniest of movements (if you have poor vision, you will definitely need to keep your glasses on) and responding in kind. And, finally, once the invitation has been negotiated, the woman will need to wait patiently until the man who has issued the invitation is standing in front of her. It is not uncommon for a foreign visitor to jump out of her chair, only to discover that the invitation was meant not for her but for the woman sitting behind her.

These codes are fairly straightforward, ensuring that the interaction on the floor runs smoothly. Other codes are more implicit yet even more essential to preserving the salon order. They are designed to keep the tango encounter safely within the boundaries of the salon. Tango is a sensual dance—a dance that brings partners together in a close and potentially volatile embrace. The spatial separation of the sexes, the circumscribed temporality of the dance set (*tanda*), and the conventions of the salon—which preclude one's hanging around on the dance floor with the same partner—all serve to keep sexual desire in check. Men do not generally go to women's tables to talk unless there is a special occasion (e.g., a birthday) or to greet someone briefly or to chat up a tourist who doesn't know any better. They shy away from inviting women who are sitting with other men, and some men even disapprove of asking a woman who has just danced with one of the men sitting at their table. For every *codigo*, exceptions can be made, of course, and this possibility contributes a bit of *frisson* to the atmosphere of the salon. For example, some husbands will dance with their wives in the beginning of a *milonga* and then stand up next to the table, indicating that now others have permission to ask her. A man who invites a woman sitting with another man may give her partner a handshake first and then compliment him when the dance is over, giving him credit for her being a good dancer.

The codes that regulate sexuality in the context of the gender regime of the salon are even more complex and implicit. For example, there is an unwritten rule that one does not dance too often with the same partner and never immediately after a *tanda* (a set). Dancers may be enthralled with dancing with each other, but unless they are prepared to "take a coffee" at the end of the *milonga*, they will do well to limit their dancing to two sets. This particular rule can be bent if the dancers know each other well enough to avoid misunderstandings. However, generally speaking, the *codigos* enable dancers to enjoy dancing without having to worry about unwanted intrusions upon their autonomy. As one of my informants explained, she had learned the hard way that it is not a good idea to accept invitations for outside the *milonga*. She was in the process of apartment-hunting, and one of her regular dancers told her that he might have something for her. They agreed to meet in the apartment. While she was looking around, he disappeared into the bathroom, only to emerge stark naked a few minutes later, arms spread wide and with a naughty grin on his face ("How about it, beautiful?"). She was able to flee the scene, but she decided that that was the last time she would agree to meet someone outside the salon. Of course, some dancers may welcome the chance to get together outside the salon and may see the *milonga* as a space where they can meet potential partners for sex or something more. The existence of codes can make it harder to arrange such liaisons, however, even when they are desired by both partners. A Canadian dancer told me how difficult it was to actually date someone she met in a salon. One of her regular dance partners—a man whom she found quite attractive—invited her to dinner. Although she was interested, she recalls having to dance four sets with him just so that they could negotiate the ground rules for a first date. As she put it, "I had to be able to trust him, and those minute intervals between dances don't give you much time to figure things out together."

The salon regime in Buenos Aires is both rigorously homosocial and organized by a separation between the sexes. Men go to the *milongas* to socialize with their male friends. They dance under the careful inspection of their friends whose respect they want to earn, and they are careful to avoid offending other men. As Jeffrey Tobin (1998) puts it, men in Argentinean tango salons dance for one another; women are mere vehicles for their relationships with one another. In the salons, relations between the men and women often seem frozen in time, regulated through rituals of male dominance and female submission. The traditional forms of machismo seem, at first glance, to still be alive and kicking today, with women relegated to the position of passive object, waiting to be asked, waiting to be led, waiting to be desired (Savigliano, 2003:189). This seemingly antiquated gender regime, however, intersects with differences in class, age, and marital status, in ways that give gender a different meaning from the one it had in the early days of tango, when single immigrant men competed with one another for the attentions of the few available women. The "rebellious broads" described by Savigliano (1995) who flouted conventional morality in order to dance tango have changed as well. Today women in the salons in Buenos Aires are likely to be younger than the men. They are usually middle-class and often professionals. Many are divorced or single. They see the salons as an activity to be squeezed into their busy schedules. In contrast, the men tend to be older, are often more precariously employed or retired, and many are married. It is not uncommon for men to "sneak off" to the *milonga*, leaving their wives at home. These differences create myriad and highly complex constellations of power on the dance floor. Men with little power in everyday life can wield control in the salon over women who would normally be unattainable for them. Independent women can abandon themselves in the arms of men they would not look at twice in their ordinary lives, secure in the knowledge that they will be leaving them behind when the *milonga* comes to an end. The class differences also mitigate the insults of having to be a wallflower. Because in most tango salons there are always more women than men, women have to be prepared to spend some time waiting to be asked to dance. Many local women attempt to soften the indignities of "wallflowering" by making cutting remarks about the local men's general lack of "cultural refinement" and "poor social skills." In this way, they use their superior social positions outside the *milonga* to equalize the gendered imbalances within the salon culture.

In Buenos Aires, the tango salon offers the opportunity for both men and women to draw playfully upon the accoutrements of a past gender regime. They can temporarily take on the stereotypical personae that Savigliano (1995) depicts in her history of tango's Golden Age. The man may display the dramatic and slightly macho behavior of the "whiny ruffian" with impunity. The women can imitate the sexy yet tragic demeanor of the "rebellious broad." However, as Savigliano convincingly argues, these gendered roles are little more than a form of ritualized play. In the *milonga*, dancers allow themselves to become objects for one another's fantasy (Savigliano, 2003:164). The regime of the salon contains and controls these fantasies so that dancers can construct a deliciously seductive, yet reassuringly safe space—a space that is separate from the contingencies of their ordinary lives outside the *milonga*.

Tango Dancing in Amsterdam

Tango made its first appearance in Amsterdam in 1913, becoming a rage, albeit a controversial one. A decade later, a second wave of tango hit the shores of the Netherlands, this time in a slightly sanitized form—the "French tango"—which soon became popular among the urban and artistic elites. A German variation of tango was in vogue during the 1930s, particularly through music imported by German tango orchestras. In 1937, a local Dutch tango band called Malando became popular with its hybrid mixture of Argentinean and German tango with some Dutch folk tunes thrown in for good measure.[12] Tango then fell out of fashion as other dances became popular, only to reappear in the 1970s with the introduction of Piazzolla's[13] tango music and, several years later, the international tango show *Tango Argentino*.

The most recent revival of tango dancing in the Netherlands[14] began with the opening of the first tango academy in 1986, bringing the complicated relationship between a past Europe and a distant Argentina to Amsterdam with a vengeance. Since then, a vibrant tango scene has emerged in which it is possible to dance tango every evening of the week. All that is required to find a place to dance is a quick look at the local Internet site. The participants are mostly local dancers and visitors from other nearby cities. However, there are invariably a handful of dancers from other parts of the world, making it hard to characterize dancers in terms of their nationality. The tango subculture in Amsterdam is a cosmopolitan mix of the local and the global, much as it is in

Buenos Aires. Its core consists of a relatively affluent and highly mobile population with the time and money to spend on leisure activities and the desire for community, a social outlet, and a taste of the exotic—all the ingredients that Argentinean tango seems to offer.

Milongas are held in a variety of venues, from schools and community centers to cafés, churches, museums, and theaters. While some of the salons capitalize on a sense of "past-ness," it is not a past that includes the shabby interiors and faulty plumbing common in the salons of Buenos Aires. In Amsterdam, salons may be decorated in a romantic style reminiscent of tango's Golden Age, replete with chandeliers, velvet curtains, candlesticks, and the ubiquitous photo of Carlos Gardel.[15] Others capitalize on being trendy, holding their *milongas* in a luxurious hotel or on a rooftop with a sea view or even in a restored *manège* where tango was danced against the décor of wooden stalls, vaulted ceilings, and the faint whiff of horse manure. The tango salon is presented as something special and out-of-the-ordinary, a place to escape from one's everyday life.

In Amsterdam, salons cater to different audiences with some favoring open-style dancing with complicated configurations of steps as well as a wide range of music genres (*neo tango*) while others are more "traditional," preferring the close embrace, smaller steps, and classical tango music. Tango dancers tend to be upwardly mobile professionals with jobs in business, education, law, health care, information and communications technology, or the arts. There are few differences between men and women in terms of class background, occupation, or educational status, and in Amsterdam one would be hard-pressed to find the octogenarian working-class *milonguero* who is such a welcome fixture of the tango scene in Buenos Aires. I remember dancing with one such elderly *milonguero* in Buenos Aires. He was considerably shorter than I, with an enormous stomach, dyed hair glistening with hair creme, and sporting several gold chains and rings. While I was always eager to dance with him, it was also clear to me that this was not someone I would be likely to encounter outside the confines of that salon. One night, after a particularly wonderful dance, he looked at me, somewhat sadly, and said: "If I came to Amsterdam, would you dance with me?" I recall thinking how incongruous he would be there and I wondered, with considerable discomfort, if, indeed, I would be as anxious to dance

Figure 1.3. La Bruja, Amsterdam. (Photo: Colin Brace.)

with him in Amsterdam as I am in Buenos Aires. By the same token, I—as a woman who is well "past [my] mini-skirted, cropped, see-through look prime" (Savigliano, 2003:154)—probably have less difficulty finding dance partners in Buenos Aires, where I am more likely to be regarded as attractive than is the case in the age-conscious, if not ageist, culture of Amsterdam. On the average, dancers in Amsterdam are more likely to be single and somewhat younger than dancers in Buenos Aires, with the average age being between thirty-five and fifty.[16] However, the demography of tango is changing everywhere as tango gains popularity among dancers in their twenties.[17]

The Amsterdam tango scene draws participants from a wide range of backgrounds, including individuals who have recently migrated from different parts of the world. Just as Buenos Aires cherishes its image as a nation of immigrants (from Europe, of course), Amsterdam also prides itself on being multicultural—in rhetoric if not always in practice—and many dancers draw upon the image of tango as a dance developed by immigrants. As one of my informants, a German construction worker who had recently relocated to Amsterdam, told me, he can't listen to tango music without automatically seeing sepia-tinted images of groups of immigrants surrounded by suitcases, just off the boat and ready to embark upon new lives in Buenos Aires. However mythical, this image enabled him to connect tango to his own experiences of feeling lonely or displaced.

Dance attire tends to be more casual in Amsterdam than it is in Buenos Aires. Women, in particular, are less likely to wear clothing that displays their bodies in an overtly sexual way. However, they adopt styles that are considerably more feminine than what they would probably wear outside the salon. It is not uncommon to see low-slung skirts with slits, fishnet stockings, and stiletto heels, alongside the ubiquitous leggings, baggy pants, and sport shoes. Thus, what might look ordinary and far from flashy in a salon in Buenos Aires, where one is used to exuberant fashions, is extraordinary and daring for Amsterdam. For women in Amsterdam, tango salons are a place where "you can wear things that you always dreamt of but could wear nowhere else" (Petridou, 2009:61).

Nowhere is this more apparent than in the passion many woman have for tango shoes. While the *milongueras* in Buenos Aires are well shod, they are considerably more concerned about comfort and less likely to talk about shoes, unless to complain about the tourists and their shoe fetish. In Amsterdam, however, being a connoisseur of shoes is a sign that you are a serious dancer; shoes are a mark of distinction, the higher the heel and the more openness of the shoe indicating greater proficiency (Littig, 2013). Women often compare their latest acquisitions, admiring one another's shoes, finding fault in the fit of a particular model, or simply sighing in relief at the end of the evening when shoes are removed and tired, aching feet are finally liberated. In contrast, taking off one's shoes publicly in a salon in Buenos Aires is likely to evoke looks of horror and is, therefore, better reserved for the privacy of the women's lavatory or the coatroom. Shoes are a public affair, however, in Amsterdam, with women enjoying exchanges about shoes and good places to buy them. It is even a way for women who do not know one another to bond. For example, I was once approached by a woman I had never met before as I was leaving the dance floor. She explained that she recognized my shoes, having bought hers at the same shoe store in Buenos Aires.

The dress codes for men are different in Buenos Aires and Amsterdam as well. The average *milonguero* would be well and truly horrified to observe the way men show up at salons in Amsterdam in cargo pants, not having bothered to change their shirts before coming to a *milonga*. "You can smell the sweat from the last salon" is a commonly heard complaint from women dancers. Many female dancers in Amsterdam grumble about the cavalier attitude their male counterparts seem to have concerning hygiene. There are exceptions, of course, but even these are a far cry from the well-groomed, casual attire of most *milongueros* in Buenos Aires. For example, in Amsterdam, some men will don what they imagine to be "typically" Argentinean tango apparel: old-fashioned suits, dress shirts, suspenders, or even a fedora. Or they wear flamboyant shoes in patent leather or bright colors. However, paradoxically, the ostentation of the shoes is also regarded as the mark of a novice dancer. As one of my male informants somewhat sarcastically noted, "The flashier the shoe, the less talented the dancer."

The salons in Amsterdam are organized in ways that are both similar to and different from those in Buenos Aires. Each time I return to Amsterdam after a stay in Buenos Aires, I find myself slightly "off center" (Creef, 2000). I begin to look through different eyes at the salon culture where I learned tango and where it became the passion of my life. Even my home salon, the one I go to every Friday, rain or shine, seems strange, somehow not quite right. For example, there is always someone at the door to greet you and in many cases you can expect a warm welcome with kisses being exchanged, just as is done in Buenos Aires. However, after paying the entrance fee, in Amsterdam you are on your own. While the host might indicate where you can hang up your coat and change your shoes, no one is ever ushered to a seat, and, indeed, reservations are unheard of in the salons of Amsterdam. Dancers are expected to find their own seats. A case in point is an Argentinean dancer from Buenos Aires who was visiting my home salon in Amsterdam recently. He seemed completely bewildered by the setup and finally made his way, somewhat timidly, to the bar, where he asked the bartender in carefully articulated Spanish where he should sit and how he should order his drinks and whether it was usual here to invite partners to dance with the *cabeceo*. After the fixed and hierarchical seating patterns in the salons of Buenos Aires, it can, of course, be a great relief to be able to move around a salon as one wants. However, there are drawbacks to this freedom, particularly if the salon is crowded. It may, indeed, not always be possible to find a vacant seat, let alone a seat in a good location, and, having found a seat, you may not be able to hold on to it. Even wraps or bags placed ostentatiously on a particular chair or table do not guarantee that the seat will not have been taken when their owner returns from a dance, nor does being a "regular" entail privileged seating. Chairs are occupied on an informal, first-come–first-served basis. It is not uncommon for an altercation to ensue when a dancer attempts to reclaim a previously occupied seat, only to hear: "You can sit anywhere," "Hey, it's a free world," or, more aggressively, "What's your problem?"

The relaxed sociality that is an integral feature of Amsterdam salons is what I most miss when I am in Buenos Aires: being able to sit with whomever I want without having to worry about violating the *codigos* or being able to chat with a male friend without eyebrows' being raised. On the other hand, I miss the sexualized *frisson* of the salons of Buenos Aires, which is absent in the Amsterdam tango scene. The segregation by sex, which is standard fare in most salons in Buenos Aires, is unthinkable in Amsterdam. There are, of course, plenty of unspoken codes in Amsterdam. However, they are less clear-cut and it is precisely this vagueness about how to behave in a salon that produces uncertainty among the dancers. For example, there is an unspoken assumption that men will do the inviting, but this is not codified as an unshakable rule as it is in Buenos Aires and it is by no means uncommon for women to ask men to dance. Most dancers would insist, in fact, that it is hopelessly old-fashioned and sexist for men to invite and women to wait to be invited, and this is often cited as one of the ways "we" do things differently "here." However, many men will admit that they don't really like to be asked to dance by women. Many of the men I interviewed complained about women "descending" upon them just as they are catching their breath or working up their courage to ask someone to dance. They described feeling uncomfortable when they enter a salon that has "too many" women because they will be assailed with reproachful looks from women who expect to be asked to dance. While *milongueros* in Buenos Aires, secure in their "right" to initiate a dance, are unlikely to give the matter a second thought, men in Amsterdam often see the situation in the salon from the woman's point of view and are worried that they will be perceived as selfish or sexist if they don't accept invitations from women.

In Amsterdam, women are also considerably less likely to accept "wallflowering"—as Savigliano (2003:189) calls the "waiting to be asked to dance" that is an inevitable part of any salon—than the seasoned *milongueras* in Buenos Aires.[18] Women are caught between wanting to be invited, and thereby having their desirability as dancers confirmed, and wanting to be able to take charge of their own fate in the salon and not be dependent upon men. Many of the women I spoke with were frustrated at having to sit out dance after dance while men either asked other women or hung around drinking beer or wine and talking ("Why did they come to the salon if they're not going to dance?"). However, taking the initiative after having been sitting too long was also done with undisguised ambivalence. It's difficult to avoid dancing with a man when "suddenly, there he is, standing in front of you, and how can you say 'no' without hurting his feelings?" It is also a source of resentment that women who ask men to dance are "butting into line before their turn." This indicates that Amsterdam is no less hierarchical than Buenos Aires, with dancers paying just as much attention to who should be asked, when, and by whom. However, as one of my informants put it, "You just want to have things clear, you know. You want to know who is going to take the initiative. So, OK, in tango, it's the men. I don't mind."

The practice of the *cabeceo* (a nod as method of invitation) that is so distinctive for the tango scene in Buenos Aires has been transported to Amsterdam, often by dancers who have already been to Buenos Aires. Having seen it in action there, they become fervent proponents, arguing that it has many advantages for both parties and is, in any case, a more "authentic" way of doing things. One enterprising dancer even organized a workshop to provide instruction in how to do the *cabeceo*, and salons will occasionally be organized—as the host puts it—"the way they do it in Buenos Aires," which means that guests are ushered to fixed tables and expected to invite one another to dance through eye contact. While these initiatives are greeted with enthusiasm by some, other local dancers remain skeptical, arguing, "You just can't make people do things that aren't in their culture."

Even dancers who insist on practicing the *cabeceo* will find that the informal seating patterns and the lack of clear demarcation between those who are and are not available for dancing in Amsterdam salons do not facilitate this form of invitation. Many of my informants explained that they would like to invite partners with a nod but that it is difficult to get their attention. As one man put it, "Some women just never look at you. They have their eyes on the floor. Even when you get their attention and you think you're all set to dance, there is always some guy who jumps in front of you at the last minute and then off she goes with him and there I am, left holding the bag." It is far more common for a leader, usually a man, to walk up to a woman and invite her directly to dance. Sometimes he will simply tap her on the shoulder or grab her hand and pull her onto the dance floor—something that would probably horrify an Argentinean *milonguera*.

Once on the dance floor, however, the music is identical to what one would find in a salon in Buenos Aires. For many Dutch DJs, this is a point of some pride; it is part of being *au courant* with the tango scene there. While the music is organized in a similar fashion (in sets of four *temas* separated by a *cortina*), couples do not have to vacate the floor at the end of a set. It is possible to hang around with one's partner without having to worry that doing so will raise expectations. Moreover, there are always plenty of opportunities for informal chatting in the salons and, therefore, little pressure to have to squeeze everything into the dance set. A real culture shock for anyone after dancing in Buenos Aires is the total absence of *piropos* and *chamuyos* (exaggerated compliments). Dancers in Amsterdam tend to find such compliments over-the-top and may react with embarrassment if a compliment is too extravagant. A typical response is a mumbled "Nice dance" or a comment about a particular step's having gone "pretty well." Some dancers apologize for missteps that occurred during the set, something that would never occur in Buenos Aires, where there seems to be less concern about whether the dance is perfect than in Amsterdam. In any case, the informal code seems to be that, however intense the dance itself, partners should waste no time before returning to "normal" interaction.[19]

In Amsterdam, the dance floor sometimes feels less organized and more disorderly than the *pistas* of Buenos Aires. This is partly due to different conceptions of what a "good" leader should be doing. In any salon, dancers are not just dancing with one another but are also aware that they are being watched. However, there are notable differences in what an audience sees as a "good" or a "bad" dancer. The *milonguero* is critically scrutinized by his (male) friends in Buenos Aires to see whether he has chosen a partner who can dance well and is able to lead her so that *she* looks good. It is to his credit if she has her eyes closed and a blissful smile on her lips. His style is minimalist, and, indeed, it is considered a sign of effeminate vanity for a man to put too much effort into his steps (Tobin, 1998:90–91). In contrast, a dancer in Amsterdam is more likely to show off his ability to perform elaborate steps. He may be less concerned about leading his partner and making her look good than in drawing her attention (and that of any onlookers) to his own repertoire of steps. Argentinean *milongueros*, who are more accustomed than their Dutch counterparts to dancing in crowded venues, are often better able to manage the interaction of the floor. While most leaders in Amsterdam are familiar with the rule that they should be dancing in the same counterclockwise direction in order to prevent collisions with other couples, they may be less adept at—or less interested in—adhering to the rules of tango floorcraft. While many men in Amsterdam complain about inconsiderate or unruly male dancers, there is no effective or socially acceptable way to control them. Even the most egregious trespassing rarely evokes more than a bit of mild grumbling, whereas outright displays of aggression in Buenos Aires are not unknown, ranging from verbal assault to vigorous shoving or the well-aimed poke in the ribs when dancers do not observe the *derecho de la pista* (the law of the dance floor). An interesting exception to this, however, was a recent experience I had in which an exuberant dancer stomped on my foot when he backed into me and my partner. I had to sit down until the pain subsided. The man came over to me later to apologize, clearly upset about what had happened. Later I heard that he had posted to a blog on the local tango site to discuss whose fault it had been—his, mine, or my partner's. Thus, while the problem of unruly—or untrained—dancers' disrupting the flow on the dance floor may be inherent to any tango salon, the techniques for managing it vary considerably. In Amsterdam, a reproach is likely to be met with indignation and a "Mind your own business" or "We're all just here to have a good time."

Tango salons in Amsterdam are organized in such a way that they are meant to replicate "tango as it is danced in the salons of Buenos Aires." However, as I have tried to show, those features of Argentinean salons that are regarded as inappropriate for the Dutch context are also altered when necessary to meet the needs of local dancers. Nowhere is this more apparent than in the ways in which "old-fashioned" or "traditional" notions of masculinity and femininity are reworked with an eye to the ubiquitous discourse of equality that pervades gender relations in the Netherlands. While men generally take on the position of leader in tango and often admit privately that they even enjoy being able to "explore [their] macho side," they also express a commitment to gender equality. Many complain about the burdens of having to lead and are sympathetic to the plight of women wallflowers. Women who dance tango indulge in displays of hyperfemininity through their clothing as well as through their mannerisms and are willing—if not always happily—to abandon their initiative in order to follow their partners' lead. However, they resent having to wait to be asked to dance, expect to be able to take the lead from time to time, and are highly critical of men who are overbearing and authoritarian on the dance floor. The (discursive) commitment on the part of both men and women to egalitarian gender relations as well as the absence of clear-cut rules and conventions often make it more difficult to manage the tensions that inevitably emerge between partners than is the case in Buenos Aires with its established salon etiquette. While the gendered tensions need to be negotiated—a point to which I will be returning in later chapters—ultimately they are contained by the tango salon itself. The salon provides a space where it is safe to abandon ordinary personae and playfully engage with one another in ways that are strange, sometimes even exotic, and yet, at the same time, eerily familiar, because they are reminiscent of a past that never was (Cozarinsky, 2007). It is this separation of the salon from ordinary life through its aura of "past-ness" and "elsewhere-ness" that links the tango cultures in Amsterdam and Buenos Aires more firmly than the specific details of seating, clothing, codes or *cabeceos*, or gender regimes could ever do.

But if this is the case, whose tango is it? If tango dancers in Amsterdam are adapting a dance from another time and place in accordance with their own needs, does it make sense to call what they are doing "dancing tango as it is danced in the salons of Buenos Aires"?

Some Reflections on Authenticity

Several years ago, I had just returned from a trip to Buenos Aires and was recounting my salon experiences to a group of tango friends in my home salon in Amsterdam, insisting that they really had to go and find out for themselves. One of my friends, a longtime tango dancer, seemed uneasy with what I had to say. Finally, she announced in an almost apologetic tone that she wasn't sure she wanted to go to Buenos Aires. When I looked surprised, she added, somewhat defensively: "I mean, you can dance tango here, too, can't you? You can dance tango anywhere. I don't *have* to go to Buenos Aires, do I?"

Initially, I found my friend's reaction troubling, but, on second thought, it was also instructive. While it had not been my intention to make her feel uncomfortable, my enthusiastic stories had clearly given rise to her concern that, as a serious tango dancer, she should automatically want to go to Buenos Aires. I had perhaps implied or, in any case, tapped into an unspoken assumption that tango in Buenos Aires is somehow more authentic than and, therefore, preferable to tango in Amsterdam. But why would dancing tango in Amsterdam be any less authentic or less valuable than dancing tango in Buenos Aires? Is the tango that is danced in Amsterdam—or, for that matter, in Berlin, Helsinki, or Istanbul—still the "real thing," and, if not, what is it? And, more to the point, perhaps, what does the "real thing" mean anyway?

Argentina is regarded as the cradle of the tango: as dance, as music, as cultural product, and as an imaginary (Baim, 2007). In 2009, the United Nations Educational, Scientific and Cultural Organization (UNESCO) included tango on its worldwide list of intangible cultural legacies that need to be preserved, protected, and promoted.[20] This in itself underscores that tango is an important symbol of *argentinidad*, of what it means to be Argentinean (Archetti, 1999). This quality is part of what attracts dancers from all over the world to dance tango, allowing them to enter imaginatively the mysterious world of the salon, to dance "tango as it is danced in Buenos Aires." The assumption that the authentic tango is situated in Argentina is what enables Buenos Aires (its historical and symbolic home) to become a kind of mecca for tango dancers. At least one pilgrimage is almost mandatory for anyone who really wants to learn how tango should be danced. This not only encourages serious dancers from different parts of the world to spend their vacations in Buenos Aires. The journey also provides them with a badge of distinction on their return to their home turf. They can situate themselves as part of the "initiated few," superior to those who, by staying at home, can be relegated to the "ignorant masses" (Petridou, 2009:70).

In Amsterdam, the salon culture is saturated by a discourse of authenticity—a discourse that is integral to the self-presentation of the dancers, the organization of the *milongas*, and the interactions among dancers, both on and off the dance floor.[21] It is assumed, for example, that "authentic tango"[22] is danced in a close embrace in a salon, with an eye to an internalized experience of connection between the partners rather than an open style with flashy performances of fancy steps. Dress codes are adopted—at least by some—that mirror styles in Buenos Aires: slit skirts and high heels for the women, black shirts for the men. Salons are decorated with an eye to the past—albeit a highly romanticized notion of the past devoid of any reference to economic disparities or the problematic aftermath of imperialist relations between the North and the South. Music from the Golden Age of tango is imported, along with rituals for organizing the interaction on the dance floor. The knowledge of the *codigos* is adopted and selectively employed to ensure that the *milonga* proceeds smoothly, as well as to instruct and criticize dancers who are either too inexperienced or too narcissistic to dance tango "properly" without causing disruption on the dance floor.

But even the staunchest defenders of authenticity—the ones who insist that tango should be danced in its most pure and unadulterated form—will admit that certain changes invariably need to be made to appease the emancipated and "modern" tastes of an Amsterdam audience. And, indeed, not every dancer wants to dance tango "as it is danced in Buenos Aires." Some consider this to be overly restrictive and based on outmoded gender inequalities. In particular, younger dancers often advocate a more open style of dancing with imaginative steps, playfulness rather than overly serious passion, and a celebration of individuality rather than concern for one's neighbors on the dance floor. They are in favor of experimenting with the music and developing more informal venues for dancing. The modernizers of tango (*nuevos*) situate themselves as a European vanguard, interested in shedding the stuffy traditions of the "old" tango so that it will remain viable and interesting for new generations and a broader, global audience (Villa, 2009). This desire for modernization and transformation, however, remains linked to a discourse of authenticity through the reference to tango's history as a dance that has always changed in the course of its travels. In other words, what is most "authentic" about tango is its capacity to reinvent itself.

What the advocates of traditional tango as well as the moderniz-ers have in common, however, is the unspoken assumption that the "authentic" tango is located firmly in Buenos Aires. Neither side enter-tains the notion that tango as it is danced in Amsterdam might, in fact, be authentic, let alone typically "Dutch" or, for that matter, "European." Dancers in Amsterdam draw upon racialized notions of authentic-ity when they claim that Argentineans have "tango in their blood" or that because they are Latinos they "dance from the heart." By the same token, the sentiment that "we" (Dutch Europeans inhabitants of the "developed" global North) are not "in touch with our bodies" or fear too much "bodily contact" not only dooms "us" to imitation (we are never quite the "real thing") but also further underscores the connec-tions among ethnicity, national belonging (*argentinidad*), and dancing tango.

This, of course, also enables tango dancers outside Buenos Aires to become the modernizers of tango, whose task is to rid tango of its out-moded conventions and transform its choreography and music in ways that will make it more appealing to a new generation of dancers. In con-trast, the Argentineans are stuck in their position as the representatives of "authentic tango"—a tango that is static, unchanging, and frozen in time and place. The discourse of authenticity leaves aside the question of whether tango did, in fact, actually exist in Buenos Aires in the form that is considered "authentic" by Europeans as well as dancers from other parts of the world. It assumes that tango has not changed much in Argentina and that Argentineans simply continue to dance tango the way it used to be danced in the past. And, finally, it imposes the task of dancing tango in its "authentic" version on *porteños*, while dancers from other parts of the world can enjoy the prerogative of choosing to dance tango in the traditional way or transforming it into something new.

But is the way Argentineans approach the "authenticity" of tango really so different?

Most Argentineans embrace tango as their own, even if they do not actually dance it.[23] However, this "ownership" is—and has always been—complicated by Argentina's fraught relationship with Europe, its tendency to view itself through European eyes and measure itself according to European ideals (Kaminsky, 2008). At different moments in time, Argentineans have celebrated tango as the pinnacle of their culture, rejected it as an inadequate representative of their achievements, and recovered and exploited it to their own financial and cultural ends (Baim, 2007; Cozarinski, 2007). In the context of the most recent revival and the dramatic rise of tango tourism, Argentineans took up tango, once again, this time, however, adopting a rather pragmatic approach. Tango is separated into its "home" variant, the authentic tango danced by ordinary folks on local dance floors in accordance with a traditional codes, and its commodified "export" variant, which financially exploits hyper-erotic staged performances of tango danced by professionals for foreign audiences (Cara, 2009:438). This conceptualization expresses the desire of contemporary Argentineans to "own" tango, while at the same time accommodating the cultural and financial economies in which they live that make tango a profitable export product.

However, the notion of "home tango" does not resolve the problem of what constitutes authenticity because it is impossible to determine what the "real" tango might look like. Even leaving aside the long history of controversy about tango's origins (see Thompson, 2005; Baim, 2007), a cursory look at the more recent past shows that tango is not danced today the way it once was. The dance, the venues, the *codigos*, and, indeed, the dancers themselves have all undergone radical changes. For example, in the early 1960s tango was an activity that was restricted primarily to family gatherings, community centers, or "clubs." Because it was still considered slightly risqué, it was common for young, unmarried women to be escorted to dances by their mothers. Dancing in these venues proceeded under watchful maternal eyes, with a certain amount of distance being maintained at all times between dance partners.[24] While dancers in Buenos Aires now employ a discourse of authenticity to define the close embrace as the emblem of "traditional" tango,[25] the close embrace is a relatively recent phenomenon, at least in respectable society (Savigliano, 1995). To further complicate matters, a new generation of *nuevo* and queer dancers in Buenos Aires has appropriated the more open style of dancing that was favored in the past and dubbed it an essential ingredient of their strategy to modernize the tango. In short, as in Amsterdam, both traditionalists and modernists employ notions of authenticity that have little real connection to tango's actual history.

The salons in Buenos Aires have changed dramatically over time as well. Even those venues that now claim to be the most "traditional" are, in fact, of fairly recent origin, initiated in the wake of the tango revival of the late 1980s. The current state of affairs in which married and single women now go to salons in Buenos Aires unescorted and sit by themselves is less a matter of old-fashioned separation of the sexes than a product of processes of modernization and gender emancipation. In this sense, Argentina is not any different from Amsterdam or other parts of the world. While Argentinean women may, like their European counterparts, advocate the hierarchical ordering of the salon as the way "real" tango is danced and willingly submit to hours of waiting until a *milonguero* asks them to dance ("wallflowering"), they are also likely to complain vociferously about relations between the sexes, and few would be prepared to accept macho behavior outside the salon (Savigliano, 1995; Taylor, 1998). Argentinean men display a similarly ambivalent stance toward "tradition." As Tobin (1998) has astutely demonstrated in his ethnography of the salon, many of the jokes that *milongueros* make about machismo are possible only in a context in which middle-class men need to distance themselves from a patriarchal past and establish themselves as suitably modern and enlightened.

In conclusion, notions of authenticity are mobilized in both Buenos Aires and Amsterdam, albeit in different ways. In Amsterdam, authenticity is discursively linked to place—the "salons of Buenos Aires." When dancers in Amsterdam dance "authentic tango," they imaginatively enter an exotic space far away from their everyday lives. In Buenos Aires, where the *argentinidad* of tango is taken for granted, authenticity is linked to a notion of the past and how tango used to be danced. When dancers in Buenos Aires dance authentic tango, they do not,

however, replicate a real past; rather, they are reenacting a sense of past-
ness outside of history in the present (Cozarinsky, 2007:40). Thus, in
both cases, discourses of authenticity enable dancers to escape the realities of the present and enter a space that is neither "now" nor "then,"
neither "here" nor "there"—as the well-known Argentinean writer Jorge
Borges famously put it—to live in the now, the then, and the future.
It is in this timeless space or this moment without a place where it is
possible to experience nostalgia for all that one has lost, while at the
same time being connected in an intensely and highly embodied way to
another person. It is "more pure than pure" (Kešić, 2012).

2

Tango Passion

Probably the most famous tango scene in the history of film appeared in *The Four Horsemen of the Apocalypse* (1921) when silent movie heart-throb Rudolph Valentino danced with darkly beautiful Beatrice Domínguez. The setting is a smoke-filled cabaret in the Boca quarter of Buenos Aires, full of leering, drunken men. He is dressed as a *gaucho*,[1] thereby representing rough, macho masculinity, while she is exotically attired in an embroidered Spanish shawl with a carnation in her hair. The dance is highly stylized and overtly sexual, with lots of glides, entangled legs, and passionate bending and swaying. Valentino has "stolen" Domínguez from her companion and he is showing off, reveling in his rival's anger. The other men display a mixture of awe and jealousy. The dance ends in a passionate kiss, which she resists. Valentino pushes her away in disgust, and she lands on the floor at his feet "in an ambivalent gesture of hatred and rapture" (Savigliano, 1995:134). This scene, which has been recycled in many more cinematic tango performances, has become emblematic for how we imagine tango.[2]

What these renditions of tango on screen have in common is the performance of passion. We see the passion in the long and sensuous way the partners gaze into each other's eyes, in the cat-and-mouse moves of approach and retreat, the teasing playfulness. We see it in the aggressive edge of the male dancer. And we see it in the woman's weak attempts to resist and in her ultimate—if ambivalent—acquiescence to being conquered by a macho man.

Passion belongs to our common sense of what tango is about. The notion that tango is about passion is integral to how it is represented— not only in films but also in the media, in performances, and in tango shows. Professional performances of tango can be found on the Internet

Figure 2.1. Rudolph Valentino dancing tango with Beatrice Domínguez in the silent film *The Four Horsemen of the Apocalypse* (1921, dir. Rex Ingram).

or in dance festivals where tango couples engage in exuberant displays of eroticism.[3] These representations draw upon universal conventions of passion, capitalizing on the explicit, the explosive, and the provocative aspects of the dance. The dance begins with the couples sensuously walking toward the center of the dance floor and sizing each other up before entering each other's arms and ends with wild gyrations, kicks, and usually a *sentada* (a brief sitting on the partner's thigh). This is not tango as it is danced in the salons of Buenos Aires; it is tango for export, staged and marketed as a spicy, exotic dance to an international audience of uninitiated outsiders (Cara, 2009).

Export tango sells the notion of tango as a *performance* to undiscriminating tourists as well as to tango dancers across the globe, who eagerly try to emulate this image of passion when they dance. It is not uncommon to see renditions of such overt displays of passion on the dance floors of Europe, where dancers adopt the clothing and moves they have observed in professional performances. Sultry expressions of longing and blatantly seductive movements are the externalized expressions directed at an audience that will then read them as "passionate." While Argentineans at home dance tango "from the heart"— a tango which internalizes passion as an intensely private experience that is reserved for those who have grown up with tango as music and dance—those who have come to tango through its exported renditions appear to be doomed to tango as performance, full of flashy acrobatics and exaggerated eroticism (Cara, 2009:441).

According to Savigliano (1998), this exaggerated performance of passion in tango goes hand in hand with the *politics* of passion. In her view, tango passion is not simply a private experience, but it is entangled in fantasies born of postcolonial economic and cultural power relations. The image of tango as a passionate dance is part of the colonializing gaze that transforms tango with its aura of an exciting and slightly scandalous confrontation with difference into something to be consumed by inhabitants of the global North. Passion is associated with the image of the sexy Latino/a and it is this image that organizes how dancers move, look, feel, and try to *be* when they dance tango. The dramatic steps, the slit skirts and fishnet stockings, and the sultry look are integral to the way many dancers believe tango should be danced. These are the imagined accoutrements of tango that are exported to other parts of the world.

However, the image of tango never quite matches reality. Villa (2001, 2009) analyzes the disjuncture that inevitably emerges between the imaginary of tango and the actual experience of dancing it and discovers that dancers outside Buenos Aires are never quite sure whether what they are feeling is what they are supposed to feel. It is not the imitation of this iconic image of tango passion that brings politics into the equation but rather the would-be *aficionado*'s inability ever to achieve the real thing that is central to the politics of passion. For Villa, this disjuncture is political precisely because it underscores the constructed character of the imaginary and opens up possibilities for experimentation and even transformation. It is here that tango can—and often does—transcend its colonial past and becomes a subversive, (post) modern, and even queer dance.

Tango scholars like Cara, Savigliano, and Villa have—each in their own way—convincingly demonstrate that when people dance tango, performance and politics go hand in hand. By uncovering the ways in which passion is performed in and through tango, they show how much work needs to be done in order for a particular rendition of a dance to be read by both dancers and their audiences as "passionate." As a result of their research, we can begin to appreciate how the political past in which tango is embedded will invariably shape its performance in the present.

As important as their linking of passion to performance and politics is, it is my contention that something important is missing when it comes to understanding tango passion. Even from my own experience in run-of-the-mill tango salons in Amsterdam and Buenos Aires (as well as in other parts of the world), I would argue that the eroticized displays of tango passion as described above and that are part and parcel of most staged tango performances tend to be more the exception than the rule in tango salons. In fact, they are more likely to occur when dancers are inexperienced and anxious to make a good impression, or when professionals try to impress (and recruit) potential pupils. What can be seen more often is considerably less dramatic and more intimate and, indeed, looks very much like what Cara (2009) calls home tango— that is, tango danced "from the heart." Thus, while passion is what many tango dancers are looking for when they dance tango, their passion is perhaps not best conceptualized as an exoticized performance à la Rudolph Valentino. This kind of conceptualization of passion does little to help us understand what it is about tango that makes dancers love to do it. It does not explain why they turn to tango rather than to break-dancing or to the Lindy Hop or even to salsa, dances that are fun and even sexy but that do not have the same cultural connection to "passion" as tango does.[4] Passion must be involved in any dance, but especially one that requires years of arduous lessons to learn and which is so difficult and demanding that many experienced dancers describe it as "bigger than us all." But what is the *experience* of passion exactly, an experience that is so rarely visible on most dance floors, yet so fervently desired by so many tango dancers?

In this chapter, I explore how tango *aficionados* make sense of their passion for tango. What kind of experience is this passion for tango, and how is it generated? And what does a passion for tango mean to the men and women who love to dance it? In exploring these questions, I focus primarily on dancers in Amsterdam. While my Argentinean informants are also passionate about dancing tango, they tend to describe tango dancing, somewhat unhelpfully, as "just something we do," end of story. In contrast, the dancers I spoke with in Amsterdam had lots to tell me about passion, once they got started. They were inclined to approach tango as novices for whom a passion for dancing was a new and decidedly unfamiliar experience that they were still trying to figure out.[5]

In my search for passionate dancers to interview, I did not limit myself to seasoned tango dancers. I often discovered a passion for tango among beginning dancers, who, while stumbling over the steps, displayed the expressions of rapt intensity that I have come to associate with a passion for tango. I could read in their faces the fantasy of what the dance would someday feel like for them. I did look for dancers who regularly visited *milongas* and for whom dancing tango was a significant part of their everyday lives and, in fact, recruited many of my informants, literally, from the dance floor, as I watched them dance and speculated on whether or not they had "it."

Because I wanted to restrict my informants to people who would be passionate about dancing tango, I avoided interviewing those whose involvement in dancing tango was limited to taking the occasional lesson or for whom tango was a casual hobby, something they liked well enough but could easily live without. I also tried to stay away from people who seemed to be frequenting the salons primarily for other reasons than dancing—for example, tango teachers who were recruiting potential students or rounding up dancers for a competing *milonga*, or people who seemed more interested in cruising the *milongas* for potential sexual partners than in dancing tango, although obviously there was some overlap there.[6]

My informants were fairly equally divided between men and women, ranging in age from twenty-three to sixty-seven, with the average age around forty-five. This corresponds with the demography of most European dance communities.[7] The age group of thirty-somethings is the most underrepresented in the tango scene, probably because starting a family and taking care of young children makes a serious commitment to the salon culture difficult. More than two-thirds of my informants were single, divorced, or widowed. While the majority were white, middle-class, ethnic Dutch, a substantial number came from families with immigration backgrounds, something that was often mentioned in the course of the interviews. This was the case when, for example, a dancer would refer to her Spanish background as a reason for liking tango music or a dancer would trace his involvement in tango to the "nostalgic streak" he inherited from his Russian grandparents. I have changed the names and other identifying features of my informants except in cases where they asked explicitly to appear in this book under their own names.[8]

I spoke with tango dancers in their homes, in my home, or in noisy cafés where we met before heading to the *milonga* to dance. As word spread through the local tango scene that I was interested in interviewing dancers, many people came up to me in the *milongas* and asked whether I would like to interview them. It is not surprising that I had no shortage of opportunities to conduct interviews because, after all, I was asking people to talk about the thing they most loved to do. What is more surprising is that I, as a researcher, never reached the "saturation point" that I have learned to expect in any qualitative research inquiry— that is, the point at which the interviews do not produce anything new and the researcher knows she has enough material and it is time to stop (Glaser and Strauss, 1967). That there was no saturation point in the present inquiry reflects the topic of passion itself, which automatically seems to elicit a longing for more. I continued to do interviews well into the final stages of writing this book, and, indeed, even now, as I put the finishing touches on this chapter, I have no sense that the last word has been said about tango passion.

Although my informants were invariably eager to talk about their passion for tango, it was not always easy for them to find the right words to describe their experiences. Dance scholars have long been familiar with the difficulties dancers have in articulating verbally what dancing means to them (Ward, 1997). What the experience of dancing means to a dancer resists being put into words. For example, when I asked informants how it felt or what they liked about dancing tango, they would say something like "Hmmm, let's see" or "That's hard, I don't know how to explain it" or "I just feel it." Many would put on tango music during our conversations to help them talk about their dance experiences. Some would jump up in the middle of the interview to show me a particular posture or movement. Several even began to cry when remembering a specific dance or a particular partner and then proceed to tell me how their dance experience resonated with the death of a parent or spouse, a divorce, or just missing their homeland. Tango passion is irrevocably embodied,[9] and making sense of it requires that the dancer imaginatively enter his or her body in order to put into words how it feels to be in an embrace, to listen to the music, to translate the music into movement, and, last but not least, to coordinate these movements with one's partner, connecting with each other and together with the music. It is not that the dancers did not know what they were experiencing. On the contrary, they knew all too well. They merely needed to find ways to talk about embodied experience "where a practice emerges as an invisible constellation of sensations, meanings, and action" (Wacquant, 2005:466) and express discursively something that was deeply felt but difficult to describe.

The experience of tango passion begins when two people hear the music, enter an embrace, and engage in a dialogue without words, and it ends with connection. This connection—between the partners and with the music—constitutes the *cuerpo de baile*, which means, literally, the "body of the tango." It is what makes tango more than just two people moving together, creating instead a "rich, multi-faceted—albeit temporary—relationship between souls" (Olszewski, 2008:69). Connection is what most *aficionados* desire and hope to achieve when they dance tango. It is the essence of the experience of tango passion, and it is also elusive and fragile. When all is said and done, there are no guarantees that a dance will lead to a passionate experience, and, indeed, many dancers dance tango without it.

Experiencing Tango Passion

It may take two to tango, as the saying goes, but the experience of passion involves more. As the philosopher and dance scholar Erin Manning (2007) describes it, tango is

> an exchange that depends on the closeness of two bodies willing to engage with one another. It is a pact for three minutes, a sensual

encounter that guarantees nothing but a listening. And this listening must happen on both sides, for a lead is meaningless if it does not
convey a response from a follower. As various tango aficionados have
pointed out, the lead can never be more than an invitation, as a result of
which the movement in response will remain improvised. This dialogue
is rich and complex, closer to the heart, perhaps, than many exchanges
between strangers and lovers. (p. 4)

In this formulation, Manning emphasizes tango as a transitory
encounter in which the outcome cannot be predicted. There are no set
sequences of steps or fixed choreographies in tango. The dance begins
when two separate bodies agree to come together, touch each other,
and listen to the music together. There are no guarantees that this will
result in a memorable dance experience. Instead, the process is paradoxically as unpredictable as it is carefully orchestrated. Each dancer
has her or his specific role to play. If they approach each other with an
eye to creating a momentary relationship through the dance by listening intently to each other's bodies, chances are they will dance beautifully together. If not, they will have difficulty "finding" each other at all
(Manning, 2007:88). Thus, it is only through listening and responding
to each other that they can create an encounter which is so intense that
it can be called "passion."

Music

Music is integral to what makes tango a passionate encounter. While
tango begins for most Argentineans with the music, for many Europeans tango music is an acquired taste. It is not music we have grown up
with, and its lyrics are incomprehensible even to a Spanish speaker.[10] It
is something we have to learn to appreciate. However, once a dancer
has become serious about tango, the music plays an essential part in the
experience of the dance.

Almost every dancer will recognize how it feels to hear the first
strains of a tango song before entering the salon. Your heart begins to
beat faster; your breath quickens. You clutch your shoe bag with a feeling of excited anticipation, but also some nervous apprehension. The
faint, oh-so-familiar music in the distance, slightly scratchy with a

whiny male voice, is full of Golden Age nostalgia, all melancholy, unrequited love, and longing. It is exactly this moment, a moment which is integral to a passion for tango, that makes many tango dancers feel—paradoxically, immediately, irrevocably, and in the most embodied possible way—at home.

How is it possible that music from another place and another time has the capacity to affect one so strongly? For Argentineans, tango is part of their everyday experience. It belongs to the "hearts and minds" of the people (Ulla, 1982; Archetti, 1999). It is something they have grown up hearing. If they belong to the generation that came of age during the 1960s, they probably wouldn't dream of dancing it. However, they would remember hearing their mother singing the lyrics while cooking dinner or seeing their parents or grandparents dancing it. They would have listened to the music on the radio, and many would know the lyrics by heart. Most Argentineans are proud of the poetical nature of tango lyrics. Unlike other forms of popular music, tango lyrics are considered works of art in their own right, unparalleled in Latin American literature. As literary and musical form, tango is part of the national identity: "Nobody could be a good Argentinean without it" (Soriano, 1987:140, quoted in Archetti, 1999:143). Tango speaks to the nostalgia for and sadness of the past as well as the dramatic experiences and frustration of the present in a way that makes sense to Argentineans (Cozarinsky, 2007).

But what does this music mean to dancers who were not born in Argentina? An example of how tango music can strike a chord in someone from a very different culture and context is provided by Marcus, a fifty-three-year-old physician, who started dancing tango ten years ago and since then has "never looked back." He explains how tango music "pulls [him] in" and makes it impossible for him *not* to dance. "There is something really almost *violent* about it. I don't know what else to call it." It "harmonizes with my bio-rhythms." When I asked him what that means, he told me that he is a second-generation child of Hungarian parents. As a child, he danced the *czárdás*, a Hungarian folk dance that has the same intensity and fierceness he associates with tango. As he puts it, tango "connected me with something really deep inside myself, with a rhythm that was natural for me and which I know is not *western* and also not *Dutch*" (his emphasis). The fact that he took his first tango lessons from two political refugees from Argentina resonated with his own family history—his father's exile during the dictatorship in Hungary and the family stories of his uncle's imprisonment after the 1956 uprising. Listening to tango music tapped into Marcus's own feelings of being an outsider and his longing for a sense of home.

Not all of my informants had backgrounds of displacement or immigration like Marcus. However, they invariably noted that the music resonated with deeply felt emotions that they linked to experiences in their lives—a dying parent, a recent bout with cancer, an unhappy love affair or divorce, repeated migrations. One of my informants recalled dancing with a young woman who suddenly began to cry while they were dancing. She later explained, smiling somewhat sheepishly, that the music reminded her of her first love. Tango music evokes sadness, and the dance provides a space where the expression of sadness is permissible and doesn't have to be explained. Or, as Discepolo, one of the most famous tango lyricists, once wrote, "a sad thought danced" (Thompson, 2005:26).

Embrace

Dancing tango requires more than an embodied connection with the music, however. It involves two bodies' coming together in an embrace. The embrace is what sets tango apart from other couple dances in which partners dance on their own or follow each other's movements without actually touching. Even when partners dance with some distance between them (open style), tango always involves an embrace, a physical connection, or, as one of my informants put it, "Tango is about giving another person a hug."

What does it feel like to enter this embrace? To begin with, one is immediately assailed with smells: a whiff of perfume or after-shave, the fragrance of shampoo, a minty odor of toothpaste, the smell of a freshly laundered shirt. How someone smells sets the stage for the dance. Many informants complained about partners who hadn't used deodorant, wore shirts that stank of old sweat ("Oh, god, the same shirt he wore last time"), or had just consumed a meal with lots of garlic and red wine. For some, how a partner smells is the bottom line: "I'm not going to surrender myself to someone who doesn't smell good. If it doesn't

Figure 2.2. Embrace. (Photo: Mirjam van Niel.)

smell good when I go into his arms, I just leave." Smell is, however, not
the only sense involved. Sound, touch, and, to a lesser degree, sight are
also factors.[11] Partners can hear each other's breathing, feel each other's
hearts beating. They sense skin against skin, the tickle of a strand of
hair or the prickle of an unshaven cheek, sweating hands, the sharpness
of shoulder blades under one's hand, the cushiony feel of a stomach or
breasts as bodies lean together. Once the dance begins, there is the feeling of muscles moving, a leg against one's own, the almost imperceptible
sighs of delight, a sudden gasp at a misstep or an appreciative chuckle
at an unexpected move. This is an intimacy without words (although
occasionally a dancer may sing the lyrics of a tango gently into the ear
of his or her partner).

In the close embrace of traditional salon tango, bodies form a trian-
gle, leaving the feet free to do steps. The partners turn as if they are on
a single axis, with communication occurring through the chest. They
dance cheek-to-cheek, the woman's[12] left arm resting across the shoulders of her partner, who cradles her firmly but gently with his right arm,
grasping her right hand at eye level.[13] The embrace is the beginning. It

brings two separate embodied individuals together so that they can begin dancing as one body to the music.

It is not easy to enter a tango embrace, however. Adele, a forty-nine-year-old photographer, remembered needing six months just to get up her courage. She had already fallen in love with the music and watched people dancing, and she was sure that she wanted to learn it. But, as she put it, "It was just too intimate. . . . I knew that it was about intimacy, not just about being touched, and I had to know that I was ready for that. . . . You have to want and accept intimacy; otherwise there is no point in learning tango."

The intimacy of the embrace is precisely what puts some people off tango dancing. As Nicolas, an engineer and fervent tango dancer, put it, it's so completely "un-Dutch" to get that close to another person. He describes conversations with his colleagues ("all nerds") about his passion for tango. "They look at me as if I were talking about Mars. If I were to say to one of them, 'Come into my arms,' they would drop dead of shock!" For Nicolas, it is a constant source of amazement that a perfect stranger would be "willing to enter your circle," to trespass into the space that conventionally separates people in social interaction.

The success of an embrace involves holding (or being held) in a way that feels right. Many of the women I spoke with described being held too tightly, having "the breath squeezed out of you" or "feeling like you are being pressed into a cage." Miranda, a divorcée in her early fifties, laughingly complained about dancers who "take you in their arms as if you were one of those inflatable dolls and fling you around the dance floor. They don't even need a real person."[14] Others send out mixed signals ("Come closer. . . . No, stay back"), indicating ambivalence about being embraced. Or they may need a few dances to get used to the physicality of the embrace, before they can enter into it. Many of my male informants described the embrace in similar terms, noting that they can feel the moment that their partner stops being tense and begins to relax. "It's as if she's saying, 'OK, now I'm ready. We can do this together now.'"

But what is a "good" embrace? Is it enough to feel comfortable in a partner's arms? Is being able to pick up each other's signals sufficient for a satisfactory embrace? Or is something more mysterious or elusive involved? According to Klein and Haller (2009), the embrace is essential to the experience of tango because this is where "presence" is transmitted—that is, the sense of a special connection that takes both partners out of their everyday lives (see also Bourdieu, 1996). It enables them to feel that they are both completely invested in the moment and prepared to bring themselves into the activity of the dance.

For Avi, a student who works with horses during his summer break, presence is a bodily awareness that allows the dancer to be clear about what he wants from his partner. To my surprise, he explained what he meant by comparing presence in tango with trying to get a horse ("500 kilos of muscle") to move. "You can't talk to the horse, so you have to be very clear with your body. You have to show the horse: 'I want to go there and I'm going to come into your space and I don't want you to kick me.'" Laughing, he added that he had already been dancing for months before he made this—admittedly—somewhat unexpected connection. However, it was "really cool" because he discovered that he could lead his partner in any direction he wanted. "That's when my teacher came up to me and said, 'You've got it!'"

From the first moment of the embrace, both leaders and followers sense whether they are sufficiently present to make the dance work. This is an embodied sensation that occurs without a word being said. The embrace conveys the sense of being free of all distractions, able to leave everything else behind. As experience, it resembles meditation. Or, as Chia, a yoga teacher and single mother of two, puts it, a good embrace allows you to be "totally in tune with yourself, free to *be* yourself. You are able to let go, and, at the same time, you are totally together with the other person." While the sensation has decidedly gendered undertones—for example, the follower needs to convey receptiveness to being led and the leader a willingness to lead—the desire to be together in the moment is quite similar. Liz, a divorced hairdresser in her mid-fifties, explains, "You can always feel whether a man is willing to zoom in on you. . . . If that willingness isn't there, I'm pretty much finished after one dance." She translates the sensation that her partner is "there" in the moment into his "being there for her," and this is precisely what is embodied through the embrace. The embrace enables both partners to *feel* their mutual desire to dance together. For Nicolas, too, the feeling that the partner is really "there" for him is what makes him want to dance:

It's more important than whether she is a good dancer. In fact, I don't even think that is important. Sure, a plus factor, it can make the dance more pleasant, but what is most important is that she does everything so that you feel she wants to dance with you . . . with you, together in the music. Without that intimacy, you are just two single people whirling around the dance floor. That doesn't do anything for me.

Dialogue

The embrace may be the starting point, but in order to be able to dance, partners have to find a way to communicate with each other. Tango requires a constant dialogue—a dialogue without words. Finding a way to understand each other, to encounter each other through the dance, is part and parcel of what the experience of tango passion is all about.

Unlike ballroom dancing, tango does not involve a fixed choreography of steps. While dancers learn some basic steps, each dance has to be improvised. It emerges from scratch, developing in that particular moment, in response to the music, through the coordinated activities of both partners. With each dance, partners embark on a process of discovering a common interpretation of the music and translating it into movement. The movement of the dance is initiated by a lead, a direction, an opening to which the follower responds. The leader will have to draw upon a repertoire of steps—translating in a split second what he (or she) hears into what he is able to do with his feet. It is not enough to provide a lead, however. He must also find a way to entice his partner into accepting his invitation.

The dialogue begins with discovering what one's partner can or cannot do, a process that occurs in the first few minutes of the dance. Marcus describes this as trying to figure out his partner's energy level and matching his own level of energy to hers:

Some women react well to a strong impulse, otherwise nothing happens. But there are also women where that is the last thing you should do. Beginning the dance is a process of taking a step and waiting, another step, maybe something fancy, and then more waiting. Then, I think: "OK, that's it." Then I can do more. If it's good, then I also get some countermovement. There's some tension and then I think: "OK, *now* we can dance."

At first glance, it would seem that the dialogue between the leader and the follower is where differences—invariably marked by gender and other axes of inequality—are bound to come to the fore. However, this is more ambivalent than one might expect. For example, the follower can set the tone by indicating how she would like to dance. Leo, a lawyer in his mid-sixties, recalled the first time he visited a salon in Buenos Aires and how he screwed up his courage to ask a well-known older *milonguera* to dance. Worried about meeting her expectations, he began by embracing her somewhat gingerly. As soon as the first dance was finished, she surprised him by giving his hand a firm squeeze, as if to say, "OK, that was fine for starters. But who do you think you are dancing with? Could we have a little more *pizzazz* now?"

For many men, their ideal dancer is so alert and focused that she can "read" their emotions without their having to say anything. The ideal female dancer is "light": She relaxes and allows herself to be carried, moving "in response to the improvised, imaginative, inspired move of her partner, thus contributing to his creative freedom" (Carozzi, 2013:28). As Leo put it, thinking about his favorite kind of partner: "She just knows everything I'm thinking and feeling. We don't have to talk."

While this seems, at first glance, to freeze the follower into a feminized position of passivity, this is not entirely the case. The leader cannot force his partner to do what he wants; he can only offer an invitation. She may accept the invitation. But, then again, she may not. Many of my informants explained that accepting a leader's invitation was easier said than done. Being able to follow is complicated, requiring months and even years of painstaking effort and practice to learn. As Miranda, an experienced tango dancer, puts it, "For a lot of women—at least, emancipated women—the hardest thing is to set your own initiative aside. That was the first thing I had to learn as follower. Not to take any initiative at all." Following entails constantly instructing the various parts of the body to relax, to wait, to be alert to the partner's signals. It is about unlearning one's impulse to act and to become, as Carozzi (2013) puts it, "light."

For women who are experienced dancers, the perfect dialogue means being able to close one's eyes and "sense your partner's movement before he makes it." It is not simply a matter of banishing one's own initiative but rather of engaging in a conversation. A follower can influence the interaction by slowing a dance down, interjecting playful embellishments with her feet, or moderating the intensity of the dance. She can refuse some of her partner's invitations or entice him into a different direction. She can make herself as light as a feather ("walking on cat's feet") or fit herself so closely to his bodily movements that he will feel as though he were "dancing with a glove on." She can let him know at the beginning that she is going to "give him a run for his money." But she can also let him understand that she is tired and just wants to be rocked gently to sleep.

This dialogue depends upon partners—regardless of their gender, age, or social background—being tuned into each other and the possibilities they have together. It is precisely at this point that the dialogue most often breaks down. Many of my male informants complained about partners who just "go off on their own," making them feel powerless as leaders. When that happens, there is nothing more they can do. While many experienced leaders do not mind dancing with a novice, the condition is that she can "let herself go." As one informant explained, "If she's able to follow, I can get her to do things she never dreamed she could do." Of course, some leaders may try to prevent misunderstandings in the dialogue by resorting to verbal instructions ("Let's try a *gancho*,[15] shall we?"). While this may ensure the successful execution of a particular step, it is not conducive to a passionate encounter on the dance floor. Discovering how to communicate without words and finding ways to make adjustments through the process of dancing itself are part of the process. Eva, a web designer in her late thirties, recalled how irritating it was for her, as a beginning dancer, when her partners insisted on telling her how she should be dancing or providing instructions. "That's the way to make me feel insecure. Totally unsafe."

While some older, experienced male dancers may attempt to "educate" younger, inexperienced women, as a strategy this backfires as soon as their partners develop confidence in their own ability to dance. Many women view such behavior as a power game, a display of dominance, rather than as a dialogue that emerges in and through the dance itself. Rosemary, a nurse practitioner in her mid-fifties who has been dancing tango for more than ten years, realized that she was becoming "just really, really fed up with men who want to put me in a box." Laughing,

Figure 2.3. Dialogue. (Photo: Mirjam van Niel.)

she adds, "Please, just give me some space. I'm still here. . . . Look, if someone tries to silence me, it's not going to work. I need space to enjoy the dance." This does not mean that she wants to abandon the division between leading and following. A strong leader is welcome, particularly at the beginning of a dance, so that the steps work. However, "There always comes a point when I start thinking, 'You've got to give me some space.' I don't want to feel limited by the boundaries he sets."

Tango involves a dialogue between two differently positioned dancers. One partner invites and the other responds, yet the movement itself should feel like something they develop together. Inevitably, the process of coming together across differences entails transgressing the boundaries of each individual. For this reason, tango invites not only intimacy, even tenderness, and mutual passion, but it is also a potential source of tension and conflict. At its worst, it feeds "an already troubled relationship between self and other, woman and man, leader and follower" (Manning, 2007:4–5).

As Savigliano (2010:139) puts it, tango produces antagonisms which are aggravated by already existing differences and hierarchies of power. The resentments and impossibilities that are part and parcel of heterosexual love invariably crop up and have to be dealt with in tango. If the leader tries to control the movements of his partner rather than invite her to take up his lead, she will be forced to follow him mechanically rather than engage in a mutual and creative dialogue. If the follower refuses to accept the lead or goes off on her own tangent, the dialogic character of the dance is disrupted as well. Through the dialogue between the dancers, these antagonisms are negotiated, invitations made and rejected, confrontations met or avoided. Leading and following require a delicate balancing act in which both partners have to reach across the multiple differences that divide them in order to create an experience of one-ness. The passion of this encounter emerges precisely because these differences are neither dissolved nor abandoned but rather momentarily transcended in a wordless, mutually sustained, and perfectly calibrated dialogue.

Connection

When tango works, it creates a unique connection. Dancers' bodies not only have to fit together in terms of their size and posture; they are required to move together in response to the music. There has to be a dissolving of the physical boundaries of two separate bodies. It is this "unique kinesthetic connection" (Olszewski, 2008:63) which engenders the "tango feeling" that dancers are looking for, the thing that makes a "good dance." Connection is the embodiment of tango passion. Or, as Marcus put it, "Connection, connection, connection . . . that's what tango is about."

Every dancer I interviewed spoke of the physical sensation of connection as becoming one body with their partner, one organism moving in synchrony to the music: "You become a monster with four legs." The connection is described by even the most prosaic and down-to-earth of my informants with words like "pure," "total," and "sublime." This sense of perfection is predicated on each person's relinquishing his or her personal boundaries, accepting a loss of self in order to become one with the other. For example, Jasper, a divorced man working as an urban planner for the city government, explained that connection is "opening up your heart to another person. It's like giving up all your secrets to her. Total exposure. It's . . . I don't know how else to put it. It's drastic. It's a relationship between souls, not just bodies."

Figure 2.4. Connection. (Photo: Mirjam van Niel.)

Connection in tango evokes an intimacy different from what one normally experiences in everyday life. Many dancers describe how the connection makes their ordinary concerns—grocery shopping, problems at work, having to catch the next train—disappear. "It all vanishes because in this moment you are totally connected to your partner. You just let go—it's like floating over the floor, together with this other person. That's all that seems to matter." Renate, a naturopathic healer in her late forties, compared the connection of tango to being rocked—an image that appeared in interviews with other dancers as well. It evokes a deeply felt and gender-transcendent longing to return to the arms of the mother and, in this way, to reinstate a lost sense of one-ness with another.

Connection is not something that is there from the beginning. Most dancers remember the first time they experienced it as the moment when "everything came together" and they realized what tango is all about. Danny, a performance artist in his mid-forties, told me that he had already been dancing for more than a year with the same woman, taking classes together and practicing steps, when it suddenly happened. They just stared at each other in amazement:

It was *so* intimate! How weird that I can be this intimate with you (I thought)! . . . I think this is what makes it so addictive; it's what we all want. We don't act this way normally, on the street . . . with people we don't know. But in tango, you can be so vulnerable, you *have* to be vulnerable, otherwise it doesn't work. You have to open your heart. And I think that's what we all want.

This intimate connection can happen with a familiar partner—as in Danny's case—but it can also happen with a perfect stranger. Indeed, many dancers were particularly awestruck by having the experience of connection with a stranger—with a person they had never seen before (and would probably never see again), or with whom they had never shared a single word or an experience outside the moment of the dance. Many dancers have embodied memories of this kind of connection. They remember dancing with someone many years ago in a strange city without knowing his or her name or even having a conversation. Yet they can still recall exactly how the person's body felt, what it was like to move with him or her to the music. The sensation of dancing with this person is relived, again and again over the years, never ceasing to surprise. The memory of a single dance can evoke a sense of connection more visceral than what they experience with friends and family whom they have known and loved for many years. The memory of a remarkable connection with a person they do not know and will probably never even see again remains imprinted on the body.

Tango dancers—regardless of gender or age or social background—invariably look for the perfect dance, the ultimate dance, the dance in which they will experience a connection with their partner with no holds barred. This is the dance in which everything—the music, the sense of being one's self, the embodied connection of the embrace, the wordless communication between the partners—comes together. Joachim, a single man in his mid-thirties, described for me his "perfect dance" in the following way:

It's when the music finishes and you don't want to leave the embrace. You were dancing, something different happened, something magic, and then it stopped. It was perfect and then it's finished. The perfect dance? You only know it was perfect when you leave it.

It is in the transitory quality of the perfect dance that an essential—and, perhaps, the most important—feature of the tango connection emerges. Connection is not only about coming together and becoming one with the other in the music. It is also about leaving. Nowhere is this more perfectly illustrated than in Samantha's story. Samantha, an attractive guidance counselor in her early forties, became interested in tango after an unhappy breakup. She enjoyed dancing, but for several years she was, as she put it, "just having fun. It didn't mean that much to me." She had heard other people talk about the "perfect dance" but had never experienced anything like that herself. And, then, unexpectedly, it happened—the dance that everyone was talking about, when everything came together.

> It was wonderful. Fantastic. But, you know, at the same time, it made me really sad because it was also like saying good-bye. I realized that I would never be able to expect this again. I couldn't ask this man to dance with me again and be sure that I would have the same experience. That's not how it works in the tango. It was the most wonderful moment, but it was also the saddest.

Taken together, the music, the embrace, the dialogue, and the connection produce the experience of passion in tango. As experience, this passion is not the same as the excitement of a sexual encounter or the butterflies-in-the-stomach sensation of being in love. What makes tango different is that it potentially allows dancers to enter what Turner (1964/1987) has called a state of liminality. They find themselves balancing on the threshold between the old (their ordinary lives and personae and social arrangements) and the new (a connection that is like no other, and yet doomed to be over in a few minutes). This experience of transcendence—of being "betwixt and between"—is what permits partners who are separate in so many ways to come together in a harmony that is unimaginable in most other areas of their everyday lives. It seems to encompass all one's most innermost hopes and dreams, making it feel like the "moment one has been waiting for all one's life" (Benzecry, 2010:5). At the same time, tango passion is, paradoxically, the saddest of all possible experiences because it is about leaving, loss, and the end of a perfect moment. The paradox of tango passion is that, in order for one to be able to surrender to it, it has to be kept within the boundaries.

Passion and Its Boundaries

Tango passion is always a bit unruly, constantly threatening to transgress the confines of the dance. For this reason, people who dance tango have to find ways to manage the feelings that tango can generate and keep their passion under control—at least for the duration of the dance, but sometimes even after the dance is over. Passion depends upon boundaries' being set if it is to be pleasurably intense, but not so intense that it will spoil the dance itself.

Nearly every dancer I spoke with, whether single or partnered, looking for a relationship or anxious to avoid commitment, acknowledged that there have to be limits to how far one can go in tango. In the midst of the most lyrical and exuberant descriptions of perfect dance moments and unforgettable dance partners, a small—often humorous—footnote would appear. For example, a dancer might compare a great dance to an orgasm, only to then assure me, "It's not a sexual one, of course." Or a dancer might describe the intimacy of a dance as "pure," "total," "perfect," or "like nothing else, ever," only to add something like "but, thank God, you don't have to crawl into bed with your partner at the end of the *milonga*." Or a dancer might insist that "tango is the perfect relationship, but it's a *mini, mini* relationship." Dancing tango is "like falling in love, but only for fifteen minutes."

As we saw in the previous chapter, the organization of the salon can facilitate the enablement and constraint of tango passion. The codes set boundaries which allow dancers to manage the tensions that are part and parcel of dancing tango: closeness and distance, connection and separation, intimacy and anonymity, the pure and the mundane. Dancers can connect in a close embrace, knowing that they will have to separate and return to their seats as soon as the *cortina* begins. They can surrender themselves with abandon because the etiquette of the salon will protect them from unwanted intimacies. They can experience the encounter as perfect and unique, precisely because they know it will be limited to the moment of the dance and will not spill over into their everyday lives. As one of my informants put it, "You fall in love with your partner, not as a person, but as a dancer, in the dance, in that moment."

It is, of course, not always easy in actual practice to manage these boundaries. Tango is a sensual dance, and the line between dance passion and a seductive preliminary to a sexual encounter is not always clear. Dancing in a close embrace can be confusing, provoking anything from inopportune erections to unwanted advances. It, therefore, requires an ongoing negotiation of boundaries, whereby each dancer has to calibrate how much distance or nearness he or she feels comfortable with. For example, Avi explained that he found it "hard to get that close to another person without it meaning stuff." Dancers who have difficulties keeping sex out of the dance may opt for a less intimate style of dancing tango in which both partners maintain some distance by dancing "in their own axes" rather than leaning into the embrace as is done in more traditional forms of tango.[16] But even if partners do not opt for a close embrace, they still will need to find ways to neutralize sexuality during the dance. Some dancers enjoy flirting during a *tanda*, but most will feel uncomfortable if their partner touches them inappropriately or becomes overtly sexual while dancing. A hand placed too close to a breast or a leg wrapped too tightly around a partner's leg can feel intrusive rather than intimate. As one of my male informants put it, "Dancing tango is not about having sex with your partner. It's a game of seduction. You're not trying to reach some particular goal, but just playing with the possibility."

Obviously, not every dancer may be able to or even want to keep the boundaries intact, or, at least, not all the time. Many dancers do socialize with each other outside the *milonga*. Others embark on sexual affairs with people they have met through dancing. Some even develop intimate relationships with their dance partners. However, crossing the line between passion in the dance and passion in everyday life does not come without a price. For example, Helene, an attractive divorced journalist, fell in love with one of her favorite dance partners. At first, having a relationship with him made their dancing even better. "I felt like I was in heaven," she said. However, after several months, the problems began. He didn't like her dancing with other men and made a fuss every time she went to a salon on her own. Initially, Helene accepted his behavior because, as she put it, "Tango is such a dance of passion, there's a lot of sensuality there and that can wake up a person's jealousy." However, to her dismay, what was much more difficult to accept was that she no longer liked dancing with him as much after they had become partners in real life:

You dance with the same man and he always dances the same. You get bored [laughs]. End of story. You start wanting another man who will seduce you all over again. And it's the same for men, you know. Who wants to dance with his wife all the time?

Danny, who lives with his longtime partner and two children, came to a similar conclusion:

Would I want to dance with my closest friend? Or with my partner, even? No. No, not really. . . . It's almost like you need to keep things separate. You need to hold on to the anonymity so that tango can stay pure.

For both Helene and Danny, having too close a relationship with one's dance partner changes the quality of the dancing, paradoxically making it less rather than more passionate.

In this chapter, we have seen how the intimacy of an embrace, the wordless dialogue between two differently situated people, and the intensity of a connection form the ingredients of passion in tango. This is what enables the unique experience of coming together, losing oneself, and finding another person in a transcendent moment outside time and space. In order for it to succeed, however, both partners need to take measures—however reluctantly—to cordon off this experience from the distractions of sexuality, the conflicts of relationships, and the demands of their everyday lives. Or, as Savigliano (2003:162) puts it, it is precisely this paradoxical state of abandoning oneself to the moment and yet remaining in control that is tango's *sine qua non*. This is what allows dancers to have their cake and eat it, too.

An Afterthought

As I was thinking about how to finish this chapter and pull together the strands of passion as performance, experience, and politics, I remembered the following incident.

I was sitting in a *milonga* in Buenos Aires. The music of Oswaldo Pugliese,[17] which is supposed to be the epitome of passion, was playing. This music is extremely slow, with sudden changes in rhythm. Whenever Pugliese is played, the dance floor takes on a different energy with everyone strutting his or her stuff. This is the music for *ganchos* and all those elaborate steps ordinarily reserved for show tango.

Personally, I dislike the way everyone seems to go wild as soon as they hear Pugliese. His music seems to invite a performance in which the excessive drama of the dancing is disconnected from what I consider to be the "real thing": the *experience* of passion. Because a mere performance of passion is not what I'm looking for when I dance tango, I was ready to sit this set out when Ricardo, a seasoned *milonguero*, caught my eye and I decided, after all, to give it a try.

What followed was—for me—a very different encounter with Pugliese. There were long, reflective moments of standing perfectly still, a step made only when absolutely necessary. And then, suddenly, there would be a playful twist or turn, a dramatic sweep or slide. I began to hear the music in a new way, as complicated and nuanced, rather than as merely theatrical. This had to be the way Pugliese was meant to be danced. Dancing like this made me feel outside myself, unaware of anything but the connection with my dance partner and the music until, suddenly, at the end of the set, Ricardo took me totally off-guard by leaning over and kissing me lightly on the lips. I must have looked shocked at this obvious violation of salon etiquette because he laughed, casting his eyes upward and shrugging his shoulders with feigned embarrassment. Clapping his hand over his mouth, he whispered, "Oops." And then, with a mischievous glint in his eye, "Pugliese!"

This encounter illustrates some of the complicated entanglements of tango passion. It had all the ingredients necessary for a passionate *experience*: the sublime connection, the sensation of being outside time and space, the pleasure of being able to lose one's self, to let everything go and surrender to the joy of the moment. However, by finishing off a dance that had already been intense with a playful but excessive performance (the kiss, the rueful shrug, the sly smile), Ricardo brought me back to reality with a jolt. He seemed to be showing me that a little irony would not be amiss here,[18] that I should not be taking this passion thing *too* seriously, that a dancer should be able to laugh at herself and take some distance. In this way, Ricardo adeptly turned the dance experience into a humorous performance and, in so doing, playfully cooled out a passion that just might be getting a little out of hand.

The encounter with Ricardo not only disrupted my previously held conviction that a passionate *performance* of Pugliese would have nothing to do with the (real) *experience* of passion but, more important, provided a troubling confrontation with the *politics* of passion. As Savigliano (1995) has so astutely analyzed, all tango dancers are complicit in processes of exotic "othering." In a move that gives a new twist to the adage "It takes two to tango," she shows how exoticism is the mutually enacted outcome of unequal encounters between dancers from the global North and the global South (Savigliano, 1995:75). From this perspective, Ricardo's transgression might be viewed as an understandable response to his being exoticized as a passionate and mysterious Latino: "If this is the way *you* see me, then this is what *I* will give you." It shows how encounters between locals and foreigners in the tango scene in Buenos Aires are inevitably embedded in complicated global geographies of desire and power. As a local, Ricardo might have taken advantage of me as foreigner who could be counted on to be unfamiliar with the *codigos* of the tango scene in Buenos Aires, thereby transforming me from desirable dance partner into naïve tourist, all in one fell swoop. Or his motives could have been even more prosaic. He may simply have seen me as a potential source of income, a visitor who might want to take lessons with an experienced local *milonguero* like him. His calling card left tactfully on my table suggested that, in any case, tango passion was not the only thing involved. For someone who wishes to see herself as a serious tango dancer, not to mention a critical feminist scholar, this realization was sobering. And yet my unease—both then, and now when I recall it—about the politics of passion does not take away the mutual pleasure that tango provides. Ricardo's roguish hint served to mediate, at least for the moment, the inherent antagonisms of the transnational encounter by pulling us together and reminding me that, when all is said and done, it is Pugliese who is to blame.

3

Tango Trajectories

For anyone who wants to understand how dramatically tango can affect someone's life, the 1996 Japanese film *Shall We Dansu?* is a perfect place to begin.[1] The film shows a successful but unhappy accountant, Mr. Sugiyama, who has a family and a house in the suburbs, looking out the window of a Tokyo commuter train one night as he is returning home from work and seeing a beautiful woman with a melancholy expression looking out the window of a dance studio. After much hesitation and many more times of watching the dancers through the lighted window as they move across the dance floor, he finally gathers up his courage, goes to the dance studio, and asks to take dance lessons. The film is devoted to his struggles to learn ballroom dancing and the complications that emerge as he attempts to hide his involvement from his wife and daughter. As his passion for dancing grows, his life takes on a new meaning, changing the way he feels about himself, his work, and his relationships. Ultimately, his secret is revealed after his wife hires a private detective to uncover what her husband has been doing. In a desperate attempt to understand what has happened to the person she thought she knew, she and her daughter attend an amateur competition in which he is participating. The end is chaotic but predictably happy, with his wife asking him to teach her how to dance. The hero enjoys a final bittersweet dance with the beautiful dance instructor whose appearance in the window so many months ago had so irrevocably changed his life.

This film raises questions that are at the heart of the present inquiry. For example, it asks why an ordinary, well-adapted, and even conventional person might become so enamored of a foreign dance that he cannot imagine his life without it. It addresses the puzzling fact that he is prepared to endure months of costly and painful lessons, put up

Figure 3.1. Still from the 1996 film *Shall We Dansu?* (dir. Masayuki Suo).

with the countless humiliations of learning the ropes of a strange dance culture, and contend with the disbelief, shock, and sorrow of his family, friends, and colleagues who wonder what has happened to the person they knew and loved. And it tackles the tantalizing enigma of how social dancing can become so irresistible and, indeed, so addictive that an otherwise normal person would be willing to push everything else aside in order to participate in it, becoming in the process a different person from the one he was before.

To be sure, *Shall We Dansu?* is not, strictly speaking, about Argentinean tango.[2] However, in many ways it captures the spirit of Argentinean tango more than many of the tango films that have been circulating since the dance began. These films invariably focus on sexual and romantic encounters, often across cultural or class boundaries, with tango providing—literally—the background music. The suggestion is that where tango is, love is soon to follow.[3] The protagonists' struggle to learn the dance is considerably less central to the plot than their struggles to work through the problems of a romantic relationship. Interestingly, even the U.S. remake, *Shall We Dance?* (2004),[4] transforms the plot into a Hollywood love story between a bored, middle-aged worka-holic (Richard Gere) and a sexy dance instructor (Jennifer Lopez). In contrast to this "feel-good romance," as one reviewer called it, the origi-nal Japanese version begins with the serious Mr. Sugiyama's unrequited love for the beautiful Mai. However, as soon as she crisply informs him that he'd better leave if his interest in dancing is motivated only by his interest in her as a woman, Mr. Sugiyama discovers that it is the danc-ing itself which is, in fact, more important for him. This is what is mak-ing him feel, as he puts it, "more and more alive every day."

Shall We Dansu? differs from other cinematic representations of tango by showing how people actually learn to dance tango.[5] We can imagine how baffled an ordinary person might be when he first real-izes that he wants to learn a dance, particularly one that is considered embarrassing or even slightly distasteful. We are not surprised that most people would have to fumble their way through lessons, unable to get the hang of where to put their feet or how to move their partners in the right direction. We can sympathize with the uneasiness that a per-son might feel at dances where there are always more women than men and where women expect to be "taken care of" on the dance floor, even by their novice dance partners. As the film progresses, the viewer can't help but become intrigued by the protagonist's determination to con-tinue his dance lessons and amused by the ways his passion for dancing changes his life and his persona: from the feet moving under the desk at work to the rhythms of imagined music to his practicing steps alone on the platform, while waiting in the rain for the next train (shades of Gene Kelly), and, of course, the ultimate reward for all his effort when he participates as a contestant in an amateur dance competition.[6] We want him to continue with this strangely improbable and yet delight-ful activity that has gotten him out of the rut he was in, dispelled his depression, and given him a taste of freedom.

In this chapter, Mr. Sugiyama's passion is a starting point for thinking about how ordinary men and women become enamored of Argentin-ean tango. His story will be transposed from urban Japan, where ball-room dancing is considered exotic and slightly disreputable, to another urban center, Amsterdam, where Argentinean tango is also considered exotic and slightly disreputable, albeit for other reasons.[7] While the his-tories of these social dances differ in both places, they are also, and have always been, entangled. As Savigliano (1995) shows, Argentinean tango has always traveled and, in the course of its travels, been domesticated for consumption in Europe, before being transported to Japan as ball-room tango. However, no matter which form it takes, tango attracts *afi-cionados* for whom its exoticism is appealing (in Japan, because it represents the "West," in Amsterdam because it is from the "South") as well as for the possibilities it offers for entering an alternative reality outside the commitments and routines of everyday life.

While the ingredients of tango passion were the focus of the previous chapter, the ways in which this passion can embroil a person in a trajectory that unfolds outside her or his conscious control are the subject of this chapter. To this end, I borrow the concept of trajectory developed by the sociologists Strauss and Glaser (1970) to describe processes that disorder a person's life, necessitating a radical reconstruction of identity. "Trajectory" was initially employed to understand processes of suffering, physical illness, disability, dislocation, or events that lead to a "downhill spiral" and "biographical disarray," but these are by no means the only possible trajectories. As Riemann and Schütze (1991) have argued, trajectory processes can involve anything from a love affair to a creation of a work of art to a new career—anything, in short, that introduces a sense of fate into a person's life and reshapes the present situation and his or her expectations for the future (p. 338). While rarely viewed as a downhill spiral, becoming a tango dancer may, nevertheless, evoke the biographical disarray, changes in identity, and altered expectations for the future that are common to any trajectory process.

In order to understand how this process works, I will be following dancers from their first tango lesson through their ever more frequent visits to local *milongas* to their finally becoming full-fledged *aficionados* who dance every evening, are prepared to travel far and wide just to dance, and, indeed, can hardly imagine a life without tango. Obviously, this process is not the same for every person who dances tango, and not every passionate dancer will end up so addicted to tango that he or she will abandon everything in order to dance it. However, some dancers—not unlike the fictional Mr. Sugiyama—will become so enamored of tango that it radically changes their relationships, their social world, and their sense of who they are. Drawing upon interviews with dancers from Amsterdam as well as dancers who have gone to Buenos Aires to dance, I explore how these tango trajectories work. Beginning with their first encounter with tango, I uncover the arduous process of learning to dance and the gradual immersion in the tango culture, only to end at the more extreme end of the continuum with the tango exiles who relocate to Buenos Aires, leaving the familiarity of home behind in order to dance. I will show how dancing tango can fulfill a person's most deeply felt needs precisely because it unsettles the ordinariness of everyday life, opening up the possibility for something new and different.

First Encounters

The initial encounter with dancing tango is often a mixture of chance, of being in the right place at the right time, and fascination with an activity or an ambience that seems strange yet alluring. Many of the dancers I spoke with maintained that their desire to learn tango was almost immediate, akin to a "love at first sight" experience. As soon as they saw people dancing the tango, they knew that this was what they wanted to do. Avi, the twenty-three-year-old student we met in the previous chapter, began dancing when he was in high school; however, he'd already known he wanted to learn it from the time he was eight years old. His parents had taken him on vacation to Paris and he remembers seeing people dancing along the river. "I didn't know what it was then, but I saw them dancing in this funny embrace and it just stuck. I always remembered it and later on I found out it was tango. I knew right away: 'This is my dance.'" When asked what it was about the embrace that made it stick in his mind for so many years, he explained:

> These people were in this different state, this dream-like state in the middle of the city, with the buzz of traffic and all kinds of things, and they were just holding each other very tight and dancing. I was really amazed by it. It really spoke to me.

Many of my informants told similar stories of observing tango by chance and becoming so intrigued that they wanted to learn how to do it themselves. For others, their first encounter with tango was less a dramatic "love at first sight" than part of a more gradual process. Some had experience with social dancing—ballroom, Latin, rock 'n' roll, or just dancing at parties. Others trace their interest in tango to their having taken ballet lessons as children. And still others attribute their interest in tango to their "nature" or to the fact that they have always liked to dance. As Rosemary, whom we met in the previous chapter, puts it, "I'm just a dancing kind of girl. Ever since I was little, as soon as you put on music, I'd start to move. Moving is the way I express myself." Others make reference to their ancestry—as Marcus did by tracing his involvement with tango to his experiences with Hungarian folk dancing as a child—thereby lending their dancing tango a kind of cultural inevitability.

Of course, not everyone regards tango as something that was "in [their] blood." For some dancers, the decision to learn tango depends more on chance and on the specific circumstances of their lives than on any "natural" predisposition. Some are pulled into tango by friends who have invited them to come along to a *milonga* ("Tango is just the thing for you"). Others hear about it only to file the information away for future use. For example, Samantha describes having been very much at loose ends. She had finished her studies, was in a dead-end job, and was recovering from a broken heart. She decided to make a list of activities designed to pull her out of her isolation in, as she puts it, this "dark period of my life."

> I wanted to do horseback riding, I wanted to try painting lessons, I wanted this, I wanted that. . . . I happened to be in this café and saw an advertisement for a tango salon and thought, "*Hey*, that's something I always wanted to try. I'll take a tango lesson."

While the actual decision to take up tango may be arbitrary, most of the dancers I spoke with describe having come to a point in their lives where tango seemed like a solution to their problems, a way to "do something about [their] situation." Their lives were not going the way they had hoped or planned; they felt they were in a crisis. Some had been working too hard and needed a hobby. Others were depressed because they had lost their jobs or were retired or their children had left home. Still others had recently broken up with a partner or become divorced after years of marriage. Some were facing a recent loss (the death of a parent or a spouse) and saw tango as a way to cope with grief or loneliness. In other words, they needed something to fill the gap. For them, tango seemed to offer a way out of their crises, a strategy for getting their lives back on track. A case in point is Marta, a stylish sixty-five-year-old dress designer and occasional actress who took up tango after her husband died. She remembers that she did nothing but cry for six months after his death, until finally some friends persuaded her to go to a tango salon with them. She started taking lessons, discovering, somewhat to her surprise, that she not only liked to dance but even liked going to *milongas* on her own. "It was a gradual process, you know. But what happened was this: Now when I start to cry, I can exchange my sadness for melancholy. It's another sensation."

Whether dancers explain their desire to dance tango as something that they have "always been meant to do" or as something they have gotten into more gradually, their accounts frame dancing, retrospectively, as a new beginning—something that is the start of something good, a new life, even a new identity.[8] Dancing tango is presented as a way to overcome a stubborn bout of depression, to (finally) meet someone they really like, or, more dramatically, to rediscover their true selves ("I've always been a dancing girl"). Wanting to dance tango is only the beginning, however; more is needed to catapult a dancer into the trajectory of a true *aficionado*.

Learning to Dance

Tango is not an easy dance to learn. For most would-be dancers, learning tango requires years of classes. It is not enough just to learn the rudiments of the basic steps, as is the case, for example, with salsa. Beginning tango dancers not only take lessons, sometimes more than once a week, but they spend hours trying out their steps at home or, like Mr. Sugiyama, practicing during their lunch breaks at work. They attend workshops with (visiting) instructors, sometimes throw in a private lesson or two, and regularly visit the *milongas* in order to "make their miles."

Beginning dancers are often warned by more experienced members of the tango community that it can take as long as five years to be able to dance tango well. Learning tango takes time and effort. Some dancers balk at the thought of such a commitment and may opt for an open style of dancing that can be less daunting to learn because it requires less balance and yields a faster result than traditional tango. Those who go for the more classic style may find themselves struggling over the basics ("just walking") for years on end and wind up wondering if the whole enterprise is not, after all, a mission impossible.

A particularly poignant example is Tim, who describes himself as "one of those people who can't make the connection between what I hear and what I want my body to do." He explains that he could not get the hang of learning to do steps and that trying to develop a whole sequence of steps on the dance floor was even more bewildering. For the first year and a half, every lesson was "pure panic." He recalls standing in front of his partner, who just looked at him with hollow eyes as if to say, "OK, now what?" He spent the first four years with his eyes glued to the floor, thinking only about steps—"not my partner, not the music, not the people on the dance floor." Going to *milongas* was even worse. That was a real "jungle"; just having to approach a woman and ask her to dance was an "ordeal." When asked how he managed to keep going, he explained, "I have taken rock 'n' roll classes and it was the exact same thing. But I always knew that, at a certain point, the ordeal would be over, so I just kept going."

While men (or leaders) typically have more problems learning tango, women do not have an easy time either. Susan, a divorced engineer in her mid-forties who has been dancing for nine years, described learning tango as a trajectory. She began taking lessons in order to get out of her post-divorce depression and start meeting men. She had already done swing dancing, but it gave her motion sickness. She decided to try tango, but she didn't "grab on to it immediately." She remembers the first few years as "just an outlet, nothing more." She was taking group classes and trying to learn the basics. After about three years, she began to go to *milongas* regularly. Tango became a more serious part of her life. She was becoming, as she put it, a "solid intermediate follower" with a good understanding of the music. She began to develop friendships with other dancers and even started to organize her own salon. It wasn't until six years into the tango, however, that her relationship to the dance changed dramatically. She became more and more dissatisfied with her dancing and unhappy with the level of dances she was getting in the salons. "I was stuck and I wasn't getting anywhere."

She realized that she needed either to abandon tango altogether or to find a way to move on. She decided to take some private lessons with a local instructor. For the first two weeks, he just had her walking up and down in front of him ("but if you're going to be good at the dance that's what you have to do"). She remembered leaving the lessons in tears on more than one occasion. However, she persisted and finally improved so much that people began commenting on how much better she had become. "It was just amazing. And that's when I thought: 'OK, this is a *lifetime* thing.'"

The more advanced a dancer becomes, the more likely he or she is to realize how much more there is to learn. Joachim, whom we met in the previous chapter, has already been dancing for several years, but the more he dances, the more he realizes that

> There is no *limit* to tango. You don't know how far you can go. You arrive at a point and you stick your head outside and there's still more to do. It's like when you travel around the world, you try to reach the horizon, but you keep on going and you just never get there. . . . I thought I was advanced. . . . I thought I was able to run and then a dance instructor told me it would probably be better to walk [laughs]. So, now I have to learn to walk again.

Learning tango is often described as a "never-ending process," and many tango dancers are prepared to spend endless hours working on their balance, improving their techniques, increasing their musicality, or just doing some "fine-tuning" with a private dance instructor. It is not uncommon for serious dancers to go back to the basics and take beginners' classes. While for some this may be a reason to become discouraged and look around for an easier dance, for others it is precisely the sense that there will always be another mountain to climb which hooks them. For these tango dancers, the process of learning tango becomes a powerful force in and of itself, driving the individual to keep coming back for more. Tango is transformed from an exciting and slightly scary possibility or a pleasant but replaceable hobby to the start of a trajectory (Riemann and Schütze (1991:337)—a "fateful history" in which the dancer begins to lose control and has no other recourse than, as Tim puts it, "to keep going until you get there."

Going to the *Milongas*

Once one begins to become a serious tango dancer, attending *milongas* is almost a must. Although some couples seem happy just to take classes or go to the occasional workshop or festival, most dancers take lessons because they want to go to the *milongas* eventually. The *milongas* are the goal of the lessons rather than just another activity. While many dancers can hardly wait for their first visit to a tango salon, dancing in public can be daunting in the beginning. Tim, for example, recalls going to his first *milonga* as a relative novice and the ordeal of having to "walk that long distance across the floor to invite someone to dance."

> And sometimes even before I had reached them, they would already be shaking their head[s]. You know, like this [he demonstrates with a curt toss of his head]. Just *no!* That's the *worst.* It was like: "Do I have leprosy? Where are my spots?"

For many beginners, *milongas* are threatening. Nicolas, whom we met in the previous chapter, spent more than a year hanging around in the salons before he dared to dance. He recalls practicing his steps on the sidewalk in front of the salon: "one-two-three. . . . I needed to know what I would be doing later before I went in."

Once dancers start going to the *milongas*, however, the *milongas* quickly become a part of their weekly routine. Some reserve a particular evening for tango ("My Saturdays are sacred, that's my salon night"). For others, one night is not nearly enough. It is not uncommon for dancers who are serious about tango to attend two or three *milongas* a week, and some may even go every night. For example, from the very first moment he began learning tango, Joachim took classes nearly every day, attending the *milongas* afterward. As soon as he had learned the basics, he began volunteering to dance with the beginners in other classes, too. "Everything that was involved with tango, I was in!"

He went to the *milongas* to dance, to watch people, to relax. Referring to the *milonga* as his "temple," he explains that this is where he goes if he has to make an important decision—anything from whether to stay in the Netherlands or move into a place of his own to breaking up with his girlfriend—or maybe just to relax and meditate. As he puts it:

During the week, it's impossible for me to organize anything else but tango. So, if there's a *milonga*, I go to the *milonga*. If there are classes, I go to a class. If I go on a holiday, I can survive without tango [laughs]. But then it's surviving, it's not living [laughs]. I can't help it. I like dancing tango.

Maya, a middle-aged physical therapist and mother of two teenagers, expressed similar sentiments, explaining that "a day without a *milonga* is a wasted day for me." For her, the knowledge that she will be dancing that night makes all the difference in how she feels during the day. Her work goes more quickly when she has a *milonga* to look forward to. While she is quick to assure me that she likes her job and is very committed to her patients, she admits that going to the *milonga* is the most important for her. "It's just the most wonderful thing I can think of. The rest I am really just doing on the side."

Many tango dancers like to travel in order to attend new *milongas*. Or they participate in workshops and festivals in other parts of Europe, including the increasingly popular tango vacations where lessons and *milongas* are offered in scenic locations, replete with sun and sand.[9] Dancers routinely combine tango dancing with family holidays or with work-related trips. Attending a conference or a business meeting in another country provides a welcome opportunity to dance. One of my informants told me that he was at an important business meeting in Japan that was followed by a dinner with his colleagues:

It was really swanky, you know, with good food and wine and formal speeches. The works. And all I could think about was wanting to dance. I kept checking my watch and waiting for the moment when I could leave. When that moment came, I jumped into a taxi and headed for the nearest *milonga*. I just couldn't wait to dance.

Just how central attending *milongas* can become in dancers' lives is, perhaps, best illustrated by what happens when they are unable to dance because of an illness or a family commitment. For example, Liz, whom we met in the previous chapter, recalls having to have an operation on her foot. She hadn't wanted the surgery, but eventually there was no way around it if she wanted to be able to dance without pain in the future. However, it meant that she had to stay off her feet for at least six weeks following the operation. And "that was the real drama," she explained. Having to stay home and miss the *milonga* felt like going "cold turkey." When her surgeon told her that she could start to dance again—"but *slowly*"—Liz was on her feet "in a flash." She remembers that she overdid it, dancing for several hours and ruining her newly reconstructed feet. "It was a bloody mess," she recalls. "I should have waited longer, but"—shrugging her shoulders and laughing somewhat ruefully—"I just couldn't!"

Danny, the self-proclaimed family man from the previous chapter, explained that his first thought at the end of a *milonga* is always: "When can I go again?" At a certain point, he was attending *milongas* so often that there were "complaints from the house-front: 'Oh, no! Tango dancing? Not again!'" Although he loves his family and rationally knows that he ought to find a balance between his home life and the *milonga*, he admits that if he didn't have a family or were single, he would totally abandon himself to tango. "I'd be dancing every day. It's probably like any addiction. You need more and more to get the kick. Like *'Oh yes. Oh wow!'* You keep needing a bigger dose."

Once dancers become embroiled in the *milonga* scene, the experience of dancing tango begins to resemble the effects of taking a pleasurable but highly addictive drug. Many of my informants used words and descriptions like "obsession," "addiction," "irresistible," and "something you can't live without" to describe their involvement with tango. Nicolas explains that he completely understands "what a junkie means about needing a shot."

> Sometimes I'm sitting in my car on my way home from a *milonga* and that feeling just overwhelms me. I feel it in my *heart*. I start longing for another salon so I can have the experience again.

It is not surprising that once this point has been reached, tango begins to take over the dancers' lives, pushing other activities to the side. It becomes a trajectory that disorders their former lives, often having a dramatic impact upon their relationships and everyday routines. This is accompanied by the awareness that they are no longer the same people they were before, and that their lives have been radically changed. Their biography becomes divided into a "before" and "after," whereby the "entitlement to see oneself under a familiar, routine-type perspective is gone, and one knows that this sort of experience can creep up . . . again any time" (Riemann and Schütze, 1991:345).

Way of Life

Tango does not "disorder" a person's previous life all once. Instead it initiates a gradual moving away from her or his everyday affairs. In the process, the person begins to realize that he or she has become a different person. When a trajectory involves unpleasant processes of illness or suffering, it can be experienced as disorienting and even frightening: The person loses all connection with her or his previous identity and no longer recognizes the person he or she has become (Riemann and Schütze, 1991:350). While tango dancers also describe their identity changes in trajectory-like terms as a growing "addiction," their addiction to tango is rarely experienced as negative.

Nicolas, as we saw above, admits that he is a tango junkie. In fact, he acknowledges that tango has completely taken over his life. He still has his job, of course, but the rest of his life involves little else than going to salons, often traveling far from home just to dance in a new place. He rarely goes to movies anymore and hardly ever sees friends who are not into tango. He realizes that that this probably sounds "one-sided," but, as he puts it, "I just can't help it. . . . Tango is all there is. There is nothing for me besides tango."

> Like now I have this enormous collection of tango music—540 CDs. Every time I go to Buenos Aires, I bring back another hundred. That's all I listen to. I used to listen to classical music, the *St. Matthew Passion*, the *Four Last Songs* by Strauss, the opera. My life used to consist of classical music, but that's all on a back-burner now. I can safely say that it's only about tango music now.

Although Nicolas is fairly sanguine about the new direction his life has taken, it is also clear that he doesn't see his addiction as entirely "normal." As Riemann and Schütze (1991) note, people talking about their trajectories often have to engage in some kind of "repair work" to justify what is happening to them. For example, they stress that the process by which their former lives have become disordered has been cumulative or gradual; it all happened slowly, little by little, until they suddenly realized that everything was different. In the same vein, many of my informants described their obsession with tango as a slow process whereby they stopped listening to other kinds of music and began spending more and more time doing tango-related activities like watching dance performances on YouTube and participating in tango blogs. Their Facebook friends suddenly all seemed to belong to the tango community, with most of their communication centering on the exchange of dance photographs and informing one another about where they would be dancing on a particular day. As Adele, whom we met in the previous chapter, puts it:

> There isn't a day that goes by that I don't watch tango videos. I watch them and listen to them, too. It's important to see how professional dancers move, different styles of tango. It has helped me put together my own tango course. I always save some time before I go to bed, but during the day, too. I'm always trying to make time for it. . . . I listen to lots of [tango] music, too. Every day. In the car. At home if I have time. Yeah, I realize now [laughs] how incredibly much time and energy I'm willing to put into it.

Tango not only drives out all other activities and interests. It also changes the way a person lives. Many dancers organize their living spaces with an eye to their commitment to tango. Tango art begins to appear on the walls of the living room and a person's collection of dancing shoes may end up artfully displayed in a glass cabinet as a kind of altar to the religion of tango. Most dancers make sure to reserve enough floor space in their homes so that they can practice their steps. Furniture is kept to a minimum or pushed safely toward the walls so that it will not interfere with dancing. One of my informants reduced his entire living room to an empty floor surrounded by a state-of-the-art sound system. With the exception of a small and decidedly uncomfortable deck chair, there was no place to sit, let alone socialize with other people. His private space was entirely taken over by his passion for tango.

Tango changes how dancers dress as well. Dancing tango can provide an opportunity for dancers to dress in ways they couldn't imagine doing in their ordinary lives. For example, professional women who normally wore understated business suits with low heels to work found that short skirts with splits, tops with *décolleté*, and fishnet stockings had effectively taken over their wardrobes. Some of my informants maintained that tango had even changed their relationship to clothes more generally. As Elly, a divorced nutritionist in her mid-fifties, explains:

> I walk into clothing stores with different eyes now. All I'm thinking about is whether this top or this skirt is something I can dance in. I'd say three-fourths of my closet is for tango now, one-fourth for the rest of my life.

A lust for shoes is pervasive among women who dance tango and can take on such proportions as to make a person unrecognizable even to herself. Many of my female informants assured me that they had had a predilection for sensible shoes before they started dancing tango. They wanted to be able to move around easily and tended to cast a disparaging eye on other women who tottered around on high heels. Many could never have envisioned wanting to own pairs and pairs of totally impractical but breathtakingly beautiful dancing shoes. Nor could they have imagined spending untold amounts of time and money on foot care, from creams and reflex foot massages to orthopedic insoles and silicon shoe pads. Dancing tango, however, transformed their pragmatic attitude toward shoes as a means to an end (walking) into a determination to possess as many fabulous shoes as they possibly could. They were more than prepared to take sore feet, bunions, or other foot ailments in stride for the pleasures of wearing beautiful shoes. As Kate, a middle-aged dancer with an impressive shoe collection and chronic foot problems, put it, "Some of my colleagues and friends can't believe the price I'm willing to pay for these shoes, but [laughs], I just think: What do *they* know?"

Dancing tango gradually changes the lives and identities of individual dancers, whereby activities, interests, and values that were formerly important suddenly seem irrelevant. Tango dancers may discover that they are losing touch with friends and family who do not understand, let alone share, their passion for tango. They may catch themselves at

Figure 3.2. Shopping for shoes. (Photo: Cody Simms.)

social gatherings regaling their non–tango-dancing friends with stories about their tango adventures, only to discover these same friends smiling politely but looking at them with a glassy-eyed expression and every bit as puzzled as Mrs. Sugiyama at the transformation in the person they thought they knew.

Take, for example, Eva, a dancer in her late thirties, who told me how delighted her friends had been initially when she took up dancing tango. It seemed to be the perfect hobby for someone in her position—a single woman with a high-powered job and not much time for relationships. As she got into tango more seriously, she began seeing her former friends less often as they became increasingly peripheral to her new life. "They just have other interests. They're all into buying houses and having babies. . . . I used to be in touch with them, calling and sending text messages, but I gave up. We're just too different now."

Maya's passion for tango was often a source of friction in her family. She recalls going on vacation with her husband (and then–tango partner), her teenage children, and her sister's family. As usual, she had already checked out where they could dance tango in the vicinity of the camping site. As soon as they had finished dinner and cleared the table, she began looking for an opportunity to sneak away with her husband. "It wasn't that we wanted to sacrifice the whole household for our danc- ing, but we figured we'd done all the chores, everyone was fed and ready for bed, so for us the night life could begin." That's not the way her fam- ily saw it, however. They were astounded: "Mom, you're on vacation!" Remembering the incident, Maya laughs, noting that there were "just limits to how far [she] was willing to go for family."

> There was just *no* way I could spend three weeks at a camping site with- out dancing. . . . So, OK, now I have a bad name in my family circle. They aren't hooked on tango and can't understand that, as nice as it might be at home with them, I'm always going to be trying to go dancing.

Like many of my informants, Maya had no difficulties admitting that tango had become an addiction. But, as she put it, "So many things are addictive. I used to smoke. . . . I tend to drink more wine than is good for me. . . . I guess you could say that I have an addictive personality. But tango is the best thing that I can think of."

Once tango is no longer a hobby, even a passionate one, and has become a way of life, individuals seem to accept the disorder it brings to their sense of self, their relationships, and their social worlds. They may adopt "adjustment strategies" (Kowalska, 2010)[10] in order to bal- ance the precarious equilibrium of their everyday lives with their pas- sion for tango. However, as with any trajectory, once they are "addicted" to tango, they may find extricating themselves from their addiction more and more difficult—that is, provided they would even want to. To be sure, their lives have spiraled out of control, yet tango is rarely perceived as the downward spiral that characterizes trajectories like terminal illness, enforced displacement, or extreme loneliness from the loss of a loved one (Riemann and Schütze, 1991:342–43). In fact, many dancers seem to welcome the disorderliness and disruption that tango produces, exhibiting a remarkable willingness to bid their previous existences farewell.

Of course, at some point, the disorder may become too much, as was the case with poor Mr. Sugiyama when confronted with his wife and daughter in the midst of his performance at the amateur competition for ballroom dancing. He was so guilt-ridden and upset that he nearly gave up dancing altogether. In order to appreciate just how dramatically tango can change the life of its *aficionados*, I now turn to the more spectacular forms of upheaval—the temporary and sometimes permanent sojourns in Buenos Aires.

Traveling to Buenos Aires

Whether or not one is a tango dancer who likes to travel, at a certain point a trip to Buenos Aires is almost obligatory. There is a palpable sense among serious tango dancers that this is the mecca, the place you need to visit in order to discover how tango should "really" be danced. Such trips are justified by referring to Buenos Aires as the place where "tango's roots are" or "where it all began." Sometimes dancers worry about whether they are ready to go, fearful—as one of my informants put it—that dancing in Buenos Aires might be "a size that's too big for me." Others adopt a more recalcitrant stance—as did the dancer described in chapter 1 who countered my enthusiastic stories about tango in Buenos Aires with skepticism, asking whether it was absolutely necessary to go to Buenos Aires in order to be a good dancer. However, in either case, the consensus seems to be that any tango dancer worth her or his salt is supposed to have been to Buenos Aires at least once. Renate, for example, who has visited Buenos Aires many times, recalls her first trip as an inevitable development in her process of becoming a serious tango dancer.

> I hadn't been dancing very long, but I was already hooked on the dance. I started taking lessons from Argentinean teachers. Suddenly it was: *Woooowwww!* And then it changed again when I went to Buenos Aires. I arrived there for the first time and I thought: Oka-a-a-y [laughs]. This is something else. I had to reset myself, you know. That you suddenly see: OK!

Renate is not alone in her view that lessons are not enough and that it is essential to visit Buenos Aires in order to really understand how tango should be danced. Many tango dancers make a regular practice of going to Buenos Aires to dance, combining these trips with a visit to Iguazú or other parts of Argentina and South America. While these trips are motivated by tango, they also provide an opportunity to learn Spanish and discover more about Argentinean culture and history. Jeanette, an artist in her late forties, has been to Buenos Aires six times. She goes every year during the winter in Amsterdam when it is summer in Argentina. She takes private tango lessons with the same teacher each year, has made friends with whom she corresponds during the rest of the year, and has learned enough Spanish to have conversations. She adores Argentineans because, as she puts it, "they live through their hearts, in the moment." However, when I ask her whether she would go to Buenos Aires if she didn't dance tango, she insists that "in the end, it's tango that brings me back. Being able to dance in so many different places in one day. Just that possibility."

It is not unusual for dancers to discover that once they have visited Buenos Aires, they want to go back. The trips can become addictive, with each sojourn lasting just a little longer. For example, a first visit might last three weeks, involving a sojourn in a tango hotel and some tourist activities in between. Later, the dancer may come for three months or even half a year, renting an apartment or even looking for some kind of freelance work. Robert, a history professor in his early sixties, arranged to give classes at the university in Buenos Aires so that he could stay for a longer period. It was idyllic, and, as he put it, he would go back "without a moment's hesitation." Shaking his head sadly, he added that that was probably not going to happen anytime soon. His wife is not a tango dancer and, while she did agree to accompany him on one of his trips to Buenos Aires, she quickly grew bored, so now he is on his own. Couples who do not share a passion for tango[11] may have to negotiate their vacations along the lines of "this year the Caribbean for you, next year we're going to Buenos Aires."

Single dancers may find it easier to organize their trips to Buenos Aires, but they still have to find ways to balance their desire to dance in Buenos Aires with the demands of their everyday lives. Take, for example, Susan, whom I met while she was on her third trip to Buenos Aires. The first two trips had been relatively short, just a few weeks each, and she had combined them with traveling around the region. However, this time she was able to come for a longer time because she was in between jobs at home. She explained that she has now gotten beyond the "eat-sleep-tango mode," has made some Argentinean friends, and has her own apartment. Although she's loved the experience, she's hesitant about coming back for a fourth visit.

> Until a few years ago, I never would have admitted to having a passion that's called tango. I'm such a boring, grounded, pragmatic person. I do my budgets and stuff. . . . I still sometimes don't admit it to myself because part of me wants to have a balanced life and when you start going to *milongas* four or five times a week, then you're forgetting about other parts in your life which I think are equally important. So the thought of committing to coming back to Buenos Aires *only* to dance is like tipping the scales too much. . . . But the passion in my heart says, "You're going to come back, girl. Just give it up. You're going to come back [laughs]."

As passionate as these dancers are about tango, they continue to struggle with finding a balance between their commitment to tango and their desire to have a life outside tango, between their longing for what Buenos Aires has to offer and their need to have a "normal" life at home. Even the most passionate tango dancers worry from time to time that tango is taking over their lives. They therefore need to reassure themselves that they are still in control and can put on the brakes if they so desire.

But what about those dancers whose passion for tango has already gone too far? Or, as Riemann and Schütze (1991:351–52) would put it, what happens when an individual is unable (or, in the case of tango, unwilling) to influence the forward rush (or downward spiral) of his or her trajectory? What happens when "escape" is no longer an option?[12]

Becoming an Exile

Most dancers find a way to integrate tango into their lives. They continue to have jobs, families, and friends who are not interested in tango. They may visit Buenos Aires frequently, but, in the end, they return home. There is, however, a small but significant group of dancers who decide to burn all their bridges and take the plunge. These are the people—known in Buenos Aires as the "regulars"—who, unlike the occasional visitor or run-of-the-mill tango tourist, have decided pack their bags and come to Buenos Aires to live.

A case in point is Paul, a sixty-five-year-old German businessman who had been living in Buenos Aires for four years when I spoke with him. He is retired and divorced, and his children are adults. He explains that he had entered a phase in his life when he felt he should be free to do anything he wanted. "And so my question to myself was: What do I *really* want to do?" He made a checklist of things he still wanted to do, and tango was one of them. After going the usual route of classes and *milongas* in his hometown, he took his first trip to Buenos Aires. He found himself "really getting into it" and realized that "tango is the way for me to indulge myself and to do what I really like to do." He began returning to Buenos Aires every three months until he reached the point where he figured he might as well pack up and move there for good.

> It's kind of crazy, but I thought: So what's keeping me in Germany? My kids are all there, so that would have been a reason to stay there. On the other hand, they have their own lives and they don't want me hanging around anyhow. So I started looking for a place . . . and the rest is history.

Many foreign *aficionados* like Paul take up residence in Buenos Aires. They come from all over the world—the United States, Europe, Japan, Australia, and other parts of South America (e.g., Chile, Brazil). Many were at loose ends in their lives. They were divorced or had been recently widowed. Some had been made redundant without prospects of getting another job. Others had freelance or independent jobs that made it possible for them to work in Buenos Aires. While some also tried to find work in Buenos Aires, the economic situation in Argentina is not always conducive to finding employment. However, many of the people I spoke with were retired with a pension or had sufficient savings to enable them to live comfortably in Buenos Aires. Others were willing to accept a more modest lifestyle if doing so meant they could live in the city of their dreams. Given global economic disparities, Buenos Aires is an attractive location for North Americans and Europeans. But even if they had the financial means to move, the decision to take up a life of tango far from home inevitably involved cutting ties with their past lives, their former relationships, and their sense of self. It was frightening and exhilarating, a head-on plunge into unfamiliar waters.

For example, Barbara, a successful Canadian professor, gave up her tenured academic position with lots of fringe benefits and an apartment in Toronto in order to live in Buenos Aires. Increasingly dissatisfied with her life as an academic ("If I have to write one more recommendation, I'll scream") and after a string of unsuccessful relationships and with most of her good friends spread out to different parts of the world, she decided that "there was just nothing really keeping me there." In a moment of daring ("I surprised myself"), she applied for early retirement, sold all her books, got rid of her apartment, and headed south.

What happens to these exiles, many of whom are middle-aged or older and have long histories of living in another place, replete with personal and professional commitments? How do they fare when they try to start over again in Buenos Aires? Some buy apartments, often less luxurious than what they had before, but as one of my informants put it, the new space doesn't have to be great, just good enough. "It has to be close to a subway stop so I can get to the *milongas* easily and I don't want to worry about coming home alone at night." Others move from one rental apartment to the next, often living out of a suitcase. They have enough money to get by, but their lifestyles have changed radically.

A case in point is Sam, a somewhat scruffy but attractive fifty-five-year-old who had given up a well-paid profession in communications technology and a house in Australia in order to live (and dance) in Buenos Aires. I treated him to lunch in exchange for an interview and watched as he gobbled down a hamburger with an eagerness that made me think he hadn't eaten for a while. He explained how he had figured out that he could "just about make it" in Buenos Aires with his early retirement and savings, as long as he kept his medical insurance from home. He has been renting a one-room apartment in the city center but is planning to move soon because the neighborhood is so noisy. At the end of the interview, he pocketed the packets of sugar and ketchup on the table, explaining that he "[hated] to let them go to waste." As we walked to the nearest bus stop, he regaled me with a list of places in Buenos Aires where I could get a reasonably priced meal ("with all you can eat and cheap beer").

While the change in the material circumstances of Sam's life seemed dramatic to me, I soon discovered that other exiled *aficionados* had similar stories to tell. Even people with nice apartments and enough money to live the way they had been accustomed to before had to contend with equally significant changes in their former lifestyles. The previously mentioned Barbara, who had been used to the workaholic routine of the typical academic, suddenly had to contend with "never getting any work done." By the time she'd finished her grocery shopping, tidied her apartment, and made a few phone calls, she already had to get ready to go dancing. Others had given up an active social and cultural life for relatively marginal existences as exiles. Helene, whom we met in chapter 2, had to come to terms with her new existence in Buenos Aires after having worked hard and having had an active social and cultural life in Paris. She recalls her former life as a rat race: "working, getting a drink after work, speaking endlessly with people about I-don't-know-what, going to movies." In Buenos Aires, her life is completely different. She paints a little, does some occasional writing, has coffee with a friend, or practices her yoga. But, most important, she goes to the *milongas*, which are "social without being social. You meet people, but that's not why I go." For her, going to the *milongas* regularly "just makes life so easy, especially if you are a woman alone."

> When I dance with a man, it's just incredibly pleasant and that makes me happy. So, I can come back home and do whatever I have to do. Read a good book, whatever. . . . It makes my life more a *life* than it was before. . . . OK, so it's superficial, but how many deep [relationships] do you have in a lifetime anyway?

The tango culture in Buenos Aires provides the would-be exile with daily opportunities for intimacy and adventure as well as a space for crafting a new identity, forging new relationships, and even developing a sense of community. Thus, while the biography of a tango exile may be—as Riemann and Schütze (1991) would put it—"disordered," it is a far cry from the suffering and despair that characterize many other trajectories. Even the tango exiles, who have abandoned their old lives and taken up often precarious existences in an unfamiliar place, are prone to describe their new lives as allowing them, paradoxically, to "come home." Nowhere is this more apparent than in the romantic words of Paolo, a twenty-five-year-old Italian art student who left home and family in order to live, work, and dance in Buenos Aires:

> Tango feels like home to me because there will always be the same old tangos playing over and over again. Probably like when you are listening to the same old story that your parents read to you when you were a child and you never got tired of listening to it. You feel safe listening to it and you fall asleep. Even if I am dancing with a new person and discovering new things, I feel safe in tango.

Losing Yourself and Coming Home

This chapter began with the story of an ordinary Japanese accountant who became so enamored of dancing that his whole life was turned upside down. Using this improbable passion for dancing as a starting point, I have shown how tango can become just such a trajectory for people from other parts of the world as well. The love of tango can initiate a process that may, in some cases, spin out of control, changing and even disordering a person's life in unexpected and dramatic ways. Clearly this does not happen to everyone who begins dancing tango. Some may test the waters only to discover that tango is, after all, not for them. Others may go to considerable trouble and expense to learn to dance but never get involved in the salon culture. And, of course, some dancers visit Buenos Aires, enjoy dancing in the salons, and return home feeling that, after all, there is more to life than just tango. However, a small but not insignificant group of *aficionados* does become so embroiled in dancing tango that it becomes a way of life. It disrupts their everyday routines, disorders their lives, and estranges them from their former selves. For them, tango becomes something "bigger than we are."[13]

How are we to understand this? What is it about dancing tango that can make ordinary, hardworking, and even conventional people like our fictional Mr. Sugiyama go off the deep end?

Taking up tango may be the start of a trajectory—that is, an unfold-ing process by which an individual gradually loses control of herself and her life, forcing her to develop new perspectives on who she is, her relationships, and the kind of life she can lead. It is tempting to compare this passion for tango to what happens to drug addicts who often begin as weekend users and gradually find that the drug is taking over their lives until they finally become full-fledged members of a subculture, alienated from the outside world and totally in the thrall of their addic-tion (Darke, 2011). While the trajectory of the passionate tango dancer does, indeed, bear some resemblance to that of the drug addict—and, as we have seen, many *aficionados* refer to themselves as "addicts"—there is an important difference. Tango dancers, while acknowledging that their passion has taken over their lives, seem to embrace the loss of control that threatens to disorder their everyday lives. They exhibit no signs of remorse or sadness at the paths their lives have taken, nor do they seem to seriously want to "kick their habit." On the contrary, many experience the process of becoming a tango *aficionado* as the "best thing that ever happened to [them]."

This suggests that the trajectory of a tango dancer might better be compared to processes by which people become passionate about something (e.g., the trajectory of becoming an *aficionado*). Such a pas-sion is not a fixed entity but rather an active process by which a person develops an intense attachment to something to the extent that she or he willingly gives up her or his own autonomy in order to pursue it. Following Simmel's lead, Benzecry (2011) argues that such passionate trajectories go well beyond just liking to do something, as in a hobby or a preferred pastime;[14] rather, they involve an "intense, embodied attachment which brings with it a particular kind of engagement with the world, whereby certain lines of action are chosen while others are discarded" (p. 184). Passionate trajectories develop in a social con-text in which like-minded *aficionados* specifically come together for an experience that does not occur or that might even be blocked in the broader society of which they are a part. Such passions provoke a person to abandon all that is familiar, while doing what she or he was always "meant" to do. In short, a passionate trajectory is about losing oneself, while coming home.

This still leaves hanging the intriguing question of why a particular group of people at a particular historical juncture might choose to dance tango over some other activity, pursued with equal passion, that could lead to a similar but equally disordered trajectory. Clearly there are many kinds of passion, and presumably they will also have the potential to produce dangerous pleasure and delightful disorder. Why, then, tango? It is to this question that I turn my attention in the chapters which follow.

4

Performing Femininity, Performing Masculinity

In 1992, Martin Brest's Oscar-winning film *Scent of a Woman* was released. In the film, a blind and cynical veteran (played by Al Pacino), who is planning to commit suicide after having one last fling in New York City, invites a beautiful young woman (played by Gabrielle Anwar), who is sitting alone in a posh restaurant, to dance tango. And what a tango it is: replete with passionate looks and flourishes, ending with her leg slithering seductively around his, and danced to an original Argentinean tango song played by an *orchestra típica*.[1] Erotic tension abounds, with Pacino seducing a reluctant ("I think I'd be a little afraid . . . of making a mistake") but nevertheless willing woman (she has been stood up by her boyfriend) onto the dance floor. When the absent boyfriend finally arrives, his girlfriend's flushed face attests to which man has won her heart—at least for the moment.

Scent of a Woman appeared on screen more than seventy years after Rudolph Valentino's (in)famous tango, which I described at the outset of chapter 2. Staged at different moments in time (one at the beginning and the other at the close of the twentieth century) and in different places (one in a seedy café in Buenos Aires, the other in an upscale restaurant in New York City), both films employ tango as a motif that can be recycled successfully to give meaning to relations between the sexes.

In both films, the man leads and the woman follows. He is active, calling the shots, moving purposively across the dance floor; she is passive, waiting for his signals, her eyes closed. The dance is sexy, imbued with erotic passion. It takes up hegemonic heterosexuality and gives it an extra, macho twist: self-confident men with chests thrust out and hyperfeminine women in revealing dresses with side splits and stiletto heels. Gender differences are exacerbated, not only in the dancers'

Figure 4.1. Al Pacino and Gabrielle Anwar, dancing tango in *Scent of a Woman* (dir. Martin Brest, 1996).

movements and their clothing but also in the lyrics of the music and the conventions of the dance floor. Men look around, decide whom to invite; women wait patiently until they are asked.

At the same time, the differences in the ways these tangos are represented suggests that the relationship between gender and tango is anything but stable. Despite the many resonances between these cinematic renditions of the tango, there are notable differences as well. Pacino, despite his slicked-back hair and Latino aura, is a blind and slightly dissolute senior and, therefore, a far cry from the vigorously macho Valentino in his *gaucho* garb. Pacino is gentlemanly, sweeping his partner off her feet with chivalry rather than with violence. He steals her away from her boyfriend, but with compliments and charm rather than with threats. Passion, it would appear, has been civilized (Elias, 2000/1939). The woman is in safe hands with Pacino as a partner. "No mistakes in tango," he says reassuringly. "If you make a mistake, get all tangled up, just tango on."[2] When the tango is over, he does not cast his partner contemptuously aside, as Valentino did, but rather returns her to her boyfriend with a show of such elegant good manners that the boyfriend looks boorish. Respect and consideration for the woman seem to have replaced competitive bravado. And the woman? She does not grovel but returns to her boyfriend and her everyday life—however, not before she has been given a taste of what tango can do. The dance has unsettled her, and we cannot help but suspect that she is just a little bit tempted, at least for the moment, to abandon her boring yuppie boyfriend for a man who knows how to make her feel feminine and attractive as well as safe and cherished.

As different as the relationships between Valentino and Pacino with their partners clearly are, when tango is danced in a film, we expect that gender is somehow going to be involved. Tangos are used in films precisely because filmmakers can rely on a global understanding of the dance as the ultimate display of passionate and erotic relations between the sexes (Young, 1996; Washabaugh, 1998; Thompson, 2005). These on-screen representations have made tango an effective and widespread metaphor for heterosexual passion. However, can we simply assume that the performances of gender in tango on- and off-screen will be identical? It seems to me that in order to understand how men and women "do" (West and Zimmerman, 1987) or "perform" gender (Butler,

1989) when they dance tango in real life, we need to explore how they negotiate the (hyper)heterosexual and hierarchical meanings of masculinity and femininity that are so integral to tango's cultural baggage. In other words, how do the historical and geographical contexts in which tango is danced shape the ways in which masculinity and femininity are performed?

Feminist and other scholars in fields ranging from performance studies, history, and literary criticism to sociology and cultural studies have turned their critical attention to the performance of gender in tango.[3] In her pioneering study, the U.S.-Argentinean performance scholar Marta Savigliano (1995) has analyzed the intersections of gender, class, and race in the history and development of tango. She situates tango in the uncertainties and tensions between the sexes in Argentina during the first half of the twentieth century as women became more independent and began entering the public space (sometimes to dance tango). She describes her own memories of her grandfather getting ready to go to the *milonga,* leaving his (respectable) wife and family behind so that he could dance with the powerful and sexy *milongueras* in the salons. In her analysis of the tango lyrics of this era, Savigliano demonstrates how gender was reproduced in the stereotypes of the man as "whiny ruffian" and the woman as "rebellious broad." Teary-eyed men sang of their betrayal by untrustworthy women (many of whom later became the victims of a *crime passionnel*) while extolling the virtues of their mothers. The sexual division of labor, the policing of women's sexuality, and the imagery of Good Woman (mother) and Bad Woman (*milonguita*) were the staple ingredients of the Golden Age of tango (Savigliano, 1995:48–69).

Savigliano is critical of tango lyrics that represent women either as the objects of male passion or as the victims of machismo, but she also finds evidence of women's rebellion. As she puts it, women were clearly making trouble by pursuing their desires for independence. If this had not been the case, "the whiny confessions would have no referents and the admonitions would have no purpose" (Savigliano, 1995:69). She gives examples of the early *milongueras'* spirited "strategies of insurgence" like, for example, running off with a *niño bien*[4] and leaving their working-class men behind, refusing to conform to the norms of sexual monogamy and marriage, cheating their pimps, and more. In short, Savigliano's history of tango is not a tale of uncontested patriarchal power. Rather, she shows a history that is antagonistic and full of constant struggle between the sexes, between rich and poor, the "whitened" and the "colored," the "civilized" and the "barbaric" (Savigliano, 1995:71).

In her later work, Savigliano (2003) shows how the contemporary tango scene in Buenos Aires continues to provide a space for "rebellious broads" and "whiny ruffians," although the underlying gender relations have changed dramatically. Tango continues to be a heterosexual gender game, but dancers have become differently aligned in terms of class, education, and cultural capital. While tango is still danced to lyrics that are derogatory toward women and the organization of the *milonga* continues to nurture male machismo, in reality women have moved up the social ladder and actual relations between men and women bear little resemblance to the gender prescriptions in tango.

> Men are patriarchal and authoritarian, but are also often economically dependent and obsessed with their looks and seductive skills. Women are frequently wealthier, better educated and more entrepreneurial than their partners, but forgiving and blinded by romance...until they become fed up and leave the men for a better catch or a more restful existence. (Savigliano, 2003:190)

While Savigliano has had little to say about men other than to disparage their obsession with the cult of macho virility,[5] she has plenty to say about the gendered stereotypes of victimized women as passive objects of male fantasy. In her view, contemporary *milongueras* are docile agents who, while seeming to acquiesce in the norms of conventional femininity, also transgress them by actively expressing their desire. The *milonguera* today is not passive but rather chooses her partners carefully. She is like a gambler who is prepared to risk waiting until the right man comes along—the man who will identify her as desirable and transform her from an ugly wallflower into a divine *femme fatale*, a "goddess for a night" (Savigliano, 2003:189).

Since Savigliano's groundbreaking analysis, scholars have drawn on her work in order to explore the workings of gender in contemporary tango scenes outside Argentina.[6] Paula Villa (2001), for example, expands Savigliano's analysis, applying it to the performance of gender in European tango salons. Like Savigliano, Villa views tango (at least in its more traditional form)[7] as a dance that is predicated on hierarchical differences between the sexes. She argues that it is impossible for a woman to become a full subject in this dance when she has already been immobilized by impractical clothing and stiletto heels. After all, how can she be anything but subservient and passive when she is forced to follow her (male) partner's lead rather than take the initiative herself? And, how can she feel anything but stifled and unhappy when she is enclosed in a small space over which she has no control and then forced to take steps backward with her eyes closed? In Villa's view, the separation of the roles in the dance as well as the gendered organization of the salon culture presupposes traditional gender norms, treating them as natural, immutable, and essential for the production of passion (Villa, 2001:249). European dancers seem to accept a retrograde gender regime as part of what makes tango "authentic"—that is, "typically Argentinean." Villa is more interested than Savigliano in why modern, upwardly mobile, non-Argentinean tango dancers would be prepared to adopt such—for them—strange behavior,[8] yet she does not analyze this beyond asserting that tango provides an exotic "gender game" for contemporary dancers who can afford to distance themselves from their normal lives in order to enact traditional gender roles from the past. As she puts it, European men and women are already so firmly convinced of their autonomy and independence that they can play with different identities in accordance with their own desires. For them, tango provides a pleasant diversion in which they can occasionally take on very different and much more restrictive roles (Villa, 2001:257–58).

Taken together, Savigliano and Villa provide invaluable insights for a critical transnational understanding of how gender works in and through the tango. Savigliano's history of the origins and early travels of tango and her ethnography of the contemporary tango scene in Buenos Aires are enhanced by Villa's analysis of the tango revival in Europe today. While Savigliano explores how masculinity and femininity are constructed in the lyrics of music, thereby providing insight into the global cultural imaginary of tango, Villa focuses her analysis on how gender is actually enacted in and through the dance itself. While these analyses have provided valuable insights into the connections between gender and tango, they also leave several questions unaddressed.

The most important—and most mundane—is whether contemporary women (and men) are, in fact, performing retrograde femininity and masculinity when they dance tango. In other words, are these performances of gender sufficiently explained by recourse to tango's past? Should the tensions in relationships between men and women from another time and another place provide the template for understanding gender relations in a very different time and place? But, even if this is, in fact, what contemporary tango dancers are doing (as Villa would argue), why would they want to do this? How do they reconcile such guilty pleasures and "politically incorrect" performances with their lives as emancipated and enlightened members of late modern society?

In order to answer these questions, I will be taking a different approach. In this chapter, I explore what the performance of femininity and masculinity in tango can tell us more generally about the complicated workings of gender and (heterosexual) desire in the present transnational context of late modernity. To this end, I draw upon interviews with tango dancers in which they describe and justify their own performances of masculinity and femininity in passionate encounters on the dance floor. While I have spoken with dancers in both Amsterdam and Buenos Aires, in this chapter the balance will tip slightly toward my informants from Amsterdam. This is not because gender relations are more "traditional" in Buenos Aires (as Villa seems to imply) but rather because dancers outside Argentina often feel compelled to explain why they are prepared to cast aside their ordinary personae as emancipated men and women in order to dance tango. It is precisely because they need to justify such "strange behavior" that they provide a good starting point for thinking about what is at stake when women and men dance tango.[9]

Tango and Femininity

It is generally agreed that a tango salon is a perfect place to observe femininity in action. It is a space where femininity is performed in an exaggerated and highly sexualized form. While there are exceptions (queer tango, *nuevo tango*),[10] in most classical *milongas* women go to great lengths to present themselves as feminine. They do this through the revealing clothes they wear, the seductive way they move their bodies, and their flirtatious interactions with their partners, on and off the dance floor.

Helene, the journalist we encountered previously, moved to Buenos Aires from France and has been living there for several years. She notes that the *milongas* always make her feel "just very much a woman." She says this with some surprise, because in her pre-tango days in Paris, she was much more inclined to dress casually. Within her circle of artistic and intellectual friends, people tended to wear jeans, even to the theater or at a dinner party. On the rare occasion when she would dress up, it would be *haute couture*—designer clothes of excellent quality, but not particularly sexy. One of the things she learned from tango dancing, however, was that "it has to be sexy." She remembers the first time she bought a new dress in Buenos Aires. It was "very *décolleté*." To her amazement, she discovered that she was getting invited to dance much more frequently. "It made a *big* difference." As she puts it, the unspoken rule in tango seems to be that "you have to show something—a bit of leg, breasts, a bare back." In Buenos Aires, local women dancers seem to have no compunctions about cultivating an explicitly feminine look— long, flowing hair, lots of makeup, lacy underwear, and bare skin (Savigliano, 2003), thereby giving European women like Helene permission to dress in ways they might not so readily adopt at home. However, even in Europe and other parts of the world, the general tendency in tango scenes is to emphasize rather than downplay femininity, even if it just means wearing your best (and tightest) jeans and your highest heels.

Adopting more "feminine" behavior requires some justification, however. For example, Susan, the divorced engineer whom we met in chapter 3, explains that she never saw herself as a particularly feminine person. Effacing her appearance was always functional in the kind of work she did. "I don't flirt, I don't wear sexy clothes, I don't let my boobs hang out." For this reason, one of the things she has always found particularly difficult in tango was being "seen." "I'm used to being invisible. Where I come from, you're invisible as a forty-eight-year old-woman. But in tango you're beautiful." For Susan, wearing feminine clothing when dancing tango was not so much, as Villa (2001) has argued, a reenactment of retrograde gender stereotypes but rather a way to "stretch herself," to explore a side of herself that has "not had a chance to grow." From this perspective, performing femininity becomes a way to express a part of her self-identity that she has had to keep under wraps in her work situation and everyday life.

Many of the women I spoke with outside of Buenos Aires took a similar stance when describing how they came to terms with the gendered division in tango between male leaders and female followers. As follower, a woman has to give up her will and accept that her partner will be making the calls. This initially feels like losing control and becoming a mere object of another person's intentions, *his* style of dancing, and *his* interpretation of the music. For some women, learning to follow can present insurmountable hurdles. As Miranda, a divorced social worker in her early fifties, put it:

> You can imagine what it's like for us more or less emancipated women . . . having to set aside our own initiative—in fact, to totally *not* take any initiative at all. . . . That was the hardest thing for me. I really struggled to learn how to do that.

Most of my female informants went to great lengths to assure me that they were used to being in control in their everyday lives, their jobs, and their relationships. Whether they explicitly described themselves as "emancipated" or "feminist," they implied that dancing tango required them to behave in ways that were antithetical to their normal behavior. However, they did not share Villa's assessment that by following in tango they were abandoning all agency. Many of the women I spoke with described the activity of following as something that could be easily combined with their identities as active subjects. A case in point is Bea, a scientist with a high-powered and responsible academic position. She explains that she has always had to take the lead—not only at work but also in her marriage, in which she is the one who generally makes the decisions. However, things have changed since she and her husband have been dancing tango together.

> I love it . . . that I can give this responsibility to him. It [tango] taught me how to give up control while not having to do things against my will . . . even being able to be myself without having to be in control.

Bea clearly situates the—for her unusual—activity of not being in control against the backdrop of her normal identity as someone who is, more often than not, the person in charge. Tango does not require that she relinquish her previous identity as competent, self-sufficient woman. Nor does her independence seem to be in any danger when she dances tango. She doesn't have to worry, as she does in other situations, about people making her do things she doesn't want to do or having to "take care of myself." Tango provides the kind of space in which she feels free to experiment, to tap into unused potentials, and, ultimately, to become a more complete person—that is, a person who can both lead and follow.

Chia, whom we met in chapter 2, takes this a step further, arguing that tango is a perfect place to negotiate difficulties in relations between the sexes. Recalling several unhappy love affairs she had before moving from Chile to Buenos Aires, she is convinced that tango has helped her come to terms with some of the difficulties she had so often encountered with men. "Tango puts things under a magnifying glass," she explains. She recalls being a beginning dancer and being desperate to dance with a particular man with whom she had had one memorable dance experience. Although he would occasionally invite her to dance, he often passed her over in order to dance with more accomplished partners. As difficult as this was for Chia to accept, she remembers having a "moment of liberation" when she realized that he was only doing what she herself wanted to do—namely, pursuing an unforgettable dance experience. This did not make her regret his unavailability as a dance partner, but it did allow her to acknowledge that it was possible for her to "feel very deeply," to experience unrequited longing for someone while at the same time being able to "let him go" and see what was waiting for her just around the corner. Since then, she has discovered that she can actively let men know that she wants to dance with them and, at the same time, accept that—as she puts it, laughing—"my insistent looks will sometimes be ignored."

Chia does not deny that the salon culture is rife with gendered asymmetries as a result of the convention that men can invite their partners to dance, while women have to wait to be invited. However, she does not regard this inequity as an obstacle. On the contrary, she presents the salon regime as an ideal space for her to pursue her own desires as well as practice behaviors she needs to learn in order to survive as a single woman in the outside world of short-lived liaisons and commitment anxiety. As Chia puts it, tango can actually better equip a woman to "get what she wants."

Of course, not all women are as sanguine about gender relations in tango as Chia is. As we saw in the previous chapters, many women—and this is certainly the case in Amsterdam—feel that they have a right to dance. They suffer when they have to wait too long for a dance and resent the privileges that men have in the salons. Many would have few qualms about asking a man to dance. Jeannette, a single artist in her early forties, complains that tango is difficult for women without steady partners. If she wants to have a good salon experience, Jeannette has learned, she will just have to ask men to dance. She is adamant that this is "only fair." However, this does not mean that she feel entirely free to ask whomever she wants. She is careful to approach men with whom she has danced before and who she knows will be friendly. "They are not going to turn me down. So I'll always have a couple of dances and my evening will be OK. But if I'm honest, I have to admit that I'd rather be asked."

Women struggle with having to negotiate their desire to dance, their sense of entitlement ("Why should I dance less than the men?"), and their—often unspoken—preference to a man's choosing them as a dance partner rather than their having to ask him to dance. This preference has less to do with any sudden lapse in their ideological commitment to gender equality than with their desire not only to dance, but to be desired (Savigliano, 2003). For most women, it is not enough just to be dancing. They also want to feel that they have been chosen out of all the other available women. In other words, women are in search of the experience, however illusory, of being the most desired and desirable of all.[11]

And how do men make women feel desirable? My informants had plenty to say about that. They explained that they needed to "feel safe and protected" when they dance and that "a partner has to be totally tuned in to who I am." "He has to be there for me, completely together with me, and not off on his own tangent." Kate, an academic and professed feminist, explains that her perfect dance is "like nothing bad is going to happen to me. I can close my eyes and just enjoy that this guy is going to take care of me and make sure that I have everything I could possibly need." Laughing, she compares it to "really perfect sex":

> I know that there are two of you and it's important to satisfy the other person. I know that's true. But I'm just telling you about my own desires here. I'd be perfectly happy to just lie back and enjoy it [sex]. I can see that in the tango, too. I have no problems with being taken care of, being pleasured.

While this seems at first glance to be the epitome of feminine passivity, Kate also positions herself as someone who "knows" that she will need to take an active role (presumably in sex as well as in tango). She also describes how she makes sure that the dance is pleasurable for her partner—for example, by helping him maintain his balance during a particularly difficult turn or doing a fancy embellishment of a step when dancing with a novice so that he will feel that he's "really able to dance tango." However, her innermost desires are not governed by the rules of equality, and tango provides a safe space for exploring these desires.

Women draw upon discourses of heterosexuality to explain their passion for tango, but they do so in ways that mix up gendered notions of female passivity and male activity. Renate, for example, recalls dancing with a well-known *milonguero* in Buenos Aires. He kept moving her from side to side, inviting her to take the lead, while murmuring seductively: "*Asi, asi. Anda, anda. Bailame.*" ("Yes, like this. Go. Go. Dance me.") "It was like he was turning himself into this beautiful object," Renate explains. Although he seemed to be handing his agency over to her, making himself the passive object and allowing her to be the active subject, this was not how she interpreted the situation, nor what made the dance so exciting for her. As she put it, he was "stimulating me to dance the way I wanted. That's what you feel, that you become the person you really are, everything that you are, everything that is part of you."

While women's dance experiences are different and idiosyncratic, many emphasize the desire to be cared for by their dance partners and of having their needs met. Being made to feel visible or beautiful or sensational as a dancer is part of what they long for and what tango makes possible for them. However, fulfilling this desire requires more than the romantic fantasy of being placed on a pedestal by one's partner. In contrast to the give-and-take of everyday life, the ideal dance partner is not thinking about himself (*his* steps, *his* appearance, *his* reputation as a dancer). Rather, he is totally focused on *her* desires, and his only goal is ostensibly to ensure that they are met. In this way, she can remain in her own private space, pampered and loved, without having to think about or take care of anyone else.

Interestingly, Bruce, one of my male informants, provided one of the most perceptive accounts of what tango means to women—at least, for women who take the follower position in tango. We were talking about the meaning of Pugliese[12] for tango and why it was so important—particularly in Buenos Aires—for women to dance the "Pugliese set."

> It's the fairy tale romantic fantasy for women.... She gets whisked around the dance floor by Prince Charming... she's got her eyes closed so she doesn't see how fat or short the guy is ... that she's started off with a toad.... You can close your eyes and go off into fairyland.... Pugliese is the pinnacle of that idea. It represents all the reasons women go to the *milonga*, all captured in the Pugliese set.

But what about the men? I ask. What does Pugliese mean for them? Laughing, Bruce explains:

> Responsibility. You've got this person who wants to go off into fairyland. Making that happen is not easy. I've talked to a lot of people, both men and women, and I think I can safely say that women tend to be more excited about Pugliese than men.

Tango and Masculinity

If women are engaged in doing femininity, what about men? How do they "do" masculinity when they dance tango? The performance of masculinity is relatively easy to spot in the salons of Buenos Aires. The good *milonguero* displays his masculinity not by executing fancy steps but by pleasing his partner. If she is swooning in his arms, eyes closed with an expression of rapture on her face, this reflects back on him. Her satisfaction shows off his prowess as a man. In the tango salons of Buenos Aires, masculinity is displayed primarily for the consumption of other men (Tobin, 1998). I remember observing a well-known *milonguero* in a salon in Buenos Aires dancing past a table of his friends. During the pause between songs, he called to them from the dance floor, making jokes, while his partner patiently waited at his side. When the music began, he literally "danced her" in front of his friends, opening up the embrace so that she could show off a fancy step. He smiled with complicity at his friends, who were cheering him on. Then he reeled his partner back into his embrace, and off he danced. Throughout this performance, all the woman had to do was to smile, look at him with admiration, and follow his lead. She made him look good by showing that she was having a good time in his arms.

In Buenos Aires, the dance, the organization of the salon along sex-segregated lines, and the codes all conspire to produce a specific form of masculinity.[13] My informant Bruce, who was mentioned above, is an ex-pat from Australia in his mid-thirties living in Buenos Aires, provided an interesting explanation not only of how these codes work but also of how they facilitate the performance of masculinity. We had been talking about what happens when there is a collision on the dance floor. The unspoken code is that the men will glance at each other and if the one who is to blame nods his head slightly, this serves as a "visual handshake" and the dancing can continue. If he neglects to acknowledge his mistake, however, the other man will stop and stare at him, looking aggressive and sometimes even balling his fists, until the apology is forthcoming. After hearing this explanation from Bruce, I explained that I sometimes try to "cool out" my partner after a collision by commiserating with him, but I have found—somewhat to my surprise—that my partners rarely seem to appreciate my sympathetic attempts to smooth over the situation. Bruce looked at me with surprise.

> But that's just so *clear*. Maybe I'm taking a lot of things for granted. I'm sorry. It's hard to know what to take for granted and what not. But look. So I'm dancing with a woman and it's my job to protect her at all costs. This precious, delicate flower who needs not to worry about anything because nothing will happen to her. And if someone bashes into me—or, much worse, bashes into *her*—this is a *huge* problem because I didn't

do my job. So my pride is injured and I have to pop up my chest and attempt to stupidly resurrect my pride through this aggressive behavior by addressing the guy's behavior. Something has to be done.

"Doing" masculinity in the tango salons outside of Buenos Aires requires men to follow conventions that are less taken for granted. Men who dance tango in Amsterdam also draw upon the discourses of macho masculinity as they imagine it is performed in Buenos Aires.[14] Argentinean men are regarded as possessing machismo "naturally" ("it's in their blood") or by virtue of their "culture." European men, however, have to learn it the hard way if they want to dance tango. They view machismo as something that enhances tango or is even necessary for its performance ("chest out, strut your stuff"). This cannot be done in a straightforward fashion, however, but has to be negotiated with an eye to their identities as enlightened European men. Thus, many of my Dutch informants explained that tango allowed them to discover their "macho side." For example, Jasper, a divorced urban planner, describes himself as a "nerdy guy" who has never been particularly successful with women. Still coping with the aftermath of a messy divorce that—as he put it—"damaged him" to the extent that he never wants to have that kind of permanency in a relationship again, he sees himself as basically insecure and unassertive. "I never thought that I was a 'macho-man.' Those were always other men than me." However, tango changed that.

> I guess I do have something macho in me. . . . At the same time, I'm not macho at all. I could use a little more of it, in fact . . . but the moment I start dancing it comes to the surface. . . . That's fantastic, don't you think?

Tango provides the possibility for men who could be considered unattractive, insecure, or even social losers outside the *milongas* to discover a new identity on the dance floor. Given the almost chronic surplus of women dancers in most salons, men who are good dancers will often find themselves in great demand. Women who wouldn't give them a second look outside the salon are suddenly vying for a chance to dance with them. As one ordinary-looking middle-aged man, balding and slightly chubby, who was retired and recently divorced, explained,

"Let's be honest, where else could a guy like me get to hold so many beautiful and terrific women in his arms every day of the week?"

Leo, the sixty-five-year-old lawyer we met earlier, describes himself as a "softie," yet he talks about his experiences with women on the dance floor in a way that clearly belies his behavior outside the salon. For example, he compares dancing with a woman to playing the violin, something he did with great enthusiasm as a teenager. "I guess you could say I have found another instrument to replace my violin. . . . In fact, I have lots of violins that I'm allowed to play now. And some violins are easier to play than others." Although Leo would seem to fulfill all the requirements of a modern enlightened man, he seems to have no difficulties comparing his female partners to an inanimate object. Even more disconcerting is the way he describes his ideal dancer as totally passive: "She won't do anything that I haven't led. Nothing on her own. It's like she's saying: 'Lead me! Do it with me! Let me experience it! You can do it! Let me do it!'"

The language of conquest is unmistakable here—he is active and she is passive. He "plays" her and she "lets" him do it. He is responsible for her dance experience. He brings her to ecstasy; her experience is, literally, in his hands. As he puts it,

> Having the reins in hand . . . that's what I like about it. Leadership suits me; I'm more a *leader* than a *follower*. That's just my character, and in tango dancing I don't have to *defend* myself on that score. It's *expected*, right? [laughs] The better you lead, the better it is. The *last* thing that you should be doing is *not* leading. As leader you have to be charming, make compliments, you have to put your lady at ease. It's part of the tango *character*. . . . You don't have to justify it.

While Leo clearly knows what he wants, he also realizes that what he wants requires some justification. In other contexts—for example, a collective work environment—leadership is complicated and almost always has to be explained. "Otherwise it's playing the boss. It has to be democratic." Even when he thinks he knows what would be best for the client or for the firm, he knows that he will always have to confer with his colleagues, making sure everyone is on board with his decision. "But in tango, you *have* to lead, you have to make choice[s], you don't have to confer. You're judged whether you do it well or not."

What is noteworthy here is not that Leo accepts the role of leader in tango. After all, someone always has to lead, even—as we will see in the next chapter—in queer tango. In Buenos Aires, it goes without saying that in most salons men are leaders. However, in Amsterdam, the shared ideological (if not always practical) commitment to gender equality and egalitarian relations between the sexes make leading something that requires justification. Dancing tango offers men like Leo, who (secretly) like to lead, permission to temporarily pursue an expression of masculinity that would be problematic outside the salon. In other words, they can engage in a kind of masculine behavior that feels central to their sense of self but that has to be toned down or suppressed because of social conventions.

Of course, not every man feels, as Leo does, that leading is part of his character, just waiting to be released by tango. For some men, taking on the role of leader, and all of the symbolic baggage that accompanies it, is an endeavor fraught with difficulties. Nowhere is this more apparent than in the difficulties many Dutch men have in explaining how they select their dance partners. Whereas in Buenos Aires the male prerogative to choose whom to dance with and when to dance with her is unlikely to evoke a second thought, Dutch tango dancers feel compelled to justify their privileged position vis-à-vis their female partners. As Danny, whom we have encountered in earlier chapters, puts it:

> I find it difficult that there is such a bad ratio between women and men. There are just too many women. As a man, of course, I am in a position of luxury. I can always dance. But, on the other hand, it can be hard, too. I feel a lot of pressure sometimes not to skip a set because there goes a chance for another woman to dance.

When I asked my male informants how they chose their dance partners, they often assured me that they were "social dancers" ("I learned from my mother to ask the women who haven't had a dance yet"). Doing a social dance is "how I earn points," one dancer told me, casting his eyes upward as though some deity were keeping track. Many men have commitments to the women who regularly attend a certain salon and must "work through" their list before going further afield. However, as one man explained, "I can service only six women in one evening. If there are more women who want to dance, I just can't do it." Although many men display sensitivity to the plight of the wallflower, they clearly enjoy having the privilege of being able to pick and choose their dance partners. Whether they want to dance with someone because "she is the better lady" ("oops, sorry, that sounds so negative") or because she is a beginning dancer ("that is sometimes fun, too"), men reveled in being the ones who get to decide.

While the performance of masculinity in tango is linked to control, many of my male informants insisted that what they most liked about tango was not so much having control but being able to lose it. Bruce, for example, goes to great lengths in a salon to ensure that he gets what he wants. He sits in the same seat, picks and choses his partners according to whom he wants to dance with and when, and is glad that he doesn't have to sit on the sidelines and wait to be asked as women do. At the same time, however, his all-time favorite dance experience is one that, as he put it, "knocked my socks off," leaving him totally confused for days afterward. "I guess you could say that's what I'm really looking for in tango."

One of the most surprising features of my interviews with male dancers was the way they framed their relationships with their dance partners. Tango transforms them into romantics longing to "become one with their partners," "reveal all their secrets," and "touch the soul of another person." As Nicolas puts it, "You have to be romantic to dance tango. It's only for people who are emotional. That just goes without saying. Otherwise it couldn't really move you." While many men may be reluctant to use the "L" word in their ordinary lives, in tango they seem to have few qualms describing tango in terms of love. For example, Miles, a divorced schoolteacher from Canada who lives in Buenos Aires off and on, explains that, while he is not looking for a relationship with his tango partners outside the *milonga*, he does want to fall in love when he dances with them. He recalls an incident in which he asked his dance partner point-blank if she could fall in love with him—"you know, just for 15 minutes?" She was completely taken aback, but he persuaded her to try it because, although they had been dancing well, there was still something missing. "I wanted her to dance as though she were in love with me. That's what I want."

This suggests that, while love and romance are conventionally associated with women,[15] tango seems to open up this unfamiliar terrain for men as well. It enables them to experience the affective intensity of a romantic attachment and, at the same time, keep it safely separate from the encumbrances that are part and parcel of relationships outside the *milonga*. In contrast to women who may sometimes describe a good dance as similar to "having good sex" or a "perfect promiscuity" and "doing something for [themselves]," men are looking for love and the experience of being "swept off their feet." Taken together, contemporary women and men appear to approach tango with different needs and expectations.

What can these differences tell us about gender relations in the context of late modernity? And, more to the point, can these differences help us understand why contemporary men and women want to dance tango?

Gender, Desire, and Tango in Late Modernity

Tango is not simply a dance performance; it involves the performance of gender as well. As Jane Desmond (1997:42) has argued, dance always entails the negotiation of hierarchies of gender, along with other hierarchies of difference like class, race, and nationality. When dances travel to other places—as has been the case with tango—it is not simply their choreographies, music, or social customs that are taken up and have to be rearticulated and transformed. They also need to be remodeled in accordance with shifting gender relations in contexts with new possibilities and prohibitions. Therefore, in order to understand the workings of gender in tango today, both in Buenos Aires and abroad, we need to explore not only how contemporary dancers borrow old notions of gender when they dance tango but also how their performance of gender mirrors the new context, giving their dancing specific and distinctive forms.

Both in and outside of Buenos Aires, the days of the "rebellious broads" and "whiny ruffians" of Argentinean tango are long gone (see Savigliano, 1995). However, masculinity and femininity continue to be performed just as persistently as they were in the past. In Buenos Aires, dancers appear to revel in displays of hyperfemininity and macho masculinity. They cultivate the *frisson* of seduction and passion in the interest of having a good dance. While machismo is familiar to contemporary Argentineans as part of their cultural baggage, old-fashioned preoccupations with virility and male supremacy have undergone considerable transformation (Savigliano, 1995:43–48). Understanding machismo in the present requires untangling the reactionary and progressive patterns in displays of masculinity, linking them to the historical and socioeconomic context of a particular culture (Mora, 2012:439). For example, contemporary *milongueros* may fool around on the dance floor, engaging in blatant displays of machismo for their friends, only to dismiss such behavior minutes later as something that shouldn't be taken too seriously (Tobin, 1998:101). By the same token, Argentinean women may complain about the machismo of their dance partners, referring to them as traditional or uneducated. However, they are quick to add, they "wouldn't want to miss the games for the world." The heterosexual gender games are, indeed, at least part of what makes tango enjoyable. In this respect, the performance of masculinity and femininity in tango resembles the kinds of performances that occur in sadomasochistic relations in which a scene of dominance and submission is played out consensually for the mutual pleasure of the participants.[16] In other words, one could argue that for Argentinean tango dancers, the performance of "traditional" gender roles is a matter of play, a slightly naughty and nostalgic "time out" from their ordinary relationships, a way to achieve the transcendent experience of being outside normal time and space that is the essence of tango (Cozarinsky, 2007). The codes and organization of the salon are intended to keep these "transgressions" of the more modern relations between the sexes, which prevail in cosmopolitan Buenos Aires, clearly demarcated and safely separate from the rest of the dancers' lives.

In Amsterdam, as in most of Europe, the tradition of the salon with its codes of behavior for men and women is missing. A strong commitment to individual autonomy militates against such strict regulation of behavior like sitting at a particular table or not directly asking someone to dance. The norm is that everyone should be free to move around as he or she likes. Moreover, the allegiance to sexual equality requires—at least in principle—that women and men sit companionably together. As a result, salons outside Buenos Aires do not create the distance between men and women that is conducive to the practice of *cabeceo* with its flirtatious glances and seductive moves.

Unsurprisingly, the performance of hyperheterosexual masculinity and femininity in tango becomes problematic in a context in which
gender equality is the norm and egalitarianism the practice through
which heterosexual relationships are negotiated. All-too-overt displays
of machismo or excessive femininity would be ridiculed in a salon in
Amsterdam. As we have seen, dancers outside Buenos Aires are often
conflicted about how to "do" gender in tango, as evidenced by their
marked tendency to explain, defend, and justify their desire to adopt
"traditional" masculine and feminine personae *within* tango against the
backdrop of their "normal"—enlightened and emancipated—identities
outside tango. As any sociologist will attest, such contradictory, discursive behavior indicates that an issue is far from settled or simple (Billig,
1987, 1988; Hollway and Jefferson, 2000). Women freely admitted to liking sexy clothes, impractical shoes, and "feeling like a woman" when
they went to a salon. However, they also felt the need to assert that this
was *not* how they dressed, nor how they behaved, at home, at work,
or just "normally." They extolled the joys of "closing [their] eyes and
relaxing" in the dance but always insisted that that was the first—and
hardest—thing they had to learn in tango because they were so used to
being in charge everywhere else. They confided that their perfect partner would be able to "protect" them so that they could "let go and leave
everything to him." However, they did not describe this as passive or
subservient feminine behavior, but rather framed it as doing something
"for [themselves]."

The accounts provided by the men showed similar signs of ambivalence. They would admit to being secretly delighted to discover their
"inner macho" through tango, yet they also went to great lengths to
explain that they were "feminist men at heart." They took great pleasure
in precisely those features of tango which constituted male privilege in
tango: having a large quantity of women at their beck and call and being
in charge, while feeling guilty that the salon was unfair to women who,
of course, should have the same rights as men. They waxed poetic when
describing their dance experiences, providing accounts of "perfect"
connections, "pure" relationships, and "ideal" love affairs. These men
seemed less like traditional macho men, worried about betrayal from
traitorous women, than inveterate romantics, longing to fall in love—at
least for fifteen minutes—but without having to jump into bed at the

end of the evening. Tango seemed to release them from their fears of commitment and open the doors for love without the complications of sexuality, shared households, or children.

These contradictory justifications permeated the accounts of the tango dancers in Amsterdam in ways that were quite different from the rueful or playful matter-of-factness with which Argentinean dancers approached the subject of gender relations in tango. This is not to say that gender equality has become an undisputed reality in Amsterdam or in other parts of the global North, any more than that gender equality is not desired by many women and men in Buenos Aires. However, for the dancers in Amsterdam, gender equality is the dominant, if implicit, norm, making any overt manifestation of inequality between men and women problematic—that is, socially unacceptable, old-fashioned, or "politically incorrect." It is not surprising, then, that they had to find ways to reconcile their commitment to gender equality with the gendered divisions that are so pervasive in tango.

What is surprising, however, is why, if it is, indeed, such a problem to reconcile the performance of masculinity and femininity with a commitment to gender equality, they would want to do it in the first place. Obviously, some men and women are disinclined to dance tango for this very reason. And, indeed, even some tango dancers, as we will see in the next chapter, have so many problems with the gendered inequities of tango that they have decided to change it in order to make it more conducive to gender equality (queer tango). But what about those otherwise emancipated and cosmopolitan individuals—the majority of contemporary tango dancers—who, despite the archaic displays of masculinity and femininity, insist on dancing traditional tango anyway? Is it tango's exoticism that attracts them? Or does tango provide a way for them to experience connection without complication? Or does it perhaps fulfill some deeper need, an unrequited longing for passion that is missing in late modernity?

An Exotic "Time Out"

The first explanation of why contemporary Europeans are prepared to adopt seemingly retrograde gender roles in tango is that they are looking for a kind of "time out" from their ordinary identities as emancipated individuals in late modernity (Villa, 2009). Tango allows them to imitate gender relations from another time and place: the turn of the twentieth century in faraway Buenos Aires. By dancing tango, they can "play around" with an exoticism that they associate with the supposedly more traditional gender relations to be found in the global South. They can, of course, do this only by virtue of their position of privilege as affluent, educated Europeans, secure in their identities as modern, cosmopolitan individuals. In this view, when people from the global North dance tango, they are living out their unfulfilled desire for completion through "dominating or conquering the exotic 'other.'" The global disparities between North and South, which have their roots in the colonial or imperial past, have made tango inevitably "an erotic game played out between unequal partners" (Savigliano, 1995:75–76).

While this explanation has many merits, it does not to justice to the contemporary conditions under which tango is danced across the globe. When tango initially arrived in Paris in the 1900s, its appeal was intimately linked to its novelty as an exotically erotic dance that was "civilized" enough to appeal to the imperialistic bourgeois mentality of modern Europeans. As Savigliano (1995) puts it: "Tango could be clothed in tails and satins. But it could also be put in its place: the place of the colonized in the process of being civilized. . . . [It] could adopt the manners of the colonizer while retaining the passion of the colonized" (p. 110). But does this colonial or imperialist mentality still apply to how tango is danced today? Could it be that the willingness of contemporary tango dancers to adopt retrograde gender roles is not simply a reflection of Europe's colonial history or, for that matter, the imperial past of the United States and Japan but rather a response to the present—that is, to the conditions and contradictions of late modernity (Törnqvist, 2013)?

Connection without Commitment

This brings me to the second explanation, which is that tango is less about the past than it is a reflection of what late modern men and women desire—namely, connection without commitment. Tango's attraction resides precisely in the kind of encounter it offers. It provides physical contact, intimacy, and emotional intensity, all without the messiness of sex, long-term obligations, and children. In late modernity, intimate alliances have become temporary, fragile, or fluid (Giddens, 1991, 1992;

Bauman, 2000, 2003; Beck and Beck-Gernsheim, 2002). With the ero-sion of the constraints of community, family values, and tradition, the "pure" relationship has emerged, undertaken for its own sake and requir-ing ongoing negotiation between autonomous agents, responsible only to themselves. Whatever the vicissitudes of these relationships, they have left modern individuals with an insatiable longing for intensity, risk, excitement, and danger (Beck, 1992; Boutelier, 2002). In this view, tango provides the perfect encounter with its endless recycling of intense con-nection followed by "easy exits" (Törnqvist, 2013). Indeed, tango could be regarded as the poster child for "liquid modernity" (Bauman, 2000).

While this theory explains why tango might appeal to contemporary dancers, it does not explain how they manage the problem of gender. It does not take into account the frictions between their normative commitment to gender equality, which is endemic to many late mod-ern societies and shared by both men and women, and the realities of a playing field that is far from level. While both men and women desire autonomy and are hesitant about embarking upon a relationship for life, men enjoy a privileged position on the sexual playing field. They can choose their partners from a wider range of ages and can afford to wait before settling down, while women have to worry about the ubiquitous effects of ageism, not to mention finding a partner before it is too late to have children. In late modernity, men's "commitment phobia" has taken on epidemic proportions, leaving women with fewer choices for partners, a larger share of the emotional suffering, and a hankering for recognition (Illousz, 2012). Thus, while the "connection without com-mitment" explanation can account for why men would be prepared to enjoy tango (because it mitigates their commitment phobia), it does not really explain why women would be prepared to forfeit their hard-won autonomy to reinsert archaic forms of femininity into their dancing.

Rediscovering Passion

A third explanation is that tango allows *both* men and women to expe-rience passion precisely *because* it reinstates gender difference. Con-temporary individuals have a longing for the passion that has been undermined through the cultural values of late modernity (equality, autonomy, rationality). This somewhat controversial argument has been put forth by Illousz (2012),[17] who, unlike the earlier-mentioned theorists of late modernity, is specifically concerned with the role that gender plays in the culture of modernity.

Modernity has produced a shared cultural worldview that includes a commitment to gender equality, autonomy, consensuality, and—above all—rationality. Men and women are expected to approach one another as autonomous individuals who will enter upon and negotiate their relationships in a consensual and transparent manner. Intimate relationships have, thus, become rationalized—that is, made stable, manageable, and predictable. While this process of rationalization has unquestionably had many advantages—not the least of which is that it has made gender relations more egalitarian—it has also had the unintended consequence of disrupting the structure of heterosexual desire.

Rationalization conflicts with the ways in which men and women have traditionally experienced and expressed passion (Illousz, 2012:185). Gender difference is embedded in men's and women's identities, producing masculinity and femininity as "thick identities"[18] that provide the regimes of meaning which code heterosexual desire. Historically, heterosexual desire has not only rested on gender difference, however. It has also been tied to gender inequality, whereby what was experienced by men and women as erotic was men's power and women's lack of it. For example, many of the rituals and practices of gender relations—like gallantry, flirtation, seduction, and the abandonment of the self to the other that are at the heart of heterosexual desire—belong to longstanding but constantly changing cultural traditions that are grounded in women's subordination to men. It is precisely this dynamic that has been disrupted in late modernity with its normative commitment to gender equality and egalitarianism. The normative commitment to gender equality makes power differentials "politically incorrect" and, in so doing, makes it difficult to engage in many of the rituals that made the performance of gender erotic and pleasurable (Illousz, 2012:192). Thus, in late modernity men and women are left empty-handed when it comes to practices for expressing desire, along with an unrequited longing for passion.

From this perspective, it is easy to see how tango might allow contemporary dancers to experience the passion that is missing from their lives. By accentuating the very gender differences that late modernity has made problematic, tango facilitates the emergence of passion. Its

Figures 4.2 and 4.3. Men and women dancing tango (Photos: Mirjam van Niel.)

rituals of invitation (the *cabeceo*) draw upon the same techniques of ambiguity—the enticingly off-the-record promise—that enable flirtation. The communication between leader and follower is reminiscent of a seduction with its playful teasing of attraction and repulsion. And, finally, the close embrace of tango allows and even demands the very abandonment of self to the other that has been lost in late modernity with its norm of autonomous individuals in control of their destinies. Tango thrives on difference, allowing partners to encounter each other across the gulf that divides them, to find a space outside time and space where all boundaries magically disappear (Savigliano, 1995). Performing masculinity and femininity enables modern men and women to discover, express, and experience passion. Yet they can do so without risk to their autonomy outside the world of tango. In other words, they can have their cake and eat it, too.

In conclusion, I would argue that tango cannot be viewed as a reiteration of traditional gender relations that existed in another time and place. Nor is it simply a reflection of relationships between men and women as they exist in late modernity. Rather, tango provides an opportunity for contemporary individuals to experience something that is missing in their everyday lives. It offers them an escape from the norms of equality that facilitates their desire for passion. Tango creates gender relations that are neither retrograde nor emancipated but rather a compensation for some of the costs of late modernity.

Nowhere is this better illustrated than in the tango scene from the film *Scent of a Woman* with which this chapter began. That scene recycles and transforms the tango imaginary that was popular in Valentino's day—an imaginary that would only make us laugh today—and substitutes an imaginary of tango that meshes with the present reality of gender relations in late modernity. Tango is presented as a momentary compensation for some of the injuries to masculinity and femininity. What could be more reassuring to modern men than the image of a lonely, aging male "loser" becoming a romantic hero, able to sweep a beautiful young woman off her feet? And what could be more comforting to a woman in a context of hook-ups, biological clocks ticking away, and male commitment phobias than to be cherished and adored after her date has just stood her up? For both, the dance is a temporary escape from life as usual, offering a glimpse of how their lives could be better.

5

Queering Tango

It was 2002 or 2003—I can't remember exactly—and I was sitting in Plaza Bohemia, one of my favorite *milongas* in Buenos Aires. The DJ was playing classical tango music from the Golden Age. The elderly *milongueros* sat together at tables drinking beer while the single women were seated on the other side of the room, waiting to be invited. Gloria, the motherly hostess of the salon, warmly welcomed the guests, bringing them to their tables and making sure they felt at home. It was all very standard and business-as-usual, until suddenly two beautiful young men, Augusto Balizano and Miquel Moyano,[1] walked out onto the dance floor dressed in revealing tops and skin-tight pants and began to dance to music by Pugliese. It was an awe-inspiring performance that I will never forget. It was perfectly executed, elegant, and moving, but with a bittersweet edge often missing from the slightly aggressive tango performance between the typical macho man in his pinstripe suit and the glamorous *milonguera* in slit skirt and stiletto heels. The entanglements of these two men through tango were sad rather than antagonistic and were performed as though the dancers were in constant danger of being pulled apart. The performance, which would now probably be perceived as prototypically "queer," seemed to capture the conflict between the reproduction and contestation of heterosexuality as norm, whereby the dancers enacted the tensions between "becoming" and "becoming-stuck," between melancholy and (the possibility of) happiness (Blackman, 2011:197).[2] I remember watching these dancers with a lump in my throat, reading into their performance what I imagined to be a long history of Argentinean machismo and homophobia.[3] But perhaps even more moving was the fact that two men were dancing together in a traditional tango salon without the regular customers' showing any noticeable signs of discomfort, let alone disapproval or hostility. Apparently, something was changing in the world of Argentinean tango. Could it be, I wondered, that tango, seemingly so embedded in the regimes of heteronormativity, was becoming queer?

Not a Straight *Milonga*

Several years after watching this performance in Plaza Bohemia, I found myself in La Marshall, the first gay *milonga* in Buenos Aires. The *milonga* had been organized in 2002 and named in honor of the actress Niní Marshall (1903–96), who had been an iconic figure for many gays in Argentina, not unlike Judy Garland in the United States. On this particular occasion, the salon was packed with tango tourists, who had attended the IV International Queer Tango festival in Buenos Aires. Compared with the traditional *milongas* in Buenos Aires, this salon was striking in its informality. The visitor was not guided to a table but was expected to find her or his own seat. There was no discernible separation by sex. Groups of men or women, ostensibly friends, were seated throughout the salon, with couples interspersed among them. The rows of women waiting to be asked to dance were noticeably absent. People moved easily from table to table, stopping for a chat or taking a seat. The atmosphere was relaxed and friendly. The crowd was more heterogeneous than what one typically would find in the straight salons: men in tight black leather pants with pecs-revealing shirts; women with cropped hair, cargo pants, and gym shoes; outlandishly dressed young people with purple hair and tattoos, along with the more traditionally attired women in sexy skirts and high heels and men in casual black with their hair slicked back. There were considerably more tourists than locals, and the crowd was younger than what one sees in the more traditional salons in Buenos Aires. The codes for inviting partners to dance were different, too. While there were plenty of instances of cruising, the *cabeceo*, the traditional method for inviting with a nod, was notably absent. Instead, dancers approached one another directly, walking over to the table, extending a hand and a straightforward "Shall we dance?" Men did not have the unquestioned prerogative of choosing with whom and when to dance; women were also taking the initiative and inviting partners for dances. But perhaps the most striking difference was the appearance of the dance floor itself. Diminutive women dancers could be seen authoritatively guiding men, while men with eyes closed allowed themselves to be led. There was every combination imaginable: men dancing together, men following women, women together, old and young, and salon dancers interspersed with professionals, including Augusto Balizano himself, performing *tango espectacolo* with its big steps and intricate moves but without the drama of the performance described above. Most of the dancers were much less proficient at dancing and seemed to be struggling with the steps, often verbally negotiating who would do the leading and who would follow.

My first dance that evening was with a young *porteño,* somewhat to my surprise, as older women are rarely invited to dance by younger men, at least not in the traditional *milongas.* He was clearly a beginner, but he had a good sense of the music and the dance was relaxed and enjoyable. As soon as the set finished, I gave him the compliment that I thought any Argentinean would appreciate, namely that he had danced with "heart." He looked at me, somewhat puzzled, and laughed, saying, "Oh, it's just tango. That's all it is. I had good *maestros."*

Although my first encounter with queer tango in Buenos Aires was a welcome relief from the rules and regime of the traditional straight *milonga,* La Marshall left me with some mixed feelings as well. As pleasant as the evening had been, I had also missed some of the elements that were part of my passion for tango: the playful flirtatiousness of the *cabeceo,* the emotional thrill of a wordless encounter with a stranger, the close embrace in which differences between partners can momentarily be bridged in a unique intimacy, and the liminal experience of being outside time and space. The matter-of-factness and consensuality of queer tango made it seem strangely chaste: "no strutting around for prey, no anxiety to be chosen, no advances to be resisted, no visible negotiations concerning sexual booties or trophies" (Savigliano, 2010:143). Of course, perhaps I had missed the undercurrents that were there but unavailable to me as a heterosexual woman. Had I become too socialized in the macho cult of traditional *milongas* to appreciate queer tango? However, if this were true, why, then, did queer tango feel so familiar, so unexceptional, and so safe? It reminded me of the kinds of social gatherings and parties that I routinely attend with my non-tango friends and acquaintances. Paradoxically, queer tango with its explicitly

Figures 5.1 and 5.2. Performances by Augusto Balizano and Miquel Moyano. (Courtesy of Augusto Balizano; Figure 5.1 by Daniel Machado.)

transformative agenda seemed more compatible with my normal life than the more traditional variants of tango. How could this be?

Clearly, the phenomenon of queer tango calls for a closer look. The term "queer," which emerged in the late 1990s as a way to broaden the field of gay and lesbian studies and politics to include all non-normative sexualities,[4] is used in a variety of ways, some of which are contradictory. It can be a trendy way to talk about homosexuality, whereby "queer" is synonymous with "gay" or "lesbian." Or it can be used to question all categories (man, woman, Latina, Jew, butch, femme), oppositions (man vs. woman, heterosexual vs. homosexual), and equations (gender = sex) upon which conventional notions of identity and sexuality rely (Hennessy, 1993:964). More generally and more radically, "queer" refers to resistance against all "regimes of the normal" (Warner, 1991:16), whereby "queer" becomes anything that is "anti-normal" or "non-normal" and destabilizes the status quo. Queer tango, both as local manifestation in Buenos Aires and as global tango community, draws upon these meanings in contradictory ways, ways that mirror some of the inconsistencies in queer theory and politics more generally.

In this chapter, I explore how queer tango has changed tango as a dance, the interactions between the dancers, and the regimes of the salon. Drawing upon interviews with *aficionados*, I address why some dancers opt for queer rather than straight tango and show how queer tango attempts to unsettle the gender hierarchies that have been so central to Argentinean tango. The most tricky question, however, is the one that has been raised not only by the *aficionados* of queer tango but also by critical tango scholars—namely, has queer tango succeeded in making tango, the most heterosexist of all dances, at long last, "politically correct"?

From Homosocial to Gay

Tango has not always been the undisputed province of heterosexual couples. In fact, the origin myth of tango invariably involves two men dancing tango together in the slums of Buenos Aires at the turn of the twentieth century. This myth is usually accompanied by the "reassuring" acknowledgment that these men were acting not out of homoerotic desire but rather out of necessity, born of the demographic imbalance between the sexes at the time. In the wake of massive immigration to Buenos Aires during this period, there was an overabundance of single men between the ages of twenty and forty (Guy, 1990:40–41).[5] The first tango dancers came from the gigantic multitude of "longshoremen and pimps, of masons, and electoral committee bullies, of *criollo* and foreign musicians, of butchers and procurers" who found themselves lonely, far away from home, and in need of entertainment (Sábato, cited in Salessi, 1997:158). These men danced together out of necessity (or so the story goes), competing with one another for the attentions of the few available women, most of whom were prostitutes working in the brothels of Buenos Aires. Their interactions were volatile, marked by rivalry, competition, and violence.

Contemporary tango scholars have taken issue with this sanitized version of tango's homosocial origins, arguing that men were not simply forced to dance with one another because of a dearth of female partners (Salessi, 1997; Tobin, 1998; Saikin, 2004). They have showed how homoeroticism is historically embedded in the cultural imaginary of the Argentinean middle classes, as a result of the intersection of discourses of sexuality and criminality with the history of immigration. As increasing numbers of foreigners arrived in Buenos Aires in search of work, the Argentinean elite became anxious to protect the "purity" of the national identity from foreign "contamination." Their xenophobia centered on the belief that immigrants were introducing undesirable criminal and sexual degeneration into the population at large—from prostitution to sexual deviance in the form of pederasty, "sexual inversion," and homosexuality (Guy, 1990). In the public imagination, tango was linked to the world of the marginal, subversive, and forbidden; and, indeed, the lyrics of the early tangos provide ample evidence of tango's homoerotic subtext (Savigliano, 1995; Saikin, 2004).

Today the official discourse in the world of tango is that the dance is for heterosexuals. Although Argentinean men may still dance with one another upon occasion, they refer to this as "practicing"—a matter of learning some steps or brushing up on their dancing skills. The "real thing" is reserved for the heterosexual couple; to really dance tango, a man needs a woman. However, according to Tobin (1998), tango's homoerotic roots, while denied, continue to inform the passion generated by the dance by creating a sense of loss, a "mourning for unlived possibilities" (Tobin, 1998:99; see also Butler, 1995). This reading is supported by the popularity of male–male tangos as public performances, whereby the origin story of men dancing together is recycled. In these performances, two men can dance tango without needing gender difference to convey the "tango-ness" (*tanguidad*) of the dance (Savigliano, 2010:141). All-male tango couples are sometimes regarded as the most "harmonious and beautiful from a stylistic viewpoint" precisely because the partners can both take up each other's proposals, thereby providing a more balanced and complete improvisation of defiance and alliance. "Male–male tangos are tangos because tango is a *macho* form" (ibid.).

In contrast to male–male tangos, female–female couples are notably suspect and discouraged in both performances and *milongas*.[6] As Savigliano (2010) puts it, while the discourse of *tanguidad* is enhanced by men dancing together, it is diluted when women dance with one another (p. 141). Not only do all-female couples evoke an overly eroticized and even slightly pornographic spectacle when seen through the male gaze, but the very essence of tango is somehow betrayed when men are no longer needed as leaders. Women's leading presumably undermines and even ruins their ability to respond to men. Thus, while women can dance tango together in dance classes or family gatherings, in a salon their dancing together is limited to rock 'n' roll or folk dances like the *chacarera*,[7] in which the seductiveness is playful and there is no direct bodily contact between partners. Taken together, it would appear that femininity is considerably less containable in tango than masculinity.

This asymmetry in same-sex dancing is reflected in the gay tango scene in Buenos Aires, where, from the beginning, the space in the *milongas* was dominated, both numerically and behaviorally, by gay men. As one of my lesbian informants, remembering the early days in La Marshall, put it, "It's not that the guys were exactly opposed to us; they just didn't see us." She describes how women dancing with women had a difficult time, often finding themselves pushed off the dance floor by the more assertive male dancers. "La Marshall is for gay men, whatever anyone says. It's a masculine space. Take the masculine energy of a straight *milonga* and multiply that by two. That's La Marshall."

Mariana DoCampo, a dancer, writer, and professor of literature, recalls how she started the first women-only *milonga* (*Milonga Mujeres*) in Buenos Aires. She was convinced that women needed a space where they could choose other women as partners, learn to lead, and generally undo the elements associated with machismo that were making not only traditional but also gay *milongas* inhospitable to women who wanted to dance tango. She began offering classes to women who wanted to learn to lead and organizing a weekly *milonga* for women.

In the meantime, Buenos Aires was quickly on its way to becoming a mecca for gay tourism, with thousands of gay and lesbian tourists flocking to the city each year. Argentina proudly announced itself as the first Latin American country to abolish restrictions on civil unions among gays and legalize same-sex marriage (Sivori, 2005). A substantial section in the Lonely Planet travel guide for Argentina was devoted to gay tourism with glowing reports on how "gay friendly" Buenos Aires had become with its vibrant gay night life and numerous hotels, cafés, and restaurants catering to gay customers. In May 2012, the official website for tourism in Buenos Aires stated that gay visitors could expect "an open reception" in the city and would feel "more comfortable than they would in Rio de Janeiro." "The gay culture of the ghetto is a thing of the past. . . . [T]he heteroculture is friendly, based on tolerance rather than discrimination . . . on sharing life styles" (http://www.bue.gob.ar).

The combination of an increased social and legal acceptance of homosexuality in Argentina and the increase in international gay tourism all conspired to bring gay tango out of closet (Cecconi, 2012). All-male dance couples were regularly being invited to give demonstrations in traditional tango salons, and most local dancers were aware, if not entirely accepting, of the phenomenon of gay tango. This is not to say that traditional salons welcomed same-sex couples with open arms, however. For example, Miranda, one of my Dutch informants, recalls that she and her female partner were dancing together in a well-known *milonga* in Buenos Aires when the organizer appeared on the floor and asked them to leave. Surprised, Miranda pointed out that they had been coming to the *milonga* regularly for several weeks. The organizer merely shrugged and said, "Sorry, but we don't do *that* here." While this incident was extreme, it is more usual for same-sex couples to be tolerated, but not included. How this works became clear to me when an Austrian friend, who prefers leading and was accustomed to dancing with women in her local tango salon, described her experiences when visiting the more traditional salons in Buenos Aires. It was "simply impossible" to find a woman willing to dance with her. "It's not that I'm not a good dancer; I am. But the women won't even look at me." After hearing this, I asked one of my Argentinean informants what she thought would happen if I were to dance with a woman in one of the *milongas*. She laughed and said, "If I were you, I wouldn't try it. It would be the end of your being able to dance there. No *milonguero* would invite you after that." It is not surprising that the discrepancy between the official discourse of tolerance toward gays and the ongoing reality of inhospitality and exclusion in the traditional tango salons contributed to the continued existence of special venues for same-sex tango dancing in Buenos Aires.

Queer Tango Abroad

Early on, queer tango had been a standard feature of the global tango revival. In Europe, it began in 2001, when the first gay–lesbian *milonga* was organized in Hamburg as a space where same-sex couples could dance tango. In the same year, the First International Queer Tango Argentina Festival was organized in Berlin, thereby introducing the concept of "queer" to same-sex dancing. Queer tango festivals have since been organized across the globe: in San Francisco, Toronto, New Orleans, Sydney, London, and Stockholm, and, much later, in Amsterdam. These festivals attracted dancers from many countries, serving as an inspiration in many local queer tango scenes in different parts of the world. They not only offered workshops and performances by celebrated dancers but also included forums and discussions, films, and lectures in their programs in order to encourage participants to think critically about how to rid tango of its heteronormative baggage and make it more receptive to a dialogue based on equality between partners regardless of gender. These festivals differed from the more commercial festivals in the straight tango scene by virtue of their ideological focus and their insistence that tango needed to be modernized (Hille and Walter, 2006).

In Amsterdam, queer tango initially had a less auspicious trajectory than in Germany. An international festival was held in 2006, and several queer *milongas* cropped up in cities outside the capital. However, in Amsterdam, queer tango as a separate dance culture was, until very recently, notably absent. One reason was that, in contrast to Buenos Aires, it was not unusual to see women dancing with women, men with men, or women leading men in most tango salons. The tolerance for anything "queer" was, in part, due to the desirability within a Dutch context of displaying one's progressive colors. The Dutch national imaginary is gay-friendly, tolerant, and cosmopolitan. Same-sex dancing, therefore, could prevent a *milonga* from seeming *too* traditionally gendered, just as people of color on the dance floor provided a reassuring touch of postracialism in a society that wanted to be perceived as color-blind. Although many salons in Amsterdam aspired to the idea of authenticity (for example, by announcing on their websites that tango is danced "the way it is in Buenos Aires"), most Dutch tango dancers were, at the same time, uncomfortable with any suggestion that they were themselves traditional when it came to gender relations, preferring instead to adopt a best-of-both-worlds strategy. As we saw in the previous chapter, it is not uncommon for a Dutch tango dancer to admit that he or she likes to "play" with traditional gender hierarchies while, at the same time, insisting that "you have to go to Buenos Aires to find the 'real' thing." Nowhere was this ambivalence more clearly illustrated than in the case of queer tango, which made its sudden, and rather belated, appearance in Amsterdam in 2008 in the form of a workshop initiated by a well-known tango instructor and salon organizer. As he put it, he was interested in tapping into a new market and attracting "fresh blood" to the tango scene in Amsterdam. For him, queer tango was something "like eating Indonesian food" in Holland—different, but tasty. He was less concerned about creating a special space for queer tango dancers than about finding ways to make tango even more trendy and fun for all dancers, straight and queer alike.

Back to Buenos Aires

The emergence of queer tango as an international phenomenon had reverberations in the gay tango scene in Buenos Aires. Mariana DoCampo recalls becoming increasingly dissatisfied with what she saw as a ghettoization of gay, lesbian, and women-only tango. With fewer lesbians wanting to attend a woman-only tango salon, she saw little future in organizing tango salons solely for—as she puts it—"homosexual life." She had participated in several of the international queer tango festivals in Hamburg and Berlin and was inspired by the developments in the queer tango scene in Europe. Through her work in the academy as a professor of gender studies, she was already familiar with queer theory, and this contributed to her conviction that queer—rather than gay, lesbian, or women-only—was the right direction to take. DoCampo soon had a new *milonga* in San Telmo up and running, calling it "tango queer." She remembers feeling like a pioneer at first:

> I thought: "I have to do this. I had to explain it. To other gay people. To Augusto [Balizano]. Even to the people in Hamburg." I think we need to think more about queer theory and about queer tango. . . . [I]t was like something that nobody knew. Then we can start to make the connections . . . to develop the ideas, to discuss . . . to think about power relations and how they are not only about gender.

It didn't take long before queer tango was "in" in Buenos Aires. Within a relatively short period, it went from relative invisibility within the confines of the gay subculture to becoming a trendy feature of the contemporary tango scene. Queer tango has been publicly supported by well-known *milongueros* and *milongueras* who not only frequent queer *milongas* themselves but have participated in queer tango festivals. In 2007, the first International Festival of Queer Tango was organized in Buenos Aires, an important milestone for the local queer tango scene. While some of the local professionals performed at the festivals,[8] it was the international connection that allowed queer tango to gain public acceptance in Buenos Aires. As Mariana DoCampo notes, somewhat drily, "Because Argentineans always think like this. If it happens outside [i.e., in Europe], they want to know what is happening. It's like that. After we were invited as the guests of honor in Germany at the queer tango festival, this became something that really makes a lot of noise here."

Thus, in an uncanny reminder of an earlier history when tango was shunned as an immoral dance for the underclasses in Buenos Aires, only to be accepted after it had gained popularity in European high society, queer tango also required a foreign connection before it could be welcomed at home. These trajectories are different, yet they illustrate how tango has always traveled, albeit not always in the same direction.

Having looked briefly at the traveling history of queer tango, I now address what it actually means to make tango "queer." How do dancers experience and justify queer tango as a specific niche in the tango community? And in what ways does queer tango translate the broader theoretical and normative debates in the field of queer theory and politics into a locally situated dance culture? In other words, how queer is queer tango, and, indeed, how queer can tango actually be?

Queer Tango: What Is It?

In order to distinguish itself, on the one hand, from traditional (or straight) tango and, on the other, from gay, lesbian, or women-only tango, queer tango draws upon queer theory and politics in different and often contradictory ways.[9] The most common way is to present queer tango as a queer-friendly space in which to dance tango, allowing individuals who might otherwise be unlikely to even consider tango as an option given their own lifestyles or sexual identities to enjoy what tango has to offer in terms of movement, expression, and passion. By drawing upon the term "queer," queer tango taps into what Walters (1996:831) calls the "new queer sensibility"—a tide of gay visibility that is sweeping the world and transforming homosexuality into a chic, glamorous, and even fabulous identity. Originating in the United States and having spread to Europe and other parts of the world as it has, the concept "queer" transforms gay tango into something cosmopolitan, lending it a trendy, international veneer.

While this representation of queer tango seems to be little more than recycling the old gay *milonga* in a more modern form, some renditions of queer tango go a step further by promising a transformation of the performance of the dance itself. This transformation not only includes how individual dancers perform tango but also generates a differently gendered tango choreography as well. Tango, like any dance performance, requires that individuals reenact the codes and conventions of gender by replicating choreographies structured by gender (Foster, 1998). While tango has always provided space for individual agency in the sense that it is improvised, its structure remains rigidly gendered. Queer tango, in contrast, not only liberates individual performers from the constraints of tango's traditional choreography, but, at its most sophisticated, it attempts to rewrite the very choreography of tango itself.[10] It severs the connection between gender, heterosexuality, and the roles of leading and following by enabling dancers to freely select the role they want to dance and the partner with whom they want to dance. Queer tango disrupts the heteronormative couple, in which the man always leads and the woman invariably follows as the *sine qua non* of traditional tango. Instead, male dancers may adopt a passive or receptive role and allow themselves to be guided along the floor with their eyes closed, while women can take on the role of leader, in charge of interpreting the music, instigating the steps, managing the floor, and being responsible for the well-being of their partners. In this sense, queer tango becomes the embodiment of "gender trouble" (Butler, 1989).

Another way to present queer tango is—at least, from a feminist point of view—more politically charged. Queer tango is a way to unsettle the notions of male dominance that not only operate in the traditional straight salon but have continued to operate in gay tango salons as well. As we have seen, all-male partners often draw upon the same macho energy that is integral to traditional tango. Because both partners take an active role in the dance, they can both make and defy each other's proposals or engage in flamboyant and mutually initiated forms of improvisation. In contrast, the emphasis on equality in queer tango compels dancers of both sexes to reenvision gendered stereotypes of dominance and submission. While this transformation theoretically affects both male and female dancers, the relevance of the shift is more momentous for women. As long as women are not given the opportunity to learn the skills that enable them to lead, they will not even have the option of dancing with other women. It is not simply a matter of being restricted to one role; the very possibility of being able to dance is extinguished. Writing in her blog, "What is tango queer?" DoCampo argues that it is precisely the "impossibility of the woman–woman formula" in both gay and straight tango that queer tango subverts, thereby challenging the structural sexism inherent in the dance. Queer tango enables anyone—gay, lesbian, or heterosexual—to experiment with gender roles, and, in so doing, it allows the "exchange of difference without power inequalities."[11]

The most radical and, at the same time, sophisticated rendition of queer tango claims to disrupt all "regimes of the normal" (Warner, 1991). Or, as DoCampo puts it, "What is 'normal' here is the difference."[12] This is more than same-sex dancing or women leading men; it abolishes all norms for tango, whether gay or straight (Cecconi, 2012). Participants are expected not just to dance with whomever they want and to take whichever role they prefer; they can also freely exchange roles in accordance with the music or their moods of the moment. They are at liberty to experiment with the choreography, open the embrace between the partners to allow more adventurous dancing, and try out different kinds of music (Liska, 2009). The assumption is that leading and following will be flexibly negotiated between equal partners according to their individual desires rather than written in stone by the dictates of traditional gender roles. In this way, queer tango liberates tango from the heteronormativity of the traditional salon with its old-fashioned regime of rules and codes that restrict how individuals communicate and interact with one another, the kind of music that is played, and the choreography of the dance itself.

Unsurprisingly, queer tango often goes hand in hand with other attempts to modernize tango—like *neo tango*, which uses music from a variety of other genres—with more open, performative styles of dancing and tango festivals that include cultural and literary events along with dance performances and lessons. In short, queer tango is not about discovering "authentic tango," nor is it confined to dancers with a specific identity. "Going queer" is about being innovative and transgressive.

Going Queer

Queer tango, in theory as well as in practice, is open to anyone who is willing to experiment with the boundaries of sex and gender, sexuality, and the dance itself. One does not have to be gay or straight to dance queer tango; one only has to define him- or herself as "antinormal." By detaching itself from both the heterosexuality of the traditional salon and the homosexuality of the gay salon, queer tango draws a wide audience of dancers: men and women who want to experiment with gender roles through tango, dancers who are tired of the strict regimes of the traditional tango salons and want to dance tango in a more relaxed way, and dancers who are interested in innovating tango. In the queer tango scene in Buenos Aires, dancers range from tourists trying out their first steps to semi-professional dancers who perform in queer tango festivals around the world. While some tango dancers start out in queer tango and never look back, the majority have already had some experience dancing in traditional salons. For them, their dissatisfaction with straight *milongas* is often their primary reason for "going queer."

Dissatisfaction with Straight Salons

For many of my female informants, the suffering and sense of injustice at being compelled to "wallflower" while men can dance as much as and with whom they want is enough incentive to look for alternatives to the rigid regimes of the traditional tango salons.

Rosemary, whom we encountered in previous chapters, explains that she initially began learning to lead ("the man's role") out of a sense of frustration that she and her friends just weren't getting enough dances in the salons. However, once she started dancing with other women, leading became a goal in and of itself. Remembering an experience in which she was visiting a (European) *milonga* far from home with a woman friend, she describes her Eureka moment:

> We suddenly just didn't feel like dancing with the guys there. So I said: "You know what? Let's dance together, we're here with each other and we're having a good time and for that we don't need men . . . and, you know, when I dance with her . . . it's always good . . . so we're really independent, we don't have to sit on the sidelines as wallflowers, with or without wrinkles [laughs]. . . . And, if you ask me, *that* is what makes tango feminist."

Particularly for dancers who have been frequenting salons for many years and who regard themselves as good dancers, it is disheartening not to be asked to dance, while younger, less proficient dancers are whisked off onto the floor.

But even for women who are asked to dance, the inequalities of the salon regime may compel them to look for a place where "every woman can dance without having to wait." Ana, an attractive lesbian in her early forties, had been dancing for many years in Buenos Aires. As a young girl, she was a regular visitor at many of the more traditional, straight tango salons. A popular dancer, she had no difficulties getting invitations from some of the better *milongueros*. However, the interaction between the men and women in the salons "turned [her] off." As a case in point, she recalls "a really traditional salon" on the outskirts of the capital (Buenos Aires) where she danced with an "old man" who was a top dancer:

> And all the women, they were all just sitting around and not dancing. I remember that they hated me. I was this young girl. They didn't want to, but they were just tired of waiting. And I wanted to break that.

While some of the more experienced *milongueras* in Buenos Aires explained that they didn't have to dance every set and were, in fact, particular about whom they danced with ("two or three good ones in an evening are enough"), they, too, were dissatisfied with being dependent on men in order to enjoy a salon. For them, queer tango provides an opportunity to feel independent *and* to dance tango.

But women are not the only ones who chafe at the restrictions in the traditional salons. For example, Paolo, the Italian art student whom we met in chapter 3, moved to Buenos Aires and initially continued his trajectory as a tango dancer in traditional tango salons. Although he describes himself as "gay but not much into the gay scene," the overbearing attitude of men toward women in traditional *milongas* and his own desire for a "less strict ambiance" ultimately led him to try queer tango.

> Tango was born in the last century but there were other social rules then. I have seen men dancing in [traditional] *milongas* who are always affirming their macho power with women in a really strong way. But I don't think tango should be like that. It shouldn't be reflecting a society more than one hundred years old. I think tango should be adapting to society's new rules.

Switching

The ability to switch the roles of leading and following is central to both the theory and practice of queer tango. The crossing of heterosexualized gender boundaries repositions the bodies of the dancers in ways that upset conventional expectations and open up new possibilities for the dance itself.

> Both the leader and the follower . . . wonder where the movement is coming from. Now the leader is no longer first identified as the physical incorporation of masculinity, but perhaps as a body of intensity, speed, precision, caring. The follower is no longer simply following but emanating a movement of her own that calls forth engagement, creativity, joy." (Manning, 2007:89)

Anyone who has watched experienced dancers performing this switch will wonder at the fluidity and ease with which they can move in and out of the roles as well as at how completely it changes the quality of the dance itself. Fairly recently on one of my visits to Buenos Aires, I had an opportunity to try it myself when one of my informants, Marlene, a flamboyant, divorced *milonguera* in her late sixties, announced that she was now learning to lead and had started going to the queer tango salon. Intrigued, I asked her if I could interview her again. She agreed, but—with a mischievous twinkle in her eye—suggested that I first take a lesson with her. "It's the only way you're going to really understand what it's about." We set off together to her Thursday night lesson, the participants of which turned out to be a mixture of locals and tourists, most in their early twenties, with different degrees of experience. We all crowded around the instructor, who demonstrated steps, snapping her fingers to the beat of the music while explaining the dynamics of leading and following. Each participant was expected to do both, and throughout the lesson we alternated roles with our partners. I literally got off on the wrong foot with my first partner because it wasn't clear who was taking the lead. He continued to initiate the step during "my" turn to lead until I finally asked, somewhat irritated, whose lead it was. The instructor came over, laughing, and explained loudly enough so that everyone could hear, "In tango queer you have to decide in advance who is going to lead. So, *always, always* ask first!"

For some, learning to dance both roles is linked to their desire to become better dancers, similar to many tango instructors who become skilled in both roles because it makes them better teachers. Many male dancers learn to follow because they think doing so will improve their ability to lead by sensitizing them to what their partners expect from them. Harry, a thirty-five-year-old heterosexual web designer from Amsterdam who travels frequently to dance tango, explained that he initially wanted to follow so that he could understand the pleasure women feel ("what it's like to dance with your eyes closed"). He remembers asking one of the organizers of a queer *milonga* (a woman) to dance, knowing that she could lead and this would give him a chance to practice following. She turned him down, saying she was too busy, but that he could dance with her husband instead. "It was my first experience dancing with a guy. It was fine—not sensual, but fine. I thought: 'OK. I've crossed that bridge now.'"

The women I spoke with often had fewer anxieties about dancing with other women, even if they defined themselves as heterosexual. However, they did regret having to give up following. Miranda, for example, insisted that she had always preferred following and always would but, nevertheless, wanted to lead so that she could dance anytime she wanted with either men or women. However, as she put it, leading turned out to be "a completely different sport," requiring a different energy and skills that she didn't have ("like fighting for my space on the floor"). One of the most daunting aspects of leading was having to deal with the men she had danced with before as a follower:

> I was dancing as a leader, but I could still follow. My former male dance partner had to lead, of course, but he couldn't always remember what to do, so I would help him. Tell him what to do [laughs]. You know where this is going, right? *That* was just not okay. He was a really nice guy, but it didn't work anymore.

Paolo also described himself as being initially resistant to the whole business of switching roles. He had been accustomed to leading and found it difficult to just relax and let his partner be in charge of everything. At some point, however, he discovered that he liked being led and even preferred it in some cases ("When I'm tired, I prefer another person to be in charge of everything . . . or if they are really good dancers, it's a way of respecting their skills"). Switching allowed him to "let" a partner who wants to lead, lead, while he could become a better dancer himself by understanding the mechanics of following. "I can make sure my partner enjoys him- or herself. And that's what tango should be about; it's a very *generous* dance."

While many dancers—particularly in the early stages of learning both roles—will negotiate the positions at the outset of the set (as described previously) and then reverse positions between pieces(*temas*), in more advanced classes partners are encouraged to switch in the middle of the dance as well. Paolo describes the process of switching in the following way:

> Usually a person invites you and asks if you want to lead or follow and the other one says: "Whatever you like." Then we play this dance with the arms [laughs], you know, showing a leader arm, a leader embrace, or a follower embrace. But when the music starts, it comes very natural. You can do it anytime, but, at the end of the *tanda* [set of three or four pieces], it's much more salient. There . . . you usually switch. You dance the first one as a leader, the second one as a follower, and so on.

Mid-dance role reversal requires careful calibration in which arms are switched and body positions altered, while staying in touch with the music and avoiding collisions on the dance floor. It is very difficult to accomplish within a close embrace, which may account for dancers'giving more attention to staying in their own axes than to the intensity of the embrace itself. Thus, it is more common in queer tango to dance in an open embrace, with eyes directed at the partner's chest.

While many dancers appreciate the same features in queer tango as they would in traditional tango—the music, the embrace, the dialogue, the connection—there is no mistaking that the switch has, to some extent, replaced the embrace as essential to its *cuerpo de baile* (Olszewski, 2008). The switching of roles is the *raison d'être* of queer tango. It is a standard feature of any performance, whether during a lesson, a demonstration at a festival, or simply on the dance floor. Switching roles invariably evokes admiring "ohhhs" and "ahhhs" from the audience. What the switch demonstrates, however, is less the embodiment of tango passion than the inherent fluidity of gender and its transformation through the dance. The connection between partners is manifested in their ability to play with different positions rather than to encounter each other in a close embrace.

How differently the connection is experienced is illustrated by an exchange I had with Marlene during our visit to the queer tango salon. We were sitting at a table observing the dancers on the floor. Having noticed that most of them were dancing open style and remembering Marlene's raving about the importance of the *abrazo* (close embrace) when I had interviewed her as a straight dancer, I asked her how she felt now about the embrace. She hesitated for a moment and then replied that, of course, it was "still important, but . . .". Before she could even finish her sentence, her eyes began to wander toward the dance floor. She gestured excitedly at one of the women dancers who had been leading before and appeared to be following now. As we watched, the couple changed positions again and Marlene exclaimed excitedly, "There— look! There it is. The switch. Wow!"

"A Nice Place to Go"

Queer tango entails more, however, than changing the way partners dance with each other. It also offers a welcome escape from the traditional regime of the tango salon. Queer tango provides a venue in which anyone who wants to dance tango can feel comfortable, relax, "just be [him- or herself]." For example, Marlene, who initially went to queer tango *milongas* because she was tired of waiting and wanted to be able to dance, gradually discovered that her reasons changed the longer she went. She found that she also enjoyed sitting with her friends, listening to the music, or just having a beer. As she puts it,

> When I go to a normal *milonga*, I have to go as a woman. Don't get me wrong, I don't like girls [laughs], but here I can just be myself. I don't have to worry about how I look or have to act in a certain way. And I don't have to take care of men's egos all the time. There is nothing at stake.

Many of my informants described the queer tango scene as a community of friends. Paolo explains that when he goes to the queer *milonga*, he feels as if he is "coming home." The first thing he does before deciding where to sit is to do the round of tables, greeting and kissing everyone. "It's a kind of family moment when you are seeing each other, the same faces, and feeling comfortable in front of everyone. The ice is broken." This ritual makes the whole process of inviting and being invited much easier and less stressful.

Ana also emphasizes the community aspect of queer tango as one of its most appealing features. As she puts it,

> In the straight *milonga*, you go alone to dance. In queer tango, you must make friends in order to dance. You will meet the same people and you will become friends. Then, if you want, you will dance. Or sometimes you will just want to sit.

In traditional *milongas*, the atmosphere is full of sexual innuendo and flirting, and the separation between the salon and everyday life is carefully policed. In contrast, many of my informants explained that in queer tango they often socialize with other dancers. It is not uncommon to go for drinks or dinner after the *milonga* or meet up during the week for a film, or even to go on vacations together. However, there is one caveat. The mixing of friendship and tango can work only by virtue of the unspoken rule of not having sex with your dance partners. For many *aficionados*, queer tango is a small community, and an affair could easily disrupt friendships and destroy the convivial atmosphere of the *milonga*. As Paolo explains:

> Sex is OK with the foreigners who come and go, but with the locals, it's like a taboo . . . the feelings of seeing each other, the discomfort of saying hello in front of everybody, trying to feel normal, as if nothing happened . . . [laughs]. It's probably because tango is already so sexual. Once you break this spell, having the real thing, you take all the things away from the tango that are its essence.

Paolo's sentiments echo those of many straight informants, singles and couples alike, who also insist that dancing tango is best not mixed with having sex. However, what is distinctive in the queer tango scene is the importance participants give to community. Dancers are less likely to separate their tango dancing from friendship and regard the tango community as a friendship network. As we saw in chapter 2, the code against mixing actual sex with dancing tango serves to protect the liminal space necessary for the experience of tango passion; in queer tango, this same code is rearticulated as a mainstay for the creation of a sustainable community. As Paolo puts it, "[T]he *milonga* is my safe place. Of course, you will be exploring new things, too, but it makes you feel safe. You feel accepted. It's . . . like family."

It is clear that dancers embark on queer tango for a variety of reasons, of which the desire to dance with a partner of the same sex is only one. What they share is a marked dissatisfaction with the rigidly gendered codes of the traditional tango salons. Queer tango provides an alternative: a relaxed ambience in which participants can dress as they please and interact in a more casual way, a place for socializing as well as dancing. And, last but not least, queer tango liberates dancers from the constraints of having to "do gender" (West and Zimmerman, 1987) and the antagonistic tensions inherent in performances of masculinity and femininity on the dance floor.

Of course, alternative practices are not only advantageous; they will also have their costs. In Savigliano's (2010) view, queer tango brings with it a different kind of pleasure. It is sensual, aesthetically pleasing, and playful, but—above all—it is about having a good time. However, keeping the "tense, erotically charged atmosphere of compulsory heterosexual *milongas* and their heteronormative dance rulings . . . in check," she argues, queer *milongas* often take on "a safe, even prudish patina" (p. 142). Ironically, while queer tango transgresses the norms of the traditional tango world, it also tames some of traditional tango's intensity—an intensity generated precisely through the erotically charged confrontations with gender difference.

What Queer Tango Leaves Behind

Queer tango does not appeal to everyone, and, indeed, not every person who regards her- or himself as queer necessarily wants to "go queer" when it comes to tango. Nora, a fifty-year-old academic involved in a

long-term relationship with a woman, explained that she and her partner had wanted to dance tango for years, but they were put off by the
idea of having to dance it with "a bunch of straight people." When they
had the opportunity to attend a queer tango workshop, they eagerly
grabbed it. Contrary to their—admittedly high—expectations, they
were disappointed. "We had to keep switching roles all the time. Every
time the instructor would shout, 'Now, everybody change roles,' we
would just look at each other and groan. My partner wants to lead and I
want to follow. We knew that right away."

Many tango dancers, gay and straight, Argentinean and non-Argentinean, have a strong preference for one role, making the principle of
switching, which is so integral to the philosophy of queer tango, problematic for them. The emphasis on role switching and the insistence
that everyone be able to dance both roles feel, to them, more like an
ideological constraint than something that corresponds to their most
innermost desires—desires that they hope to express in and through
dancing tango.

A case in point is Shani, a passionate Dutch tango dancer in her early
twenties, who started out as a follower and later decided she preferred
to lead. Her ambivalence about queer tango, despite her defining herself
as a "pretty queer" person ("I really hate how masculinity or femininity steers what we can do or can't do. . . . [T]here is so much gray"), is
instructive for understanding some of the costs of queer tango. Shani
was adamant not only that queer tango held no appeal for her personally but that it destroyed the very "essence" of tango. For her, the roles
of leading and following each require their own kind of presence that
is necessary in order for one to dance well. "Tango is about being masculine and feminine. . . . I hate to say it, but it just *is*." Because tango is
what she most wants to do, she feels she has no other choice than to
accept the premise of distinct and different genders even though she
finds this problematic in the rest of her life. In her view, it is easier to
develop the kind of "gendered presence" she needs to dance tango in a
traditional, straight salon than the presence she would need for queer
tango:

> In a queer salon, you have to try and find out if that man over there is
> wanting to dance with you because he likes to dance with men or because

he wants to lead you or because he wants to be led by you. You have to *find* that *out* [laughs]. You know, that's a lot of work. It requires more cerebral action and that's something that is not relaxed. You have to ask, you have to talk, you have to think. And what often happens, because it's not clear what you are and what you want to be, [is that] you have to come up to somebody and ask them. So, there's this person, already in your space, and it would be very rude to say no.

For Shani, the switching of roles found in queer tango destroys the thing she most values in tango: finding a connection with her partner without words. This connection is enhanced by mobilizing the "universe of possibilities" that the gendered positions of leading or following contain.[13] In other words, engaging with gender differences enhances connection in tango, while getting rid of these differences makes the connection shallow. Or, as Shani forcefully puts it, "We don't need to revolutionize tango. It doesn't really need to be changed. If you need to break down some walls in order to look for a state of perfection, you are looking in the wrong direction."

Undoing Gender: Transgression or Taming?

At the outset of this chapter, I raised the question of whether queer tango can sanitize tango of its gendered asymmetries and heteronormativity, transforming it into a "politically correct" way to dance tango. This question has not only intrigued tango dancers anxious to modernize tango, but it has been the subject of some scholarly debate among feminist scholars and queer theorists as well. I will, therefore, now take a look at how critical (tango) scholars tackle the thorny issue of just how queer the practice of queer tango actually is.

As we have seen, queer tango performs the undoing of gender on the dance floor. It begins by enacting the hierarchical gender positions of leading and following that are central to tango and then undermining them as the partners switch roles. Queer tango relies on the reiteration of this playful and often highly aestheticized performance of gender and its undoing. In this sense, queer tango has all the makings of a gender performance à la Judith Butler—that is, a performance which imitates heteronormativity and, through parody, denaturalizes it (Butler,

1993:230–32). In Butler's vision, a performance is queer not because it is devoid of gender but because it calls attention to the constructed-ness of gender roles. In this way, a gap emerges between the norm and the actual practice of gender, thereby allowing for the possibility of subversion, resistance, or "gender trouble" (Butler, 1989, 1993).

Paula Villa takes up Butler's notion of performativity but comes to a slightly different conclusion when she applies it to queer tango. Villa (2009) suggests that traditional Argentinean tango has already been queered simply by its having been taken up by new generations of (non-Argentinean) dancers who are not willing to live up to the gendered norms represented in traditional tango. They are, in fact, constantly transgressing traditional forms of masculinity and femininity when they dance tango. They do this, for example, when they don androgynous sport shoes and cargo pants or when women refuse to sit patiently and wait until men ask them to dance, or when a follower interjects her own steps during the dance. In Villa's view, queer tango merely takes these more routine instances of "gender trouble" a step further. According to Villa, queer tango represents an even more radical subversion of the norms of gender because it disrupts the gendered binary between leader and follower. By doing so, queer tango not only de-naturalizes gender but also de-genders tango (Villa, 2010:162).

> If it is no longer determined in advance who walks forward, who does the overseeing, or who keeps time in the movement, if it doesn't matter which "role" one dances (because there aren't any) and when it doesn't matter if one holds his right arm so or so, if she wears high or low heels, a dress or pants, then—and only then—would the reason for failure [to meet the norms of gender] really not be meaningful at all. (Villa, 2009:120) (my translation)

Thus, Villa elaborates Butler's notion of "queer" by suggesting that "queering" does not require a reiteration of gender but can abolish gender altogether. She takes issue with the notion that gender difference is necessary for tango, arguing, instead, that it is precisely the ongoing transformation of tango which is and always has been its most defining feature. In fact, as she puts it, "if tango were ever to come to a standstill, then it would be dead" (Villa, 2010:163).

Putting aside for a moment the issue of whether de-gendering tango would make it more transgressive, the question remains whether it is possible to take gender difference out of tango. Indeed, some of the critics of queer theory and politics have expressed doubts about replacing "gender" with "queer" (Hennessy, 1993; Martin, 1994; Walters, 1996). Blurring or challenging the conventional boundaries of sex and gender does not automatically efface the complex embodied histories of desire and the identifications upon which desire is based. The parodic rebellions that are the specialty of queer politics may destabilize gender by exposing its artifice, but that is not the same as overthrowing it. Queering is an act of cultural politics which does not eliminate the structures of power that colonize the unconsciousness and recruit desire and pleasure to the service of domination and subordination (Hennessy, 1993; Martin, 1994; also Walters, 1996:866). As we have seen, both straight and gay dancers may identify with a particular role (leader or follower) for reasons that are linked to their own bodily experiences, histories, and identifications, all of which are shaped by gender. They may be willing—and, indeed, even wish to—forfeit their desire to lead or to follow in order to feel relaxed, to be part of a congenial community, or just to have a "time out" from always having to behave like a "real" man or woman. Not everyone desires the same thing in tango, and this includes the experience of passion. However, for those who do desire the experience of passion in tango, the ideological commitment of queer tango toward disconnecting tango dancing from gender and partner choice may, paradoxically, curtail rather than enable it.[14]

As we have seen in previous chapters, tango passion seems to thrive on encounters with difference(s) in a close embrace and with a wordlessly communicated dialogue. While gender is, of course, not the only difference that might be salient for creating a passionate encounter, it offers a rich history of meanings and behaviors that can be drawn upon in the experience of passion in tango. But even if other differences do the job just as well, the question remains whether queer tango can do without gender difference. The queer theorist Biddy Martin (1994) has, for example, argued that casting aside gender difference and erotic specificity as ideologically problematic (i.e., constrained by heteronormative gender) can make individuals' finding ways to express the complexity of their own specific desires more, rather than less, difficult.

Thus, it may be that, despite its insistence on being subversive, queer tango may, by eliminating gender difference, end up ridding tango of precisely those ingredients it needs to generate passion. Savigliano, who is highly critical of the gendered asymmetries in tango and appreciative of the relaxed ambience of queer tango, also questions whether abandoning traditional tango's aggressions toward otherness and the (im)possibilities of requited heterosexual love may leave the erotics of queer tango too subtle and even a little "lame." As she puts it, queer tango not only transgresses the norms of the tango world but also tames tango's aggressions toward "otherness" (Savigliano, 2010:143). In other words, too little space for "difference" within the dance itself may eliminate what is essential for the experience of tango passion.

But does queer tango have to be tame or even lame, as Savigliano suggests? Theoretically, it should be possible to embrace the erotic possibilities outside heteronormativity and use tango to engage with the tensions and antagonisms of queer desire. In this vein, Lisa Blackman (2011) has suggested that queer performances might be enriched by moving beyond seeing performativity as either reproducing or contesting of the norms of gender (p. 196). As example, she draws upon the film *Happy Together* (Wong Kar-Wei, 1997), which portrays the fraught relationship between two gay men from Hong Kong who travel to Argentina together in order to start over.[15] Tango appears (how could it not?) as the backdrop and metaphor for both their unraveling relationship and more generally for the problems of creating intimacy within neo-liberalist, capitalist societies, one of which postcolonial Hong Kong has become. In a memorable scene, the two men encounter each other in an ecstatically tender tango, danced in the kitchen of their apartment to the brooding tones of Piazzolla's *Tango Apasionado*. It is an extraordinary moment in an otherwise abusive relationship in which the long-suffering, nurturing Lai temporarily accepts his promiscuous and indifferent lover, Ho, into his home and into his arms. The relationship is doomed because they each have such different needs and expectations, and yet the moment they dance together captures something that makes tango such a good metaphor for passion: the sense of perfect togetherness and inevitable loss, that it will last for eternity, but only as a memory (Kraicer, 1997). Taking this film as a case in point, Blackman argues that queering tango requires more than the performative undoing of

Figure 5.3. Two lovers dancing together in the 1997 film *Happy Together* (dir. Wong Kar-Wei).

heteronormativity or a utopic attempt at de-gendering (as Villa would suggest). Rather, she argues that queer performances need to engage with the complicated geopolitical histories of gender, heteronormativity, and desire. Tango as a dance enables the performance of separation and coming together and, therefore, thrives on a context marked by difference, "otherness," and antagonism. As such, it provides an ideal space for playing out and interrogating difference as a volatile mixture of desire and longing, sadness and aggression, joy and desperation.

In conclusion, the poignant tango in *Happy Together* and the dramatic dance performance I described at the outset of this chapter both demonstrate that tango is not inherently heterosexual; it is also eminently suited to the passionate engagement with the complexities and dynamics of homosexual desire. Is this rendition of queer tango more "politically correct" than traditional straight tango? Perhaps. But if it is subversive, it is not so by virtue of having eliminated (gender) difference or reinstated equality and consensuality between the dance partners. As these queer performances demonstrate, the dance partners embrace dangerous differences, take risks, and play with the forbidden. This is what passion in tango is about—whether straight or queer, traditional or modern—and it is this passion that, ultimately, makes tango always and everywhere just a little queer.

6

Transnational Encounters

In 1997, the British filmmaker Sally Potter's *The Tango Lesson* was released.[1] In the film, Potter plays herself, showing how she becomes enamored of Argentinean tango. As an antidote to a crisis in her work (writer's block with her latest film script), she sets off for Buenos Aires, where she becomes immersed in the tango scene, taking lessons and visiting salons. There she meets and falls in love with her dance instructor, played by the famous Argentinean tango dancer Pablo Verón. While the film is organized as a series of tango lessons, its primary focus is Potter's tumultuous love affair with Verón and her struggles to reconcile her identity as a successful and emancipated professional woman with the machismo of the dance and of Verón himself. After many separations and reconciliations, involving trips to London, Paris, and back to Buenos Aires, Potter is eventually invited by Verón to perform as his partner in a tango show. She, in turn, asks him to star in her film. Ultimately, however, it is the cross-cultural romance that does not survive. In the final scene, we see Potter and Verón dancing their last, bittersweet tango together along the waterfront of the harbor of Buenos Aires, to a tango song composed and sung by Potter.

The Tango Lesson was a controversial film, evoking both positive and negative responses from critics and scholars like. Initially, it drew attention from feminist scholars for its critical exploration of the heterosexist dynamics of tango as well as for its validation of women's right to pursue their own desires (Fisher, 2004; Guano, 2004). In the course of exploring her passion for tango, Potter provided ongoing displays of her resolve not to let the machismo of the dance get the better of her. For example, we see her in her first tango lesson in Buenos Aires dancing with two well-known tango dancers, Gustavo Naveira and

Fabian Salas. While both men remain amiable as Potter demonstrates her resistance to the male lead and pushes against the constraints of having to take the female role as follower, they also beg her to tone it down. This has little effect, however, because Potter's agency—as Guano (2004:465) notes—"keeps shining through" as she makes her way into the "unchartered terrain of tango." Potter continues her struggle against the formula of male authority and female acquiescence in her tango and love relationship with Pablo Verón. She cajoles him into accepting her lead and teaches him to engage in some—presumably for him—rare self-reflection, even managing to further appropriate tango by singing and writing her own lyrics.[2] Ultimately, after protracted relational skirmishes, Potter turns the tables. As she puts it, "I've been following you in the tango. But to make a film, you have to follow me."

With her emphasis on women's agency, Potter not only upset the heterosexual conventions around tango, but she engaged in some reversals around age, gender, and ethnicity as well. The very idea of a forty-something woman who—as one reviewer put it—is "no babe" having a love affair with a younger and very sexy Argentinean man evoked reactions ranging from disbelief to outright disgust ("some things are better kept private").[3] It was hard for some critics to fathom how a famous *maestro* like Verón could invite a middle-aged tango novice like Potter to be his tango partner on stage, let alone embark on a romantic/sexual liaison with her. While it would be less difficult to imagine a middle-aged European man with a much younger Argentinean woman, the reversal of roles, it would seem, is more difficult to swallow.[4]

But perhaps what generated the most controversy among critical scholars was whether a film about a white European woman's passion for Argentine tango and her cross-cultural relationship with an Argentinean man perpetrated a colonial gaze thinly disguised in feminist robes. Although Potter was aware of the economic disparities between North and South,[5] her film comes perilously close to replicating the colonial project of nineteenth-century Europeans who embraced the exoticism of "their" colonial subjects for their own entertainment (Savigliano, 2003; Guano, 2004).[6] For example, Verón is presented as a stereotypical Latino—macho, sensual, self-absorbed—whom Potter literally puts on display for an international audience (Podalsky, 2002; Savigliano, 2003; Guano, 2004). Beyond his desire to be in the

Figure 6.1. Sally Potter and Pablo Verón in *The Tango Lesson* (dir. Sally Potter, 1997).

film and his loneliness as an exile in Paris (something Potter exploits by comparing it to her own ancestral Jewishness), Verón's motives are not explored in the film. It is Potter who is the center of attention. She portrays herself as a professional woman looking for a way to get out of her head and reconnect with her body. Her pursuit of her passion for tango and romantic adventure draws upon racialized binaries that equate Europeans with mind and rationality and non-Europeans with bodies and sensuality in ways that resonate with international audiences. Thus, Potter not only places the cultural product of another nation in the service of her own narcissistic fantasy and project of self-realization, but she evokes deep-seated Enlightenment notions of European superiority that reaffirm the "self-defined 'rational' European's gaze vis-à-vis what it constructs as its sensual Latin American Other" (Guano, 2004:472). Some critics wondered whether "cultural imperialism" was the price for Potter's appropriation of Argentine tango as "raw material for her own artistic and 'first world' packaged product" (Hopkins, 2002:123). As Podalesky (2002) notes, *The Tango Lesson* fails because it does not unravel the representational legacies of colonialism and imperialism.

For any encounter across national and cultural borders to be a true "project of mutual self-discovery," it would be necessary to interrogate the historically unequal power relationships that structure representational conventions as well as interactions between individuals from the global North and South. Potter's tango adventure does not do this. Instead, it remains locked in a discourse which gives her privileges that she neither acknowledges nor holds herself accountable for (Savigliano, 2003:224).

I have discussed *The Tango Lesson* at some length precisely because its content, intention, and the controversies it generated provide a welcome introduction to the topic of this chapter. The film and its critical reception raise questions that have haunted this book so far—namely, whether the global revival of tango at the end of the twentieth century is simply a replay of the colonial impulse on the part of people from the United States and Europe to exoticize the "other" and thereby keep their own superiority intact, or whether it can better be situated in the present context of globalization with all its pitfalls and possibilities. In other words, "Are we dancing to the same old tune, plodding through the same tired steps, and positioning ourselves and the 'other' in the same old ways?" (Podalsky, 2002:20). Or should tango better be seen as a cosmopolitan site that provides possibilities for mutually beneficial encounters between global citizens, creatively hybrid practices, and new ways of imagining the world (Cheah and Robbins, eds., 1998)?

In order to explore these questions, I will treat tango as a contact zone for transnational encounters, whereby differently located people come together in a space that is "already invaded" by a history of affiliations across borders (Clifford, 1998:367). My focus will be on how the most recent tango revival gets played out in Buenos Aires, undisputed home of the tango, and on the local dancers who, even if they have stayed at home, are, nevertheless, faced with an influx of strangers into their dance venues who are searching for a particular kind of tango experience. Drawing upon Michael Burawoy's (2000) framework for thinking globally, I will first show how social, political, and economic forces generated the most recent revival of tango as a global dance. I then turn to the actual encounters between tango tourists and locals in Buenos Aires and describe how the locals experience and negotiate their contacts with strangers. And, finally, I address the imaginary of tango as "authentically Argentinean" or "universally global" and what this means on both sides of the Atlantic.

Tango Revival in a Global Perspective

While the tango has a longstanding history of moving across national and cultural borders, its most recent revival as a global dance is usually situated in 1983, when a group of thirty-three tango singers, musicians, and dancers flew to Paris to perform *Tango Argentino*.[7] They were determined to resurrect the old traditions of tango, combining them with the *nuevo tango*[8] music of Pugliese and Piazzolla. The cast of the show arrived in an old military plane, surrounded by gruff soldiers in uniforms, and with only one meal under their belts. They weren't expecting much—a week's run in the Theatre Châtelet and probably "an audience of homesick Argentines from all over Europe" (Thompson, 2005:266). To their surprise, however, the show was sold out the first night and for many nights afterward, with people sitting in the aisles and many more outside the theater, wanting to get in. Their tour was extended from a week to a whole season, after which they returned to Buenos Aires in style, only to discover that no one in Argentina had heard of or read about their stunning success.

The press probably didn't find the show worth paying attention to, because in Argentina tango had long fallen out of fashion. Tango had been embraced by Peronists prior to the military regime as a way of cementing its political ideology about the national identity of *argentinidad*, as represented in the lyrics of tango (Anzaldi, 2012a:97–140). While tango as music could be heard on the radio and many of the lyrics were incorporated into the everyday speech of Argentineans, by the mid-1960s, rock 'n' roll had arrived from the United States and Great Britain, becoming a popular dance for the younger generation. As Damian, one of my Argentinean informants, put it, "Tango dancing was totally, totally out."

> It was something for my parents' generation. I remember my Dad, when I was twelve, saying to me, "OK, it's tango time and I'm going to teach you how to hold a woman." And I said, "Oh, no, Dad, I don't want this." And he saw that I was not going to do [it], so he didn't insist.

The demise of tango in Argentina was exacerbated[9] by the military *junta* that came into power in 1976, initiating a period of repression and terror. Even for those who might still have wanted to dance tango, the atmosphere was not conducive to meeting in public places. Or, as one of my informants assured me, "No one felt much like dancing."

Although tango had become almost ancient history in Argentina, a "genre from the past without a future" (Anzaldi, 2012a), with the international production of *Tango Argentino* it was off and running everywhere else. The show was performed to enthusiastic audiences in New York, Rome, Berlin, and many other cities around the world, sparking a veritable renaissance of tango music and dance. This, together with the growing popularity of *nuevo tango*, transformed tango from an old-fashioned, slightly dusty national tradition to an exotic, avant-garde dance, attracting a global audience of cosmopolitan *aficionados*.[10]

With this new interest in tango and its emergence in urban centers across the globe, Argentineans themselves also became interested in taking it up again. Some were political refugees who saw tango—the dance or the music—as part of their survival strategy in conditions of exile. Based on her interviews with Argentineans in exile, Cara (2009) writes that many people who did not dance or listen to tango at home found that when they were abroad it provided them with a powerful sense of home. The loss, melancholy, and nostalgia that are common themes in tango resonated with a deeply ambivalent national identity, shaped by more than a half-century of failed political and economic projects. Tango seemed to have the capacity to encapsulate both the tragedy and poetics of Argentinean society without denying its traumatic history, making it a perfect metaphor for the alienated but nostalgic Argentinean in exile (see also Taylor, 1987; Viladrich, 2013).

An example of how this nostalgia worked in practice is the story of Mirta Díaz, an Argentinean tango dancer who helped initiate the first tango school in Amsterdam in 1986. Her story is not atypical.[11] She had been living in a refugee center in the Netherlands with her husband and small child after they escaped persecution for their political activism in Argentina. She realized that if she was going to stay in the Netherlands, she would need to do something. She joined a theater group with other people from Latin America and, in one of their productions, performed a tango. This performance elicited so much enthusiasm that she was asked to give tango lessons. At first, she was reluctant. Tango had been part of her life in Argentina. She had listened to it every day, knew how to dance it, but she had no idea how to give lessons. But, as she put it, even though tango "meant something very different here than it meant in Argentina," she, paradoxically, saw it as a way to reconnect with her lost culture. She became co-founder of the Academia de Tango, the first Argentinean tango school in Amsterdam, and she organized several tributes to *maestros* of the tango, including Pepito Avellaneda, Antonio Todaro, and Oswaldo Pugliese. As "*la dama del tango*," Diáz received a royal honorary ribbon in 2003 for her contribution to the introduction and dissemination of the Argentinean tango culture in the Netherlands.[12]

By the turn of the twenty-first century, tango was in full swing throughout Europe, North America, and parts of Asia (Japan, Korea, Hong Kong, Taiwan, Singapore) and Australia. Tango schools and dance salons had sprung up in most major cities, and, along with them, a growing demand emerged for tango music, tango shoes and clothes, and, last but not least, Argentineans who knew how to dance tango and could teach others to do it. The international stir around tango, coupled with recurrent economic crises, including the disastrous collapse of the dollar economy in 2001, made tango dancing interesting to people in Argentina after a long period of abstinence. It rekindled a small but enthusiastic local dance community and encouraged would-be tango entrepreneurs to create dance shows, workshops, and performances for an international audience. A growing group of Argentine tango professionals emerged and began to make their living by giving classes or private lessons to visitors in Buenos Aires and by touring and offering tango classes abroad.

The first generation of these tango entrepreneurs consisted of older *milongueros* who had learned to dance tango in their youth. While they knew how to dance, they lacked any kind of formal training.[13] As one of my informants put it, "They just danced and you were expected to do the same the best you could." They were soon followed by a second generation of dancers who were more familiar with the technicalities of dancing. Many even had some training as professional dancers and had performed in tango shows. They knew how to tap into notions of passionate exotic eroticism that distinguished tango for export from tango at home (Cara, 2009). Unlike the earlier tango dancers, however, this new generation of professionals had figured out exactly how to teach tango to students who did not know the music and had no dancing experience. In short, they were able to teach tango in a way that was custom-made for their students abroad, while having the exotic "perfume" of being taught by "real Argentineans."[14] Currently, tango is attracting ever younger and more entrepreneurial professionals who are able to combine the elements of traditional tango with more show-style techniques, fancy costumes, and elaborate performances. They know how to mobilize the new social media to market themselves to an international audience through YouTube videos of their performances, websites, and blogs. Many have developed their own special niches in the tango scene, such as "Tango-Pilates," "Tango-psychotherapy," "Romantic tango," "Zen tango," or simply "real tango: Tango Milonguero."

As more and more professional tango dancers from Argentina were invited to give workshops, master classes, and performances in special shows for audiences of tango dancers abroad, transnational institutional and friendship ties also emerged. However, this was by no means a one-way street. In return, many of the tango *aficionados* from Europe, North America, and Asia began traveling to Buenos Aires in order to learn what was viewed as the *authentic* tango—tango in the place where it had originated. This pilgrimage to Buenos Aires became a "must" for any tango dancer with professional aspirations as a dancer, teacher, or performer. These trips allowed them to cultivate contacts with professional Argentinean tango dancers, who could then be invited to Europe (or North America or Asia) to give workshops and performances and who would, they hoped, reciprocate by inviting them to perform in Buenos Aires. This exchange among professional dancers became a calling card for salons across the globe, lending them an air of borrowed authenticity ("This is where tango is danced the way it is in Buenos Aires").

While the global contacts among tango instructors and salon organizers were essential for initiating and maintaining the new tango revival, it was the tourist industry that cemented the globalization of tango. Buenos Aires has become an international tourist hub, surpassing Rio de Janeiro as the primary tourist destination in the region (Subsecretaria de Industrias Culturales, 2007). The tango industry has tripled since 2001, drawing a direct income of US$135 million in 2006 and an indirect impact of nearly a half billion U.S. dollars.[15] While tango is not the only reason for tourists to visit Buenos Aires, it is one of the main cultural attractions in the tourist economy. The current mayor of Buenos Aires, Mauricio Macri, compared tango to Argentina's most important export in his opening speech at the Tango World Championship in 2010: "Tango is the soya of Buenos Aires" (cited in Anzaldi, 2012b).[16] Without a doubt, tango has become one of the most important ingredients of the new symbolic economy of the city of Buenos Aires. Downtown areas of the city like San Telmo have been revitalized and reinvented as historical tango districts. No trip to Buenos Aires is complete without the obligatory visit to a tango show. On an average day, 3,000 tourists visit a tango dance show and more than half of the international tourists attend at least one show during their stay in Buenos Aires. While the shows make up much of the revenue of tango tourism,[17] the tango industry also includes tango clothing stores, tango shoe shops, tango hostels and guest houses, tango travel agencies offering specialized tango tours through the city, and tango art, including posters, postcards, and other tango souvenirs. International tourism has also had a major effect on the local tango scene. There were few places to dance tango before the late 1990s. Since 2001, however, there are more than 300 *milongas* a week in 120 different locations in Buenos Aires with nearly 2,500 dance instructors and an estimated 35,000 dancers.[18]

This latest tango revival was hardly coincidental. Rather, it was part of a specific constellation of social, economic, and political forces that provided the conditions for the reemergence of tango in Buenos Aires as well as its global proliferation as an "authentic" Argentinean dance in other urban centers across the globe. On the one hand, the revival could not have taken the shape it did without an interdependent global economy with its increased mobility of people, information, and commodities (Burawoy et al., 2000). The contemporary shifts in Argentina—the end of military dictatorship; a collective desire to, if not entirely forget the past, at least regain a positive sense of *argentinidad*; and a crippling series of economic recessions culminating in a total collapse of the dollar economy in 2001—offered a context in which tango could reemerge locally as an important cultural product, social practice, and national symbol. On the other hand, the new tango revival depended upon the conditions and costs of late modernity across the globe, which produced an audience potentially receptive to what tango had to offer. It was contingent on a population of highly mobile individuals who were affluent enough to spend time and money on learning to dance tango. They needed to have the cosmopolitan lifestyles that would allow them to integrate tango into their everyday lives (for example, attend salons and immerse themselves in an unfamiliar music and dance culture). While tango is not only about tourism (there are certainly committed dancers who never leave their home cities), it is impossible to understand the contemporary global revival of tango without taking tourism into account.

I will now turn my attention to what the globalization of tango through tourism means for actual interactions among dancers in Buenos Aires. What kinds of possibilities and pitfalls do these encounters offer them? To put it a bit differently, does the globalization of tango simply generate transnational encounters that are "totally enclaved" within the economic sphere, as many postcolonial critics fear, or can it provide opportunities for genuine and mutually beneficial interaction between differently located individuals as well (Burawoy, 2000:140)?

Transnational Connections on the *Pista*

At the outset of this book, I described my first travels to Buenos Aires in order to dance tango. As these trips gradually became more oriented to my research, I found myself increasingly observing the interactions between local and visiting dancers less through the eyes of a tango *aficionada* and more through the lens of the feminist postcolonial critique of tango. Encouraged by my readings of Savigliano (1995) and others, I assumed that the histories of economic disparity between the global North and South would be played out in one way or another on the dance floor. For example, I imagined that many local dancers would treat the tango tourists as a potential source of income.[19] Moreover, I expected to discover examples of Argentinean *milongueros* and *milongueras* presenting themselves as erotic, exotic objects for the colonizing gaze of the tourists. I imagined that their survival strategy in difficult times would be to gain the admiration and, consequently, the support of affluent foreigners by engaging in what Savigliano (1995) has called "auto-exoticization." In this way, they would appeal to the erotic and ethnicized fantasies that foreigners inevitably entertain about Argentineans as sensual, sexy Latinos while maintaining a hold on tango as part of their culture, their *argentinidad*. Remembering the silencing of Pablo Verón in Sally Potter's *The Tango Lesson* and the unease it generated among the critics of the film, I suspected that local dancers would be cynical or even bitter about being "othered"[20] and would, if given an opportunity to voice their opinions, probably have plenty to criticize about the current flood of tourists from different parts of the world into their *milongas*.

To my surprise—and initially to my disappointment as researcher—this is not what I discovered when I began talking to local dancers. Their criticisms of tourists turned out to be considerably more nuanced than I had expected and their assessment of the tango revival far less bleak than I had imagined. In fact, for the most part, they seemed remarkably welcoming of foreigners, easily able to forgive their transgressions on and off the dance floor, and quick to emphasize how much they not only *liked* foreigners, but *needed* them in the salons.

In the next section, I will explore how my local informants negotiated the problems that could be expected in their interactions with visiting tango *aficionados*—problems that stem from the economic disparities between the global North and South, from ambivalent feelings about practices of exoticism, and, finally, from the legacies of the colonial and imperial past in the present realties of the salon.

Economic Disparities and "Impossible Romances"

Let me begin with the problem of economic inequality between locals and visitors, the inevitable starting point of current critical tango scholarship. While scholars like Savigliano tend to situate Argentina in a postcolonial framework[21] in order to explain disparities between the global North and South, Argentina has not, in fact, been a colony since 1816, when it achieved its independence from Spain. Indeed, in the first half of the twentieth century, when tango became prominent, Argentina was one of the wealthiest nations in the world. Since then, the nation has gone through a series of dramatic economic and political crises, the most recent one being in 2001 when the dollar economy collapsed, virtually wiping out the middle class and making life even more precarious for the poor. While the economy has become more stable in recent years, it would be difficult to find a *porteño* (an inhabitant of Buenos Aires), including the (for the most part) middle-class dancers who frequent the *milongas*, who doesn't chafe under the problems of inflation and complain about the state of the economy in general. Travel, in particular, is difficult for everyone given the fact that the national currency (the *peso*) cannot be used outside Argentina and the government restricts the purchase of dollars needed to pay for international travel. While many of my informants grumbled about not being able to travel easily (although not necessarily in order to dance tango),[22] professional dancers—that is, dancers who had made tango their livelihood—were most likely to frame these difficulties in terms of inequalities between Argentina and the rest of the world.

Take, for example, Mariana DoCampo, whom we met in the previous chapter and who earns her living by giving tango lessons and organizing a salon. She is regularly invited to perform at festivals in other parts of the world. While she is quick to underscore how important and inspiring the international tango community has been for her, she also notes that there are "some problems we need to be thinking about":

> You know, when Germans come to dance in Buenos Aires, they can just dance, see places, travel. But when an Argentinean goes to Europe, the situation is not the same. We can't travel just to dance. If we go to Germany, we have to work. Otherwise we can't do it. To treat tango as if we are just one big community ignores the way power works, that it's the Argentinean who has the tango and the European who has the money.

While this may be somewhat simplified—ignoring, as it does, the difficulties all professional dancers usually have trying to make a living from tango—it does display DoCampo's ambivalence about her peers from Europe. She is disappointed at their lack of awareness of the constraints under which Argentinean professional tango dancers operate and expects them to be more attentive to the differences in their respective situations.

The disparities among international tango professionals are only a small part of the story, however. Many of my informants told horror stories about tango dancers' mixing business and pleasure. For example, I was regaled with tragic tales of "innocent European women" who were taken in by wily *milongueros* who would shower them with compliments, making them feel beautiful and desirable. Once the romance had begun, however, it lasted only a few weeks before these women were being asked to pay for everything. As an Australian ex-pat, Sam, who had been living in Buenos Aires for several years, cynically puts it, "ninety percent of these guys are on a fishing expedition." While Sam's sympathies are clearly on the side of the duped women, who "think they have this lovely man from South America who has told them how beautiful they are and how nice they dance," Marlene, a local *milonguera* whom we met in previous chapters, provides a different take. In her view, many of the tourists are "just plain stupid." Recalling a fifty-year-old Canadian woman who came to Buenos Aires and fell head over heels in love with a taxi driver she met in a *milonga*, Marlene notes with undisguised irritation:

> I warned her. "Take care," I said; "he wants something." But she said: "Oh, no. . . . It's me." I couldn't believe it. I thought: Are you stupid? . . . I mean, a man dances with you *all* night. He speaks with you. He tries to teach you a little about Argentine culture. And then he tries to get a little money. It's not that he charges—we're not rude—but, you know, he'll say: I have a problem. I need money to repair my car . . . but she doesn't know what's going on and she gets involved with her heart and thinks he really loves her, that it's true. But it's not true. I can't believe it. It's so *obvious* to us, but for these tourists . . . what are they thinking?

These stories testify to what Törnqvist (2012, 2013) has described as the "impossible romances" that emerge when European tango tourists look for passionate encounters in Buenos Aires without taking into account the dramatically different conditions under which many of the locals live. She situates such liaisons in the framework of sex and romance tourism,[23] which is invariably constrained by global socioeconomic injustice. Based on her analysis of the stories tango tourists have told her, she suggests that it is better to steer clear of romance across transnational borders altogether (Törnqvist, 2012:103). However, locals may have a more nuanced view of such relationships. Like Marlene, they scoff at tourists who are not "streetwise" enough to protect themselves, but they also find fault with local *milongueros* for "selling their souls" by dancing with tourists who "can't put one foot in front of the other." Viewed from this perspective, both visitors and the locals are to blame for spoiling what tango has to offer. As Marlene puts it, she wouldn't go so far as to label such encounters on (or even off) the dance floor as impossible—"Let's just say that it's *complicado*."

Of course, many encounters between local and visiting dancers do not extend beyond the safe confines of the *milonga*. Moreover, many of the local dancers are themselves sufficiently well-off that they can come to the *milongas* to dance rather than to boost their income. Their encounters with dancers from other countries are, therefore, less likely to involve the kinds of financially motivated "fishing expeditions" described above. However, this does not mean that even middle-class Argentineans do not have their own fantasies about visiting dancers.

Sofia, a psychoanalyst in her mid-fifties, explained that many *porteños* dream of "escaping" with a wealthy foreigner who will rescue them from all the economic and political problems that make their everyday lives in Buenos Aires so difficult. In my view, this fantasy can be seen as the Argentinean equivalent of the tourist's longing for a "passionate encounter with an exotic Latino," albeit with an important difference. While the tourist—à la Sally Potter—probably envisions a temporary encounter, a vacation romance that will end when he or she returns home, for Argentineans, the fantasy, born in a context of limited mobility, seems to entail leaving home altogether.

Exoticization: Who "Others" Whom?

The second potential problem in transnational encounters on the dance floor concerns the role played by exoticism in tango. The postcolonial critique of tango divides contemporary tango dancers into "exoticizers" (usually Europeans or North Americans) and "actual exotic others" (the Argentineans) (Savigliano, 2010:138). While this critique does not necessarily reduce local dancers to totally passive objects of the colonial gaze of exoticizing visitors, it does presuppose that Argentineans will be oriented toward the fantasies that foreigners have about them rather than to the fantasies they have about themselves, let alone about their foreign visitors. It leaves little room for the possibility that Argentineans entertain (exotic) fantasies and engage in practices of exoticizing themselves. In short, the postcolonial critique does not address the ways Argentineans actively participate in, give form to, and contest the transnational encounters that take place in their local tango culture.

To be sure, the postcolonial critique of exoticism has much to recommend it, but the lack of attention to the perspectives and experiences of local dancers is a serious lacuna. It does not do justice to the self-identity of many Argentineans, nor does it take into account their own fantasies about foreigners. More generally, the postcolonial critique tends to emphasize international networks of power and exclusion while overlooking the contradictory patterns of resistance and desire that take place in actual practice (Nava, 2002:87). In short, the postcolonial critique seems to be more ideologically motivated than empirically grounded in concrete contexts of social interaction.

In what follows, I adopt a more ethnographical approach to the issue of exoticism, treating it as an integral feature of transnational encounters in and through tango. It is my contention that this will help us to understand how the exotic/erotic fantasies and desires of both Argentineans and their visitors are mobilized in complicated ways—ways that are both problematic and mutually beneficial.

Visitors, especially those on their first trip to Buenos Aires, often arrive with a thoroughly exoticized and ethnicized view of Argentineans as Latinos. They expect Argentineans to be more "sensual," "natural," and "closer to their bodies" than they themselves are. They are, in short, looking for something "different." This is, after all, why they have come all the way to Buenos Aires just to dance tango and it is, therefore, not surprising that they describe local dancers in exoticizing terms, as "other," to themselves. A case in point is Paul, the retired German businessman we met in chapter 3, who has been living in Buenos Aires for several years:

> I'm generalizing now, of course, but for Argentineans, tango just comes naturally. In Europe, there is always some holding back, but here they are much more comfortable with body on body, with hugging and kissing. It's because it's a Latin country.

Ironically, however, most of the Argentineans I spoke with went to great lengths to establish their connections to and connectedness with Europe rather than to Latin America. The last thing *they* want is to be seen as "Latino." This is not surprising given the long and convoluted history of "whitening" the national identity of Argentina through encouraging migration from Europe while eradicating indigenous people in the interior.[24] Argentina has tended to define itself as a European outpost in the South, while distancing itself from other Latin American nations and, more generally, from any kind of "swarthy third-world otherness" (Kaminsky, 2008:214). Many of my informants spontaneously supplied detailed genealogies of their families' histories of migration, explaining that they were originally from Italy or France or Russia. For example, Juan, a divorced dentist of sixty, told me that he didn't consider himself a very "good example of a *porteño*" despite his having been born and raised in Buenos Aires because, as he put it, "I guess I feel more comfortable with foreigners. My family all came from Germany and Austria so I'm just more used to being with Europeans."

A desire to present themselves as "Europe's same" (Kaminsky, 2008) by displaying an affinity with European tastes, habits, and ideals is clearly reflected in the stories my informants told me about their origins and their identities. However, while it was quite common to establish a European connection, as it turned out, for some Argentineans not just any European will do. For example, Carmen, a fifty-year-old businesswoman, explained that she, like most of her generation, grew up loving anything and everything that was European—that is (she added), "*except* Spanish or Italian. They are *too* much like us."

While many *porteños* distance themselves in no uncertain terms from anything that might be regarded as "Latino," this does not keep them from exoticizing themselves upon occasion. Their auto-exoticization takes, however, a slightly different form from that which the postcolonial critique would suggest. While rejecting the stereotype of the "sexy Latino," some local dancers have few qualms about positing their "special" relationship to tango by virtue of their identity as *porteños*. While many local dancers have, in actual fact, learned to dance tango fairly recently and may have considerably less training and dancing experience than many foreign visitors,[25] they, nevertheless, go to some lengths to establish their qualities as tango dancers, emphasizing that dancing tango is not just about skill and certainly not about steps. Rather, it is about the nebulous quality of *corazón* (heart) and having a deeply affective connection to the music and lyrics of tango. By exoticizing their *argentidad* as responsible for their unique connection to tango, local dancers can enhance their attractions for those visitors in search of authenticity.

This form of auto-exoticization appears, for example, in the compliment that local dancers sometimes give visitors: "You dance like a *porteña* [or *porteño*]." Both locals and visitors regard this as the ultimate accolade because it implies that the visitor is more than "just a good dancer"; he or she has finally "gotten" what tango is "really" about.[26] In this way, the local dancers who give this compliment underscore that the visitor will only ever be able to dance "like" an Argentinean and that, at the end of the day, the "real thing" belongs to them.

Another common example of auto-exoticizing can be found in the way locals draw attention to the importance of understanding the lyrics for properly dancing tango. This is often done *en passant* while dancing. The local dancer casts his eyes toward the ceiling and sighs, "Ahhh, the *letras* [lyrics]. . . . What a shame that you can't understand them." In the eyes of many Argentineans, foreigners may learn how to dance tango, to pick up its beat and rhythms, and even to dance with some feeling. However, they will never be able to understand its essence. Or, as Archetti (1998:159) puts it, Argentineans are more than happy to share tango with the rest of the world, but they reserve the poetics for themselves.

The most important elaboration of the postcolonial critique of exoticism, however, is not that Argentineans are exoticized and exoticize themselves in ways that are more complicated than the "sexy Latino" stereotype would suggest. They also take up the position of exoticizer vis-à-vis foreigners in their salons, thereby blurring the hard and fast distinction between exoticizer and exoticized. Many of the local men visibly perk up when dancing with foreign visitors. This may be due to the fact that the visitors tend to be younger than the locals, and it is not unusual to see a very old *milonguero* dancing with a foreign woman young enough to be his granddaughter. As one elderly dancer, Carlos, explains, "You just really want to dance with one of those *chicas*; you want to know what she feels like in your arms." Male Argentinean dancers often rave about French women, whom they regard as "elegant" and "stylish," while they value Asian women for having "perfect technique" and dancing "like feathers."[27] I remember being asked to dance a waltz with a local dancer, who explained to me later that he *always* dances the waltzes (reputedly the most romantic of tangos) with "a European woman."[28] The object of this exotic fantasy is the white European as symbol of old school elegance and high culture. As a North American (the other half of my dual nationality), I probably would not have had nearly the same symbolic cachet as dancer, given the negative stance many Argentineans have toward the U.S. *gringos*.[29]

Many of the local women I spoke with insisted that they preferred dancing with visitors, as long as the visitors can dance.[30] In their view, foreigners—at least, the Europeans and North Americans—are taller, better dressed (white shirts!), more cultured, better educated, and more likely to be good conversationalists in between dances. But, most important, foreigners are "*caballeros*" (gentlemen). As Elsa, a divorced psychotherapist, put it, the foreign tourists generally have a "higher level" than the local men. She explained that she cannot even imagine having coffee with a local *milonguero*, let alone exchanging e-mail addresses or having a friendly relationship outside the salon. "I would never do that. Never." The counterpart to this is, of course, that many European women may need to exoticize their less educated Argentinean partners in order to feel comfortable surrendering themselves to an intimate embrace with someone of a lower-class background. This was brought home to me rather forcefully when I took some non–tango-dancing friends to a salon in Buenos Aires and saw how dismayed and even a bit disgusted they were to see me dancing with some of the local *milongueros*. One friend told me later that *she* would never be able to dance with "someone like that." She did not explain whether the "that" referred to the differences in our ages, educational levels, ethnic backgrounds, or social classes, but what she clearly saw was not exotic, but only unappealing, difference.

These examples show that both Argentinean and non-Argentinean dancers exoticize each other by drawing upon stereotypes of European superiority and Latino inferiority. However, the practices of exoticization displayed in them are less a remnant of the colonial past (as the postcolonial critique would suggest) and more a result of the specific ways in which gender and class intersect in the present context of the tango salon in Buenos Aires. This brings me to the third problem in the postcolonial critique—namely, the emphasis on the past rather than on the present in the ways transnational relations take place on the dance floors.

Colonial Past or Cosmopolitan Present?

The salons of Buenos Aires have changed from the Golden Age of tango (1935–52), which Savigliano (1995) describes as a period in which proletarian *milonguitas* attempted to escape their impoverished milieux by dancing with an upper-class *niño bien*, while their male counterparts sang a whiny tango, drowned their sorrows at a bar, or perhaps engaged in a knife fight with their rivals. For the most part, the women today who attend *milongas* in Buenos Aires are well educated and fully employed in professions (e.g., psychotherapy, law, or medicine). The men, while not without income, are often more precariously employed than the women, tend to work in service or blue-collar jobs rather than in professions (e.g., taxi driving, recreation, sales), and are, on the whole, older and more often retired. While the men have an advantage in the salons both numerically (there are almost always more women than men) as well as symbolically (the *codigas* of the salon favor dominant masculine behavior), local women draw upon their class privilege of being "more cultured" or "better educated" than the men, thereby mitigating the masculinist culture of the salons. For example, Marta, the Argentinean dress designer we met in chapter 3, describes the local men as "good men, of course. But primitive."

> There's a very big difference between the men and the women in the *milongas* here. You can find many women like me, but you will not find the same with men. You can look for them through a microscope. You will not find them.

While local men and women clearly have to negotiate the class and gender tensions in the contemporary tango scene in Buenos Aires, they do not so much replicate the past as make strategic use of historically constructed convictions about European superiority in ways that make sense in the present. Exoticizing visiting dancers enables local women to situate themselves as closer to foreigners in terms of class and educational background, thereby giving them an edge over their less "cultured" compatriots. Similarly, local men can reinstate their dominance over local women by dancing with admiring tourists, thereby avoiding demands for commitment and accountability as well as easing some of the "hidden injuries of class" (Sennett and Cobb, 1972/1977).

Even this brief look at the transnational encounters on the dance floors of Buenos Aires suggests that, while fantasies and practices of exoticization shape the interactions between visitors and locals, they do so in ways that are both more contradictory and more mutually beneficial than the postcolonial critique would suggest. Postcolonial critiques emphasize the authoritative gaze of the colonializer that presumably is exercised, intentionally or not, by anyone hailing from the global North. When North–South encounters are viewed through this lens, the focus is primarily upon the injuries caused by differences in power rather than upon the contrary patterns of desire that emerge as differently located individuals participate in what has become a global dance culture.

As we have seen, Argentina's complicated history precludes local tango dancers' seeing themselves (and allowing themselves to be seen) as "Latin lovers," passively awaiting the exoticizing colonial gaze from inhabitants of the global North. While economic disparities and historical discourses of exotic "othering" shape how tango is perceived across the globe, Argentinean tango dancers play an active role not only in how they exoticize (and ethnicize) themselves but also in how they exoticize (and ethnicize) others. They draw upon imaginaries of European whiteness and refinement as well as the sensuality and embodiedness of the South, yet they do so in ways that have, at least if not more, to do with managing the local gendered and class asymmetries in the *milongas* of the present than any real or imagined colonial past.

The stories of locals and visitors illustrate how exoticization is part of a mutual process in which both locals and visitors draw upon and rework their differences in order to make their encounters desirable and exciting. Exoticization—or the construction of an exotic "other" as dance partner—enhances tango precisely because it allows a momentary escape from the "sameness" that stands on uneasy footing with passion (Nava, 2002:91).[31] The tourist who desires to dance with a "real" Argentinean finds a kindred spirit in the *porteño*, who also yearns for something different. It is precisely this desire for a taste of the "else-where"[32] that shapes encounters between visitors and locals on the dance floor in ways that may have less to do with an actual or even-metaphorical colonial past than with a very real cosmopolitan present.

Global Imaginaries

Tango is a global dance, taken up by *aficionados* from all over the world. Yet it remains firmly linked to Argentina—not only in name (*Argentinean tango or Tango Argentino*), but historically (through its travels), economically (through tourism), and symbolically (through its representation in popular culture and music). Some scholars have even argued that the complex sentiments (sadness, happiness, fear, love, pride, shame, and honor), often framed in the local language (*lunfardo*) of Buenos Aires, are probably truly accessible only to Argentineans (Cozarinsky, 2007). As it has in the past, tango today continues to speak to the emotional problems and dilemmas of Argentineans, making its texts a key element in their national identity (Archetti, 1999:144). But, if this is true, what does the global popularity of tango mean for the local *porteños* who dance it? How do they situate themselves as the devoted practitioners of something that has become global and yet remains central to their understanding of themselves as Argentineans?

Given the complicated struggles around Argentinean national identity in the past, it is not surprising that local tango dancers display some ambivalence about tango as a global dance. As Anzaldi (2012a) has convincingly shown, Argentina has two different and contradictory understandings of what it means to be Argentinean.[33] The first conception of *argentinidad* is inward-looking, rural, and traditional. It entails a wariness of economic, political, and cultural dependency on Europe and North America and a desire to avoid anything that smacks of foreign influence and cultural imperialism (Anzaldi, 2012a:80). Viewed from this perspective of national identity, tango is the expression par excellence of what it means to be Argentinean: its roots, its soul, its essence (Anzaldi, 2012a:88–89). One can find echoes of this version of *argentinidad* in the proprietary stance many Argentineans have toward tango music (Archetti, 1999:130–32). It is also mirrored in the 2009 United Nations Educational, Scientific and Cultural Organization (UNESCO) declaration of tango as cultural heritage in need of protection from globalization.[34] And, somewhat paradoxically, the postcolonial critique of tango takes up the notion of ownership when it tackles the exploitation of Argentinean culture by the imperialistic global North.

The second version of Argentinean national identity is very different. It is urban, modern, and cosmopolitan. This conception of *argentinidad* belongs to Buenos Aires with its international trade relations, its educated middle classes, and its cultural life, which is heavily indebted to European influences. Viewed from this perspective, tango may have originated in the slums of Buenos Aires, but it was its move to Paris that made it, literally, *salonfähig* (presentable) for the respectable middle and upper classes of Argentina. In fact, tango's global popularity and its ability to provide Argentina with a much-sought-after cosmopolitan identity are precisely what make it such a valuable symbol of *argentinidad*. Taken together, it is this tension between tango as a *local* Argentinean tradition and tango as a *global* phenomenon that offers the discursive framework within which *porteños* will have to make sense of the new tango revival, the burgeoning tango tourism in Buenos Aires, and, most specifically, their interactions with foreign *aficionados* who come to Buenos Aires to dance.

Contemporary Argentinean tango dancers are, therefore, ambivalent about tango as a dance that belongs to them. On the one hand, they have no compunctions about referring to tango as something they have "in their blood" or are able to do simply by virtue of their national or cultural identity. They often distinguish themselves from foreign visitors as the only ones who can truly understand the essence of tango and fend off any criticisms—for example, about their tendency toward self-absorption or their unwillingness to listen to what visitors have to say[35]—with an indifferent shrug and a "*Somos así*" ("That's just the way we are"). In this way, their national character is mobilized as protection against any attempt to absorb them into a broader community.

On the other hand, contemporary Argentineans display unmistakable pride at tango's popularity outside Argentina as well, regarding it as proof of the unique capacity of the music and the dance to inspire people in different places all over the world. They are touched by the determination shown by so many visitors to learn a dance from Argentina. Many are surprised that some visitors can dance tango better than the locals and many even go so far as to attribute the very existence of tango today to its capacity for travel. A case in point is Oscar, a *milonguero* in his early seventies and a fixture in the salons of Buenos Aires. He began dancing tango as a young boy and can remember the days when the big-name orchestras like those of Biagi and Di Sarli played in the clubs. He credits the recent tango revival in Europe for reanimating a tradition that had long been and, to some extent, still is dead in Argentina. He is, therefore, grateful to foreigners for giving tango back to him, making it possible for him to enjoy tango again—the way he could before it disappeared in the 1960s. For him, there is no doubt that the global interest in tango is what has allowed it to survive.

Many of my Argentinean informants echoed Oscar's appreciation of tango's global popularity. They explained that they liked dancing with people from other parts of the world because doing so gave them a chance to dance with someone different. The conversations between the dances were interesting, and many appreciated the international contacts that tango made possible. Carmen, for example, announced proudly that she had met people from Europe and the United States whom she corresponds with regularly. Elsa, a psychoanalyst who likes to travel, explained that she loves to practice her languages in the salons with the foreign visitors: "French and English are easy, but I'm taking German now and it gives me a chance to brush up on that, too." Even some of the older *milongueros* are beginning to learn English because, as one of my informants explained, "They want to be able to have a conversation with the tourists, too." But, most of all, my Argentinean informants appreciated the fact that tango has become global because it has changed their local tango culture for the better. Many locals—men, women, gays, and young people—feel encouraged by visitors to be more critical of the ingrained machismo in their own tango culture, finding support for the rejection of overly restrictive codes and salon etiquette. Many dancers in Argentina show a marked readiness to engage with the new and the different—something that Nava (2002) refers to as the popular consciousness of cosmopolitan modernity. Given that so many Argentinean dancers proudly embrace the widespread dissemination of tango across the globe, treating it as an authentic expression of Argentinean culture and national identity does not do justice to the ways in which Argentineans imagine and experience themselves as cosmopolitans participating in tango as a global phenomenon.

If Argentinean dancers display a cosmopolitan disposition toward tango, what about *aficionados* from other parts of the world? In chapter 1, we saw how tango communities outside Buenos Aires tend to embrace the notion that tango is typically Argentinean. They do this whether they admire and try to emulate tango in its most authentic form or, alternatively, present themselves as modernizers whose mission is to transform tango. Nevertheless, in my conversations with dancers from Amsterdam and other parts of the world, I discovered a similar, albeit inverse, ambivalence to what I had seen among Argentinean dancers. They also had to reconcile their participation in tango as a global dance with their acknowledgment as non-Argentineans that tango's roots lie in Argentina. Unlike the *porteños* who dance "their" tango at home amidst throngs of admiring visitors, dancers from outside Argentina need to explain their passion for something that belongs to another culture with their desire to participate as equal partners in a shared community of *aficionados*.

As we saw in chapter 2, even serious tango dancers are ambivalent about having to go to Buenos Aires in order to dance "real" tango. For example, Marcus had already visited Buenos Aires four times before he decided that dancing tango there was, after all, "not the alpha and omega of all things."

> You can compare it to Beethoven. His music was composed in a certain period in a certain place—and, yes, in a certain culture—but no one would say now that only the people in Vienna can play the real Beethoven. . . . [T]he strength of tango is that it's not local, but that people here, or in Istanbul, or anywhere can do it.

While he acknowledges that Buenos Aires is the source of tango, he isn't convinced that he has to go there in order to experience the real thing. Nor does he feel he has to dance with "flesh-and-blood Argentineans" in order to have the kind of dance he desires.

As we saw in chapter 3, many dancers from Amsterdam—and this is also true of those from Europe more generally—frequently travel in order to dance, often attending salons or festivals far from home. For some, going farther afield is a way to experience how tango is danced in different places. For others, traveling is a way to keep in touch with a broader tango community than the one they belong to at home. As Harry, the web designer whom we encountered in the previous chapter, puts it, "I know people from all over who dance tango. We're like a family of tango nomads." He keeps in touch with his international tango family through Facebook, where they keep one another informed about which festivals and workshops they will be attending. He has already been to Riga, Helsinki, Budapest, and Istanbul. Smiling, he says, "I haven't been to Buenos Aires yet, but I'd like to go there, too."

Even dancers who are committed to taking regular trips to Buenos Aires argue that they can dance tango just as well at home. For example, Leo, the lawyer from Amsterdam who has appeared in previous chapters, goes to Buenos Aires as much as twice a year "just to dance." However, he claims that he can find what he's looking for in his home salon in Amsterdam, too. "It's different, but it's also the same." While he admits to missing the energy of the salons in Buenos Aires and would much prefer that dancers in Amsterdam also practice the *cabeceo*, he explains that things have gotten better in that respect. He can now usually invite his local partners with a glance and a nod, just as he does in Buenos Aires. The reason for this: "Because so many Dutch people have been to Buenos Aires and have experienced tango there. So they bring it back here."

Corine, who has been organizing a salon in Amsterdam for several years, explains that she is really happy with the way tango is danced in Amsterdam. As she puts it, people have "finally *gotten* what makes tango so magical." She feels proud when she observes people in her own salon, just watching the "flow" on the dance floor and the way they have learned to dance tango.

> They are beginning to realize that they don't *have* to go to Buenos Aires because they can create it here. Themselves. Tango is in *yourself*. You don't have to travel that far in order to find it.

Tango dancers—whether they are *porteños* who have never set foot outside Buenos Aires or tango nomads who travel miles to dance tango in far-flung places across the globe ("a wallet, a ticket, a pair of shoes, that's all you need")[36] or *aficionados* who prefer to dance at home under the motto that "you can dance tango anywhere"—all participate in the transnational culture space that tango has become. Tango dancers look for new experiences in different places, knowing, at the same time, that there will always be an element of the familiar—the well-known music, the imagined embrace, or the recognizable ambience of any tango salon. But tango dancers can also stay at home and still enjoy a taste of "elsewhere" in their own local tango communities. This is what makes tango a global phenomenon. The global-ness of tango is not simply that the dance has traveled across national borders, nor that individual dancers themselves will travel far and wide in order to dance it. Tango is, above all, experienced as a global dance, even by those dancers who have never traveled at all. The very activity of dancing tango enables any person to enter a transnational cultural space, knowing that like-minded dancers are participating in similar kinds of spaces all over the world. Tango has become an imagined community of *aficionados* whose centers are everywhere and boundaries nowhere.

Contemporary scholars of globalization have spent considerable time thinking about such transnational cultural spaces.[37] Moving away from the stalemate in debates in which globalization is either vilified for exacerbating worldwide economic inequalities or exalted as opening up unlimited possibilities,[38] Burawoy and others[39] have argued for a focus on "globalization from below"—that is, on the actual effects that the increased mobility of people, practices, and ideas has on people's everyday lives, their aspirations, and how they view themselves in increasingly globalized societies. This has meant starting from the actual experiences of people in different parts of the world in order to show how they interact across national borders, participate in shared practices, and identify with imagined communities. Without discounting the obvious fact that transnational connections are invariably "shot through with unavoidable distances and indifferences, with comparison and critique" (Robbins, 1998a:3), this perspective on globalization suggests that it is possible for people to have transnational, along with national, cultural, and other, affiliations.

In this vein, cosmopolitanism has become the way in which many people in different locations make sense of their lives. In her analysis of everyday cosmopolitanism, Nava (2002, 2007) has provided a convincing argument for treating cosmopolitanism as a structure of feeling that is very much part of life and culture in a globalizing world. It can no longer be viewed as the sole privilege of the Western elite who can afford to embrace an identity of "citizen of the world" by virtue of having independence, the means to satisfy their expensive tastes, and a globe-trotting lifestyle (Robbins, 1998b:248).[40]

In a globalizing world, cosmopolitanism has become a valid "mode of belonging." As Robbins (1998a:3) puts it, even people with less affluent and ostensibly sedentary lifestyles can develop attachments at a distance—attachments that can be combined with more local or nationalistic bonds. Globalization does not necessarily require actual mobility, but it does demand a different disposition—something Nava (2007) calls "visceral cosmopolitanism." This is the disposition that people from very different places and with very different histories display when they desire passionate encounters with difference and yearn to exchange the ordinary for the unfamiliar, at least for the moment.

What does this "globalization from below" mean for how we should think about tango? At the very least, I would suggest that in order to explain why people passionately seek to enter into something larger than their immediate culture—as they do with tango—the imperial or colonial past may not be the best place to look for understanding their feelings, motivations, and experiences. The postcolonial critique of tango by Savigliano and others with its emphasis on the reverberations of colonialism in the history of tango and the lyrics of its music does not do justice to the transnational cultural space that tango has now become. This does not, of course, mean that tango is free from the North–South divisions produced by global capitalism, nor that asymmetries in power shaped by race, class, and gender come to a halt at the doors of the salon. However, a cosmopolitan disposition rather than the colonizing gaze may more accurately describe what links wildly disparate and differently situated individual dancers in the world of tango. The transnational connections generated by tango as a global dance are perhaps less an "impossible romance" á la *The Tango Lesson*, whereby unequal partners come together in a love–hate embrace with colonial overtones, than a passionate encounter across many different borders between dancers with a shared desire for difference and a taste of "elsewhere." These encounters are often problematic, but they are also full of the possibilities that tango makes available in the emergent transnational cultural space of the present.

Epilogue

Should a Feminist Dance Tango?

This book is the result of a personal and intellectual journey of many years into the transnational cultural space in which the recent revival of Argentinean tango has emerged. Armed with my own experiences as a tango dancer, I spoke with other *aficionado/as* who were equally and sometimes even more obsessed with dancing tango than I was. I have used my observations of the tango scene and my interviews with dancers to help me figure out what it is about tango that makes it so compelling for so many people across the globe and why they are willing to pursue their passion for it, often at considerable cost to themselves, their friends and family, and even to their previous understandings of who they are and what their lives should be like. The reason for undertaking this journey was not, however, simply a desire to make sense of my own and others' enthusiasm for dancing tango. I have also been motivated by an uneasiness that began with the reactions of disbelief I received from some of my friends and colleagues about my involvement in tango ("But, Kathy, you're a feminist. How can *you* dance tango?"). It came to a head, however, as I began to immerse myself in the scholarly literature on tango and discovered to my dismay that, when seen through the academic lens of critical feminist and postcolonial theory, a feminist's dancing tango appears, at best, rather odd and, at worst, disreputable and decidedly "politically incorrect." Thus, with my credentials not only as feminist but as critical scholar on shaky ground, I became even more motivated to disentangle the normative assumptions that make tango and feminism seem so incompatible.

The first assumption concerns the relationship between passion and tango. Argentinean tango invariably evokes the image of a woman being swept off her feet and forced by the passion of the dance to surrender herself to her male partner. This image has been informed by and has informed myriad performances of tango in movies, from the sultry Rudolph Valentino to the more gentlemanly Al Pacino to, last but not least, Sally Potter's exotic encounter with a sexy Argentinean tango dancer. These cinematic renditions of tango, while aesthetically pleasing and wonderfully titillating, are—at least, for the critical viewer—a far cry from what an autonomous feminist, who is ever wary of attempts to usurp her control over her own body, might be expected to enjoy.

The second assumption concerns the relationship between gender and tango. Women and men who dance Argentinean tango seem to be locked in the performance of the most traditional and hierarchical gender relations imaginable. Tango seems to be saturated with hypermasculine machismo and seductive, subservient femininity. Such blatantly asymmetrical relations between the sexes rest on uneasy footing with gender equality, which is the undisputed norm in many late modern societies. It is, therefore, difficult to imagine why a feminist, who is presumably committed to egalitarianism and consensuality in gender relations, would willingly engage in a dance that so openly flouts these norms.

The third assumption concerns the relationship between transnationality and tango. Tango is generally seen as "typically Argentinean." It even belongs, according to UNESCO, to Argentina's cultural heritage as an artifact in need of protection. The critics of the recent global revival of tango assume that when non-Argentineans, particularly those coming from the global North, participate in this "typically Argentinean" dance, they do so as outsiders who want to experience something different and exotic. By dancing tango, they, wittingly or unwittingly, tap into the discourses of exoticism that are the legacy of colonialism and imperialism. Given the injustices of the past and the economic disparities of the present, anyone with a critical awareness of North–South power relations should view a feminist who dances tango with skepticism, if not outright disapproval.

Taken together, these assumptions place tango and its recent global revival in an explicitly political perspective—a "politics of passion," as Savigliano (1995) has so aptly called it. The focus of a politics of passion is on the gendered, ethnicized, and geographical disparities that tango as a hopelessly traditional heterosexist dance with colonial overtones represents. This perspective treats encounters between men and women on the dance floor as sites for the exercise of hierarchical and heteronormative power relations. Moreover, it situates all interaction between

Argentineans and non-Argentineans in a context of exotic "othering," cultural imperialism, and economic exploitation.

Given the misgivings of the critics of Argentinean tango, there can be little doubt as to the answer to the question of whether a feminist should dance tango. The answer is loud and clear: A feminist has no business dancing tango and should, therefore, steer clear of it altogether.

Hmmm. Maybe. But, no, wait just a minute, I think. . . . The reality is that many feminists *do* dance tango and even become committed and passionate *aficionado/as*. As convenient in some ways as a politically correct take on tango may be for the critical feminist scholar, it does not do justice to the realities of tango on the ground. More seriously, however, it prohibits certain questions from being asked, let alone seriously explored. For example, what is it about tango that makes people, many of who are feminists, desire to dance it with such passion? How do women and men, both inside and outside Argentina, with their commitments to gender equality and feminist sensibilities, justify their own participation in such a retrograde, heterosexist dance? And what happens when differently situated dancers from different parts of the world encounter one another through tango? How do they cope with the asymmetries and disparities that are inevitably part of North–South relations and yet still manage to dance with one another with pleasure and passion? In view of these questions—questions that are central not only to understanding why a feminist would want to dance tango but also to why thousands of *aficionados* and *aficionadas* worldwide would as well—I became convinced that a less ideological and a more empirically grounded approach was needed, after all.

In what follows, I will, therefore, return to the normative assumptions about tango, gender, and transnationality and address the politics of passion and the assumptions that underlie it in light of what I have learned in the course of my exploration of the experiences, interactions, and encounters of the people who dance tango passionately.

The first thing I learned is that dancing tango in reality is different from the slightly scandalous performances of heterosexual passion that we see on stage or screen. Tango scholars have given precedence to these performances, showing how they are bound to jar feminist sensibilities. In so doing, however, they have ignored the most basic ingredient of why people dance tango—namely, the desire for an affective, embodied connection with another person as a way of being together in the music. As we have seen throughout this book, dancing tango fulfills a deep-seated need to transcend the boundaries of the mundane, to leave one's ordinary life behind, and to enter a liminal, in-between kind of space. Dancing tango enables a person to momentarily dissolve the border between the self and another and, indeed, even to lose oneself altogether. Passion has, of course, the troubling tendency to slip out of control. It can unsettle a person's routines, disrupt her or his sense of self, and upset previously held principles and beliefs. It can lead to a longing for more, both inside, but sometimes also outside, the context of tango. However, as with any passion, the passion that emerges through dancing tango is usually considered well worth the risks and dangers precisely because it provides something a person believes he or she needs in order to feel truly alive. Passion is, one could argue, what makes life worth living; a life without passion is a life that is bland and boring, little more than marking time.

If passion is what gives a person's life meaning, then we can hardly disparage feminists for wanting to have passion in their lives. Indeed, why shouldn't a feminist be susceptible to the lures of passion and determined to pursue it, whatever the cost? Of course, passion rarely fits in neatly with the beliefs and commitments that govern one's everyday life in rational and predictable ways. It is, therefore, hardly surprising that for a feminist, one of the dangers of a passion for tango is that it may require her to put her discursively held political convictions temporarily on hold. She will have to do something that feels slightly naughty and a little bit out of character. And, indeed, why shouldn't she be just as willing as the next person to take such risks and dangers in stride in order to pursue her passion?

But perhaps there is an alternative. Some tango critics have argued that it may be possible, after all, to dance tango without being "politically incorrect." However, this requires making some radical changes in the way tango is danced. As we saw in chapter 6, the filmmaker Sally Potter is an example of a feminist who attempts to conquer tango by mastering the performance, taking the reins in hand, and doing battle with the inherent machismo of the dance. However, after having accomplished her mission, she appears to have returned home to a tango-free existence, left with only a film *about* tango to keep her company. This cinematic example provides little guidance for someone who wishes to dance tango passionately for the length of her days. Another alternative is queer tango, which, at first glance, does seem to provide a more effective remedy to the feminist predicament of combining tango and politics. By dismantling the link between gender and the positions of leading and following and demanding that partners equitably agree to switch roles, queer tango seems to have rid tango of its worrisome heterosexist underpinnings. It appears to offer the best of both worlds—the opportunity to dance tango as often as one wishes while at the same time maintaining one's credibility as a feminist. But something may still be missing. However pleasurable and passionate this egalitarian switching of roles can be, equality may, paradoxically, not be what a feminist is looking for when she dances tango.

This brings me to the second thing I learned in the course of my journey—namely, the crucial role that gender plays in tango. It is difficult, if not impossible, to sever tango from its gendered underpinnings. This is not only because gender has played such a significant role in the history of the dance, its music, and the symbolic imaginary of its representations in the media, literature, and film. Gender also shapes the very mechanics of tango as a dance because it requires a leader (coded masculine) and a follower (coded feminine) in order to be performed at all. But, even more important, gender appears to be intimately and deeply connected to the kind of passionate encounter that many dancers yearn to create. Gender is entangled in the meanings and behaviors that inform (hetero)sexual desire in asymmetrical ways. This includes everything from gallantry to flirtation and seduction, to longing and unrequited love, to the abandonment of self to another person. Most dancers—straight and gay, men and women, Argentinean and non-Argentinean—draw upon these meanings when they dance tango, using them to express an experience that has become all but obsolete in late modernity with its normative commitment to individual autonomy, gender equality, and rationality.

While feminist critics have explained such seemingly archaic behavior as an (irrational) longing for traditional gender roles (when men were men, and women were women), the dancers I spoke with were firmly rooted in the present and not at all eager to return to the past. The men showed little interest in becoming domineering macho men outside the tango salon, nor did the women display any inclination to abandon their identities as independent women and surrender themselves to a man in their ordinary lives. Both men and women made a clear distinction between the world of tango and their lives outside the salon, where they wanted to hold on to their autonomy and favored consensual relationships with their partners where arrangements could be made and appointments kept.

Tango was a different story, however. Here, they seemed to revel in precisely what they rejected in their everyday lives. They embraced the very differences that would be an anathema to them in other circumstances. Rather than rebel against gender inequality, they seemed to enjoy playing with power asymmetries. They used the slightly antagonistic encounters with their dance partners as a space to explore and experiment with a host of feelings and desires for which there is no place in late modernity with its norms of gender equality and egalitarian relations between the sexes.

Seen in this way, a (feminist) woman who dances tango can engage in behavior that she secretly longs for and yet, for ideological and practical reasons, would firmly reject in her ordinary life—from wearing impractical high heels (bad for the feet!), to donning revealing clothing (sex object!), to flirting with her dance partner (no more massaging men's egos, please!) to closing her eyes and surrendering herself to a man (no comment!). She can do all of this, safe in the knowledge that, at the end of the evening, she will leave it all behind and take up her usual persona as critical feminist subject, as though nothing had happened at all. In short, tango lets her have her cake and eat it, too.

Gender is, of course, not the only difference that plays a role in tango. Passion in tango, as it turns out, thrives on encounters with difference. Of course, many differences can be mobilized in the pursuit of passion, gender being only one. This brings me to the third way in which the present inquiry has addressed the normative assumptions underlying the feminist critique of Argentinean tango. Tango as global dance mobilizes North–South divisions—divisions that are shaped by economic disparities and histories of colonialism and imperialism. The critics of tango emphasize the tensions and oppositions that such divisions are bound to produce between Argentineans and tango *aficionados* from other parts of the world. A picture emerges of narcissistic and Eurocentric tourists from the affluent North who take up tango in order to reconnect with their bodies and passions, thereby forcing economically disadvantaged Argentineans into the position of exotic/erotic "other" for their imperialistic consumption. For anyone with critical feminist and postcolonial sensibilities, tango, therefore, has to be seen as a politically problematic encounter between unequal parties, rife with possibilities for economic exploitation, exoticization, and ethnic "othering."

While I do not deny the importance of the geopolitical disparities between the global North and South, my journey into the transnational world of tango has led me to paint a more nuanced and less bleak picture. The contemporary tango revival has created a vibrant and ever changing transnational cultural space for encounters between differently situated dancers across the globe. For Argentineans, this has necessitated some juggling—of their desire to keep tango as part of their own culture while at the same time enjoying the benefits, material and immaterial, that its global popularity has brought. As we have seen, they are, for the most part, anything but negative about the global revival of "their" tango. On the contrary, they participate actively and eagerly in the transnational encounters that tango generates. They are much more inclined to emphasize their cosmopolitan outlook as citizens of the world than their exotic particularity as Latinos. This does not mean that they are exempt from the game of exoticism, however. They, too, take up the role of the exoticizer when they define foreign visitors in exotic terms, as more cultured and educated than the run-of-the-mill Argentinean. As I have shown, such exoticizing practices enable Argentineans to manage the tensions of class and gender in their own local contexts. As global dance, tango is, therefore, much less a relic of the colonial past than a contemporary cultural phenomenon that brings together differently situated dancers in passionate encounters with difference and the "elsewhere." Tango allows both Argentineans and non-Argentineans a welcome escape from the sameness and routines of their ordinary lives that so often numb or even kill desire. This is the case whether tango is danced at "home" in the salons of Buenos Aires or "abroad" in tango centers across the globe. In both cases, Argentinean tango as global dance draws dancers into a community of *aficionados* who participate in a complicated, ambivalent, but mutually beneficial transnational space.

Where does this leave us with regard to the question posed at the outset of this Epilogue: Should a feminist dance tango? The question is a rhetorical one, and most readers will be inclined to answer: Why shouldn't she, if that is what she wants to do? Many feminists do dance tango, the author of this book included. So why bother asking such a question if the answer is already so obvious?

One of the uses of rhetorical questions is to draw attention to meanings that might otherwise go unnoticed and reconsider them—somewhat playfully—in a different light. By asking this question, it was my intention to initiate a reflection not on the real (im)possibility of a feminist's dancing tango but rather on the apparent contradiction between tango dancing and critical feminist inquiry. What is it about tango as an embodied, passionate experience that makes it seem antithetical to (postcolonial) feminist scholarship?

Dance always entails the negotiation of gender along with other hierarchies of difference and power, and tango is no exception. It carries a long and convoluted history of gender asymmetries and heteronormativity. Moreover, it is complicated by tensions and antagonisms produced by other differences as well—class, ethnic, generational, national belonging, and more. As a dance that has always crossed and continues to cross borders, tango will never be entirely free of the histories of colonialism and imperialism and the present realities of global economic disparities.

However, this is not the whole story, and it is a story that threatens to subsume the contradictions, entanglements, and possibilities that emerge through tango when differently situated individuals encounter one another passionately in a close embrace. In the course of this book, I have argued that we cannot pretend we already know what passion means unless we talk to the people who actually experience it. For the critical feminist scholar, the challenge is to find ways to make palpable the experience of passion, to explore how it actually feels, what it means, and the consequences it has for women and men in their everyday lives. This means linking people's narratives of their experiences to the broader social, cultural, and geopolitical contexts in which they live. And it requires a refusal to be satisfied with overly ideological explanations and a willingness to confront the inherent messiness and contradictions of passionate encounters.

Passion as experience tends to be seen as the embarrassing or even shadow side of rationality, almost like a beast that needs to be tamed or contained. This perhaps explains why many scholars shy away from studying passion, preferring instead to focus on the choices people make, their preferences, deliberations, and justifications for their actions. Even feminist and postcolonial scholars who have a long tradition of problematizing the gendered underpinnings of rationality as product of European Enlightenment philosophy are—ironically—at a loss when passion as embodied experience unsettles their own critical paradigms and discourses. The feminist who dances tango highlights the disjuncture between experience and politics: She desires something that she knows she shouldn't. Her passion for tango overrules her ideological or normative commitments, makes her uncomfortable, and yet still she dances on.

It has not been my intention to discount the postcolonial feminist critique of the politics of tango. Rather, my aim has been to provide a modest provocation in the direction of critical scholarship that places politics before experience. In other words, I question whether we should draw upon the discourses of feminism and postcolonialism to explain passion while ignoring what is its most basic ingredient— namely, that people love what they are doing so deeply that they cannot help themselves and have to keep doing it. It seems to me that this is precisely where we need to start as critical feminist scholars, whether we are analyzing a passion for tango or any other passion that is unsettling and even disruptive, but so pleasurably intense that it is simply irresistible.

NOTES

INTRODUCTION

1. This is the U.S. usage. In the UK, the adjective "Argentinian" is used, and, somewhat archaically, the term "Argentine" is used for a particular person. I have used "Argentinean" throughout the book, but the reader should be aware that the matter of tango's geographical and musical origins is far from settled. Uruguay, for example, also lays claim to being the place where tango began, and the earliest version of tango has its roots in Afro-Cuban dance and music (Thompson, 2005). While I begin with the term "Argentinean tango" to distinguish it from the ballroom dance version of tango (a point to which I will return later in this chapter), I have also used the term "tango" throughout the book. Unless otherwise designated, this refers to "Argentinean" rather than to ballroom tango.

2. I have used "global North" and "global South" throughout this book as a shorthand way to refer to social, economic, and political divisions that exist between wealthy, developed countries (often, but not always, in the Northern Hemisphere) and poorer, developing countries (often, but not always, in the Southern Hemisphere). Contemporary scholars have rightly criticized the use of the North–South divide, given the shifting economies of nations across the globe, and have noted that affluence is not limited to the North, nor poverty to the South. However, it remains helpful for understanding some of the economic and political problems facing Argentina today as well as the way it is positioned ideologically by the relatively affluent consumers of tango in Europe, North America, and—to a lesser degree—Australia, and parts of Asia.

3. San Telmo is one of the oldest neighborhoods in Buenos Aires. It is renowned as a tourist center, providing many possibilities to discover tango: street dance demonstrations, tango shows, dance venues, clothing and shoe stories, and myriad tango hotels and guest houses.

4. "Thick description" is a term initially used by the anthropologist Clifford Geertz (1973) to indicate that a description should include sufficient contexualization of practices, behaviors, and situations that they become understandable to outsiders.

5. Crossley (1995) differentiates between sociology of the body and carnal sociology. The sociology of the body is intended as an antidote to the traditional

neglect of the body in sociology. Sociology of the body addresses the ways in which the body is constituted as a meaningful object within specific discourses and as the subject of a regime of practices that regulate or transform it in specific ways. Its focus is on the epistemological, ethical, and aesthetic technologies that discipline, adorn, punish, or celebrate the body. In other words, it is concerned with *what is done to the body*. In contrast, carnal sociology addresses the active role that the body plays in social life. It is concerned with *what the body does*. Its focus is on the embodied basis of social formations—that is, with revealing how self, society, and the symbolic order are constituted through sense-making, embodied practices.

6. *Milongas* refers both to a particular kind of tango music and to dance venues. *Milonga* music has a lively syncopated beat. *Milonga* as a venue refers to a place and time for dancing tango, usually with a DJ and sometimes live music. I have used the term *milonga* interchangeably with "salon," another frequently used term for locales where tango is danced. *Practicas* are *milongas* specially set up for learning and practicing steps with teachers available to help.

7. *Argentinidad* refers to the quality of Argentine-ness and is often used as a synonym for national identity.

8. Julia Ericksen (2011) has written an interesting study of ballroom dancing that highlights its similarities to and differences with Argentinean tango. While ballroom tango also draws on associations with a sultry, exotic Argentinean underclass, in fact it has its origins in Parisian social dancing during the 1920s. The most striking difference with Argentinean tango resides in the embrace. In ballroom dancing, partners arch their upper bodies away from each other, while maintaining contact at the hip. In Argentinean tango, partners dance chest-to-chest with their heads touching or very close. See also Cook (1998) for the history of ballroom tango.

9. The list of tango histories, ranging from the popular to the academic, is long. Some focus more on the music and lyrics, others more on dance. See, for example, Taylor (1976), Jakubs (1984), Collier (1993), Savigliano (1995), Thompson (2005), Bergero (2008).

10. *Candombe* was brought from the Congo to Uruguay by slaves. Its strong beat and foot stamping can still be found in the dance form *milonga*. See, in particular, Thompson (2005:7–9, 87–91) for a good discussion of its history and how it evolved into contemporary forms of tango.

11. Anzaldi (2012a) provides an insightful analysis of the polarized political situation in Argentina between Peronism and anti-Peronism in which tango functioned as a unifying cultural symbol, binding warring factions together. I will return to his argument in chapter 6 when I discuss the ways in which tango is mobilized within Argentina as a symbol of both its cosmopolitan culture and its national identity or *argentinidad*.

12. The "Dirty War" refers to a period of state terrorism in Argentina aimed at militant urban and rural guerrillas, left-wing political groups, union activists, students,

journalists, and almost anyone with socialist sympathies. More than 10,000 people were imprisoned, tortured, and "disappeared." See, for example, Robbens (2005) for an excellent history of this period in Argentina's history and its aftermath.

13. The *compadrito* was an immigrant, either from the interior or from abroad, who lived in the urban slums of Buenos Aires, often working as a pimp. He was daring and aggressive, a successful seducer of women, and in competition with other men, often engaging in knife fights. See chapter 2 for a stereotypical rendition of the *compadrito* in Valentino's performance of tango in the film *The Four Horsemen of the Apocalypse* (1921).

14. See Marcus (1995) for a seminal discussion about the strategies involved in doing multi-sited ethnographies. His work is a methodological forerunner to Burawoy's (2000) more programmatic formulation of global ethnography, which has been central to the present inquiry. For an approach that compares a wide range of tango communities in the "diaspora of tango," see Pelinski (2000).

15. I have also drawn on representations of tango in films and documentaries, publications from tango communities, tango blogs and websites, and the growing genre of tango memoirs.

16. The *Oxford Dictionary* definition of "passion" is "a strong feeling (especially love or anger)" as well as "a strong enthusiasm for a thing or for doing a thing."

17. The anthropologist Victor Turner (1964/1987) introduced the concept of liminality to describe a threshold that distinguishes certain experiences from everyday life. These experiences have the status of being transitional—between the old (which has not been totally abandoned) and the new (which cannot be fully embraced). For Benzacry, the opera house provides a space for such experiences and—as I show in the chapters that follow—so does the tango salon.

CHAPTER 1. SALON CULTURES

1. *Scent of a Woman* (1992), directed by Martin Brest, was not only the recipient of Academy Awards for best actor (Pacino), best director, and best film, but the tango scene has become iconic, part of the cultural imaginary of tango. See chapter 4.

2. These terms refer to men and women who have mastered the art of dancing tango.

3. Readers interested in ethnographies of other tango cultures outside Buenos Aires are referred to Savigliano (1992, 1995) for Japan, Klein (2009) for Germany, Törnqvist (2013) for San Francisco, and Viladrich, 2013 for New York.

4. See also Dreher and Figueroa-Dreher (2009) for a nice analysis of the rituals that go into creating a tango "community."

5. This is understandable given that some local men will dash off to dance with female tourists decked out in clothes and fancy shoes that ordinary Argentineans cannot afford, leaving local women waiting on the sidelines.

6. Tango music tends to be organized by orchestra, and dancers will have their particular favorites (Di Sarli, Pugliese, D'Arienzo). Much of the music currently

played in salons, both in Buenos Aires and Europe, comes from the Golden Age (1935–52) of tango, when tango enjoyed a revival in Buenos Aires. See Thompson (2005) and Baim (2007).

7. One of the well-known tango magazines, *B.A. Tango. Guia y Agenda Porteña*, has a regular column for compliments exchanged on the dance floor under the heading *"Mentime que me gusta"* ("Lie to me, I like it"). See also Melul (2007).

8. *Porteño/a* refers to a resident of Buenos Aires.

9. Many tango websites in Europe offer lists of these codes in order to help tourists negotiate the *milongas* without mishap. See, for example, http://tangochoseme.com/2010/07/11/tango-codigas-milonga-floorcraft/ and http://mytangodiaries.blogspot.com/2010/01/why-we-argue-about-codigos.htm. Similar websites in Argentina provide explicit guidelines for correct salon behavior. See, for example, *PractiMilonguero* (http://practimilonguero.wordpress.com). Tango magazines across the globe as well as Internet blogs offer ongoing discussions about the "ins" and "outs" of salon etiquette.

10. Interview by Monica Páz with Juan Carlos Pontorielo, 8 February 2011. This interview was one of a series called *PractiMilonguero*, conducted by the Argentinean dance instructor Monica Paz, whose project is to retrieve traditional or authentic tango from the onslaught of foreign tourists whom she sees as corrupting it with their exaggerated steps and lack of attention to the etiquette of the salon. By interviewing older *milongueros* about their experiences, she demonstrates how tango should be danced: respectfully, in a close embrace without exaggerated steps, in accordance with the *codigos*, and with an eye to the flow on the floor.

11. Because I am talking about the more traditional salons in Buenos Aires, I am assuming that it is the man who invites and the woman who accepts the invitation. In the less traditional salons and in queer tango, these codes are much looser, and, in many cases, the *cabeceo* and the gender-specific roles of leading and following have disappeared altogether, as I discuss in chapter 5.

12. As an illustration of how these seemingly irreconcilable elements seemed to converge in tango, Groeneboer (2003:52–53) cites the popular tango song with the strange title *"Twee emmertjes tango halen"* (Collecting two buckets of tango), which was a hit in Dutch dance schools. See Groeneboer (2003) for a history of Malando, in particular, and the tango in the Netherlands, in general.

13. Astor Piazzolla was a composer and *bandoneon* player who revolutionized traditional tango music by adding elements of jazz and classical music.

14. See Ferrer and Brave (1989) for a history of the latest tango revival in the Netherlands.

15. Carlos Gardel (1890–1935) is probably the most popular representative of Argentinean tango. He was a singer, songwriter, and actor who has become a national icon. His smiling image can be seen in nearly every tango venue, and most visitors pay homage to him by visiting his tomb in La Chacarita cemetery in Buenos Aires. See Castro (1998) for an interesting analysis of Gardel's significance to tango.

16. This is the same for other parts of Europe. See, for example, Villa (2001, 2009) and Klein (2009).

17. Many young dancers have taken up tango as a potentially commercial enterprise, selling their services as DJs, performers, and instructors. While this is particularly true in Buenos Aires, where international tourism has transformed tango into an important export, European dancers have followed suit. I will be returning to this international circuit in more detail in chapter 6.

18. Savigliano argues that this difference is due in part to the different meanings attributed to the wallflower. In Buenos Aires, the term is a verb (*planchar*) and refers to the (non)activity of not dancing into which an aspiring dancer has just happened to fall. In contrast, in Europe and North America it refers to an identity and, therefore, implies that the person is not being asked to dance because of who she is (and perhaps never will be asked to dance). While *milongueras* may be frustrated about not dancing or complain about the behavior of men in the salons, they are less likely to take their nondancing as a reflection of their worth and desirability as dancers more generally. In fact, many of my Argentinean informants regard waiting as a sign of being a good dancer, someone who picks and chooses her dancers rather than "just [dancing] with anyone the way the foreigners do."

19. This is not to say that the *piropos* in Buenos Aires do not have a similar function. One could argue that their exaggerated quality is precisely what sets the dance apart from the dancers' more mundane lives outside the salon.

20. See "Tango gets UN cultural approval," BBC News, 30 September 2009. Ironically, the UNESCO proposal was submitted jointly by Argentina and Uruguay, yet tango continues to be associated much more strongly with Argentina than with Uruguay.

21. Tango is not the only dance that draws on a discourse of authenticity. Kešić (2012) has convincingly argued that Dutch flamenco, another example of a dance that has traveled around the world, is characterized by a preoccupation with authenticity.

22. There are various terms for describing authentic tango (*tango tradicional, tango salon, tango milonguero*).

23. Many Argentineans, particularly those who live outside the capital, are far more likely to prefer folk dances like *chacarera, salsa, cumbia,* and *paso doble* to tango. Even within Buenos Aires, the number of locals who actually dance tango is quite small. This does not, however, diminish the symbolic (and economic) importance of tango for the national identity, something to which I return at length in chapter 6.

24. See the interview by Monica Paz of Juan Carlos Pontorielo, 8 February 2011, in *PractiMilonguero*.

25. Even Paz's interviewees are somewhat skeptical of the term, noting that what they used to dance was "just tango. That's all there was."

CHAPTER 2. TANGO PASSION

1. *Gauchos* were nomadic cowboys who roamed the vast interior of Argentina, herding cattle. The association between *gauchos* and tango is historically misleading, but in the film it lends Valentino an even more exotic air and enhances his macho-ness.

2. Just a few of the more well-known examples: Brest's *Scent of a Woman* (1992) with Al Pacino; James Cameron's *True Lies* (1994) with Arnold Schwarzenegger; Madonna's improbable tango with Antonio Banderas (as Che Guevara) in *Evita* (1996); Sally Potter's *The Tango Lesson* (1997); Carlos Saura's *Tango* (1998); the erotically antagonistic tango danced to the tunes of the song "Roxanne" in *Moulin Rouge* (2001); Robert Duvall—in real life a tango *aficionado*—directing and starring in *Assassination Tango* (2002); Richard Gere and Jennifer Lopez performing tango together in *Shall We Dance* (2004); and Antonio Banderas, once again, in Liz Friedlander's *Take the Lead* (2006).

3. For readers who would like to check for themselves, just enter "Argentinean tango" in YouTube's search field for more than ample evidence of passion as eroticized performance.

4. See, for example, Osumare (2002), Urquía (2005), and Wade (2011), all of whom describe dance as an activity that participants passionately like to do but that differs from tango in terms of its association with and performance of passion. I will be exploring this distinction between a passion for an activity in the next chapter.

5. I was, in fact, reminded of the well-known case of Agnes, which Garfinkel (1967) presented as an illustration of how gender is "done." Agnes, who was in the process of transitioning from male to female, has more to say about what gender is about than many men and women for whom it is completely taken for granted. See also Kessler and McKenna (1978/1985).

6. The tango scene in Amsterdam, which is a city with many single inhabitants, attracts many dancers who are interested in finding sexual partners or developing relationships outside the tango salon. This is also true of Buenos Aires, where a large number of male dancers, including those who are married, regard tango as an avenue for sexual encounters, material advantage, or professional advancement.

7. Klein and Haller (2008), Klein (2009). See also chapter 1.

8. Interestingly, many of my informants had no desire to be anonymous and even indicated that they would prefer to appear in this book under their own names. One dancer, for example, explained that he had nothing to hide, this is "who [I am]," and he wanted to keep his name. Another dancer compared appearing under her own name to receiving credit for her ideas, similar to the importance an academic would give to citing other people's work in scientific texts.

9. Some of the commentaries have suggested that Wacquant's carnal sociology is especially suited to activities in which the body is involved in a dramatic as opposed to a routine way (Eliasoph, 2005). I have some reservations about this.

It seems to me that every activity is embodied. Moreover, I am not convinced that tango passion is, by definition, more embodied than other kinds of passion.

10. This is because tango lyrics are often a combination of Spanish and *lunfardo*. *Lunfardo*, which means, literally, "thief," was originally part of the patois of the lower classes in Buenos Aires and later became the language of choice for many writers of tango lyrics because of its expressive and metaphoric qualities. See Baim (2007:29–35).

11. It is interesting that, whereas sight is the privileged sense in Western modernity (Bowman, 2010), this is disrupted to some extent in tango. Although appearance still plays a role in partner selection, it is possible to be a popular dancer without meeting the conventional beauty norms. In this sense, how dancing with a particular dancer "feels" has priority over how the dancer "looks."

12. I have used "woman" here because the majority of followers are women. The neutral use of "followers" and "leaders" in tango is an innovation to traditional tango that is associated with queer tango and *tango nuevo*, something I will be dealing with at more length in chapter 5.

13. See Thompson (2005) for a delightful history of the tango embrace, including not only the variations in how it has been performed but also the meanings attached to it.

14. This comment resonated eerily for me with a practice I frequently observed in Buenos Aires—namely, men dancing tango with life-sized inflatable dolls. They provide a highly popular form of entertainment and can be seen in Plaza Dorrego dancing for tourists or in *milongas* as a performance for the dancers.

15. A *gancho* is a move in which a dancer hooks her or his lower leg around the partner's thigh.

16. This is not the only reason to dance in a more open style, of course. Open-style tango allows partners to dance more performatively because they do not have to struggle with their balance and can execute more elaborate steps. Dancing tango in this way enables them to display eroticism without having to contend with the erotic feelings that dancing intensely in a close embrace can evoke.

17. Osvaldo Pugliese (1905–95) was a tango composer and pianist, famous for his dramatic arrangements.

18. See Gill (2007:266) for an interesting discussion of irony as an antidote to taking oneself too seriously.

CHAPTER 3. TANGO TRAJECTORIES

1. *Shall We Dansu?* was directed by Masayuki Suo and first appeared in Japan in 1995, where it was extremely popular, winning 14 of the Japanese equivalent of the Academy Awards. It was released in the United States a year later, with 26 scenes having been cut, reducing its running time from 136 to 119 minutes. The voiceover narration at the beginning of the film for Japanese audiences introduced the history of ballroom dancing, with an accompanying shot of

Blackpool, since 1920 the site of the most prestigious ballroom dancing competition in Europe. This narration is replaced in the U.S. version with an explanation of why ballroom dancing is "enveloped in prejudice" in Japan, where hugging in public is "uncomfortable" and dancing together, even for husbands and wives, is "embarrassing" (cited in Goldstein-Gidoni and Daliot-Bul, 2002:69).

2. Social dancing was brought to Japan during the 1930s by British dance instructors for the ex-pat community. It later became popular with the new Japanese middle class and was augmented by the French tradition of social dancing that had been inspired by Argentinean tango. According to Savigliano, the two traditions had a common goal of "westernizing" Japan (Savigliano, 1992:242; see also Savigliano, 1995:169–206).

3. This format can also be found in the growing genre of tango memoirs in which tango provides the backdrop for romance. See, for example, Palmer (2006), Cusamano (2008), Saraza (2008), Chen (2009), De Vries (2009).

4. Directed by Peter Chelsom.

5. See, for example, Sally Potter's *The Tango Lesson*, which I discuss at length in chapter 6. Aside from being a rather typical example of a film that uses tango in order to depict a love story, the film misrepresents how difficult it is to learn tango. Potter, who is also the protagonist of the film, apparently mastered the dance in just a few weeks and was even asked by the famous Argentinean maestro Pablo Verón to be his partner on stage.

6. See Ericksen (2011) for the history of competitions like Blackpool as well as a nice analysis of the importance of such competitions for amateur dancers.

7. Dancing is not only distasteful to some people in Japan; it is distasteful to some Europeans as well. As I wrote in the Introduction, the responses of my own colleagues suggest that they found it a bit embarrassing that a feminist academic like me would want to participate in a sexist dance like tango.

8. Giddens (1991:74–86) would place the decision to learn tango within the calculative strategies that modern individuals routinely deploy to plan their lives, while keeping an eye to the future. Such strategies are necessary in the context of late modernity, where identities are less fixed and are not governed by social and familial constraints. Today, individuals have to figure out for themselves how to build and manage a coherent identity. See also chapter 4.

9. Tango vacations draw upon the same rationale that is used for cosmetic surgery and others form of medical tourism in exotic locales. See, for example, Connell (2006).

10. Kowalska (2010) is concerned with the kinds of adaptations that individuals with transnational biographies have to make when confronted with unexpected situations in which they have to fit old and new relationships into new contexts and reimagine their futures. Adopting global scenarios can help them make sense of their lives. A tango dancer who becomes part of a global dance community can be viewed as a good example of how such "adjustment strategies" work.

11. Some couples may share a passion for dancing tango but still entertain reservations about going to Buenos Aires together where, in order to participate in the salon culture, they will have to face the choice between either sitting together and dancing with only each other or splitting up, sitting solo, and having to contend with the general flirtatiousness of the dance scene.

12. Of course, it is easier to talk in terms of not being able to escape the dynamics of a trajectory when we are dealing with illness or dying. A sense of fatality is missing with dance, or even with other kinds of addictions—for example, to drugs or alcohol. However, as Riemann and Schütze point out, "escape" can also mean reconstructing new networks that neutralize or reduce the compelling force of a particular trajectory, making it, therefore, applicable to tango as well.

13. This frequently heard expression is used by *aficionados* to explain why, once one has started dancing tango, there will never be an end. It is also a way to curb signs of inappropriate hubris, suggesting that however good a dancer becomes, she or he will never completely master this dance.

14. Benzecry takes issue with sociologists who conflate passion with power or status rather than ask the obvious question: How do people come to *love* doing something? Simmel (1958), in contrast, had an eye for people's longing for a personal adventure that could take them outside the realm of profane, quotidian life.

CHAPTER 4. PERFORMING FEMININITY, PERFORMING MASCULINITY

1. The song was "Por la cabeza," one of the most popular tangos, composed and performed by Carlos Gardel in 1935 with lyrics by Alfredo Le Pera. The title— "By the head of a horse"—is taken from the world of horse racing and compares the addiction to gambling on horses with the addiction to beautiful women.

2. Cited in Zhao (2008:640). See also Young (1996).

3. See, for example, Guy (1990), Desmond (1997), Tobin (1998, 2009), Archetti (1999), Villa (2001, 2009), Fisher (2004), Saikin (2004), Viladrich (2006, 2013), Manning (2007), Törnqvist (2011, 2012, 2013), and Carozzi (2013).

4. A *niño bien* ("nice boy") is a wealthy young man who leaves his sheltered milieu to dance tango in the slums of Buenos Aires.

5. See Tobin (1998), who suggests that most women who write about tango prefer to leave the topic of machismo in the hands of its devotees or allow it to die of its own accord. This was for him, as "man and outsider," enough reason to "plod right in" (p. 102). His perceptive and even-handed analysis of masculinity in tango is, indeed, well worth reading.

6. See Pelinski (2000), Klein and Haller (2008), Klein (2009), Petridou (2009), and Törnqvist (2013).

7. Villa argues that queer tango does manage to abolish gender hierarchies—a position with which I will take issue in the next chapter.

8. Villa implies that this dilemma does not arise in Buenos Aires. However, as I have shown in chapter 1, Argentineans also have to manage the tensions that

are part and parcel of gender relations in late modernity. While they also "play" with traditional forms of masculinity and femininity when they dance tango, they are no more frozen in the past than their European counterparts.

9. See Billig (1988, 1991) for a good analysis of why everyday rhetoric is a perfect place to uncover the workings of ideologies.

10. I will discuss this in more detail in the next chapter.

11. Shades of *Snow White* and the well-known scenes in which the queen, Snow White's wicked stepmother, stands anxiously in front of the mirror asking who is the "fairest of them all." See Barzilai (1990) for an interesting feminist analysis.

12. See also chapter 2.

13. See, in particular, Tobin (1998, 2009) for an excellent discussion of men's salon behavior and the meanings of masculinity in the contemporary tango scene in Buenos Aires. For a more popular and quite perceptive perspective from a male tango tourist, see Winter (2007).

14. Machismo is a contested concept and one that has generated considerable controversy (see, for example, Balderston and Guy, 1997). Savigliano (1995) defines Argentinean machismo as a "cult of authentic virility fed by a sense of loss" (p. 43). Jeffrey Tobin (1998) expands Savigliano's discussion of the homoerotic roots of machismo in tango, critically drawing upon the work of Judith Butler (1995) on heterosexual melancholy. Based on his ethnographic research in tango salons in Buenos Aires, Tobin argues that he could not find the "ungrievable loss of homosexual desire" in his informants' masculine displays (p. 101). Instead, he discovered straight men playfully engaging in hyperbolic displays of masculinity and being quite comfortable talking about latent homoeroticism. This behavior, I would argue, is less available to men dancing tango outside of Buenos Aires.

15. There is a substantial body of literature on the relationship between women and romance. See, for example, Modleski (1982), Radway (1984), and, for a postfeminist take on romance, Gill (2007:218–48). See also Illousz (1998, 2012), to whom I will be referring later in this chapter.

16. See, for example, Hopkins (1994) and Stear (2009) for interesting discussions of how sadomasochism can be regarded as compatible with the desire for gender equality and women's autonomy.

17. Controversial because she is a feminist. Her work could easily slip into an alliance with the anti-feminist backlash that bemoans what it sees as the negative effects of women's emancipation.

18. Illousz (2012:184–87) uses this term to refer to how gender identities become overloaded with meanings—meanings that make them feel not only natural but also essential to one's sense of who one is. The fact that these identities are historically sedimented and strongly coded means that they do not have to be constantly negotiated, making them well suited to the ambiguity of seduction, eroticism, and the aestheticization of power and (hetero)sexual desire.

CHAPTER 5. QUEERING TANGO

1. Augusto was later to become the co-founder of La Marshall, the first gay *milonga* in Buenos Aires, and one of the organizers of Queer Tango festivals, which have become a regular occurrence in Buenos Aires.

2. The notion of "becoming stuck" is drawn from Butler's (1989, 1993) work and refers to the manner in which members of society become invested in certain norms in ways that make it difficult to transform and create livable lives in relation to normalization. See Ahmed (2004) for a further elaboration of "stickiness" as applied to the affective dimensions of heterosexuality, which can be notoriously resistant to change.

3. See, for example, Salessi (1997, 2000) and Saikin (2004).

4. It is impossible to do justice to the massive corpus of literature in the field of queer theory and politics. Some of the most frequently cited are Butler (1989, 1993), Sedgwick (1990), De Lauretis (1991), and Warner (1993). For a nice overview, see also Walters (1996).

5. The census records of 1914 showed that nearly 78 percent of male adults were foreigners, with the total number of resident foreigners 78,046. Of this number, women made up 23,572 while men made up 54,474 (Salessi, 1997:159). Between 1914 and 1936, for every 100 women there were 150 Argentinean men and 125 foreign men in the city (Guy, 1990; see also Pellarolo, 2008:417).

6. While there was a small tradition of female tango singers during the Golden Age of tango, they also tended to cross-dress in order to avoid any suggestion that a woman would sing lyrics directed at another woman. Even today, in all-female tango performances, the leader will don male apparel. See Viladrich (2006).

7. Salons in Buenos Aires routinely offer one set of *chacareras*, often toward the end of the *milonga*. While folk dances are particularly popular in the interior of Argentina, they are popular as well in Buenos Aires, where they are regarded as representing the rural and more authentic counterpart to urban, cosmopolitan tango as symbol of the national identity. See, for example, Delaney (2002).

8. A case in point is Aurora Lubiz, whom many of my informants referred to with undisguised reverence as "our patron saint." Lubiz was one of the first professional local tango dancers to openly endorse queer tango and to perform regularly at queer tango festivals.

9. In addition to North American and European studies on (queer) tango (Villa, 2009; Savigliano, 2010), there has emerged in recent years a growing body of Argentinean scholarly research on queer tango in Buenos Aires that makes abundant use of Anglo-American queer theory (Arrizon, 2006; Pellarollo, 2008; Liska, 2009; Cecconi, 2012), thereby providing an illustration not only of how cultural and social practices like tango dancing move from place to place but also how theories travel.

10. See Horowitz (2013) for an interesting critique of queer performativity as a special kind of performance. She argues instead for a perspective that treats

queerness, straightness, femininity, and masculinity as always and equally embodied, whether on stage, in the street, in the classroom—in short, wherever people interact with one another through their bodies (p. 318). This perspective is more in accordance with the argument I make in this chapter.

11. See http://www.tangoqueer.com/.

12. Ibid.

13. Shani's use of the term "universe" resonates with Illousz's (2012) analysis of gender as a thick identity of historically sedimented and strongly coded meanings. This was discussed in the previous chapter.

14. Not every tango dancer is looking for passion when she or he dances tango, of course. Many tango dancers, queer and straight, engage in social dancing, not to mention doing the occasional "mercy dance" for reasons that have nothing to do with passion. I am indebted to Judith Stacey for reminding me of this.

15. See Manning (2007:19–48) for an excellent discussion of the way in which the trope of "starting over" is enacted through dance in the film. She argues that the improvisational quality of tango allows space for developing queer forms of relationality.

CHAPTER 6. TRANSNATIONAL ENCOUNTERS

1. *The Tango Lesson* (1997), directed and written by Sally Potter. The film won several awards, including Best Film at the Mar Del Plata international film festival in 1997 and an American Choreography Award.

2. This is itself transgressive. While there have been many female tango interpreters since the 1910s, very few tangos have actually been written by women. Indeed, many female performers assumed male attire when they sang in public and used humor and sarcasm to undermine the demeaning portrayal of women as victims of violence or traitorous *femmes fatales*. See Viladrich (2006).

3. Quoted in Hopkins (2002:121).

4. This is substantiated by the growing body of literature on international tourism in which affluent men from the global North embark on sexual and economic transactions with younger local women from the global South. See Pritchard et al. (2007) for a good overview. An illustration of what happens when the roles are reversed can be found in the recent film *Paradies Liebe* (2012), by the Austrian filmmaker Ulrich Seidl, which portrays older European women ("sugar mamas") who seek out African boys for romantic encounters. Seidl combines his well-taken critique of the exploitative relations that emerge through economic, political, and social disparities between the global North and South with the portrayal of these women as naïve, racist, obese—and indeed, ridiculous.

5. For example, Potter collaborated with several other national production companies in an attempt to be less territorial about her film. Her idea was that the film should belong not to her but to each participating company, envisioning it as a multinational co-production, much in the spirit of tango as a global dance. See Hopkins (2002:126–27) for a critical discussion.

6. See, for example, Torgovnick (1990), Young (1990, 1995), McClintock et al. (1997), and Stoler (2002), to name just a few.
7. Thompson (2005) provides a lively and engaging description of this event, including an elaborate description of the dance routines and the dancers.
8. *Nuevo tango* refers to music that incorporates classical and jazz with traditional tango music. It can also refer to new styles of dancing that include off-axis moves, playfulness, attention to rhythm and melody, and emphasis on a greater improvisational skill of women in dance.
9. Taylor (1998:187) links tango with its "absences and sorrows" to the violence perpetuated by the military regime during the "Dirty War." While her analysis can help to explain some of the emotions contemporary Argentineans may experience when they dance tango in the present context in which the nation is trying to come to terms with its violent past, I am doubtful that it says much about what tango meant to those who danced it at the time of the military dictatorship.
10. Throughout this book, I have used the term *aficionado* to refer to Argentinean and non-Argentinean tango dancers with a passion for the dance. "Tango tourists" refers to people who visit tango shows, buy shoes, or listen to tango music while visiting Buenos Aires without being dancers themselves, while "visitors" or "visiting dancers" are foreigners who go to the local *milongas* and take an active part in the local tango culture.
11. Interview in the anthology edited by Babette Niemel (1977:77–92), who places Diáz's experience in the context of that of other political refugees, fleeing conflict situations in their homelands.
12. *La Posta*, no. 2, May 2003, p. 1.
13. In the Netherlands, Pepito Avellaneda and Antonio Todaro, both legendary dancers, were influential in the early years of the tango revival. See Groeneboer (2003) for a more elaborate history.
14. Interview with Marianne van Berlo and Arjan Sikking, 18 September 2011.
15. Subsecretaria de Industrias Culturales, 2007, p. 16 (quoted in Anzaldi, 2012b).
16. Soya is Argentina's most important export product and is important for earning foreign revenue (dollars). Tango, however, is what Buenos Aires exports—it is the city's equivalent of soya, its "green gold."
17. Subsecretaria de Industrias Culturales, 2007, p. 42 (cited in Anzaldi, 2012b).
18. Ibid., p. 15.
19. See the Introduction for an example of this.
20. Kaminsky (2008) provides a particularly convincing theoretical analysis of this, arguing that Argentineans have historically both desired to be noticed by Europeans and yet been resentful of being exoticized as different from Europeans.
21. Lund (2001) is critical of postcolonial perspectives more generally because they fail to adequately theorize Latin American exceptionalism. The cultural elite of Argentina has always desired inclusion within Europe and displayed a marked preference for Eurocentric discourses that privilege Western knowledge

and culture, thereby allowing its members to distance themselves from Latin America's culturally and materially disenfranchised. Because Argentina does not have a colonial past and considers itself an exception vis-à-vis its neighbors, it has a much more complicated relationship with Europe than the critiques of colonialism and cultural imperialism would suggest.

22. This is significantly different from tango enthusiasts in other parts of the world (Europe, North America, Japan) who regard traveling to salons in other locations as part of their tango identity (see chapter 3). For Argentineans, the desire to travel is less associated with dancing tango, probably because Buenos Aires is generally considered the home of tango and the best place to dance it.

23. Much of the scholarly literature on sex and romance emphasizes the exploitive features of relationships between tourists and locals. An interesting exception is Meisch's (1995) study of relationships between young foreign women and Ecuadorian men. She argues that these alliances are less classic examples of First World exploitation than contradictory cases of two groups' being fascinated by and using each other. She does not deny that such relationships involve gendered and ethnicized power asymmetries. However, she does suggest that mutual fascination should be part of the analysis.

24. For this history, the reader is referred to Nouzeilles and Montaldo (2002). The merit of this comprehensive and multi-faceted collection of original texts is that it provides a nuanced critique of the stereotype that Argentina is "like Europe and not like the rest of Latin America." See also, Kaminsky (2008:99–121) and, for a more jaundiced but nevertheless provocative view, Naipaul's *The Return of Eva Perón* (1974/1980).

25. Aside from the oldtimers who have been dancing tango for years, some of my informants, particularly the younger ones, admitted that, while they had danced tango as children, that was "just something we did, not with steps or anything." They really learned how to dance only when they started frequenting the *milongas*, often taking a few lessons to brush up their dancing skills. In contrast, many of the foreign visitors dare to dance in Buenos Aires only after they have several years' worth of lessons under their belts and feel good enough to brave the dance floors there.

26. For visitors, of course, this compliment allows them to distinguish themselves from other foreign dancers, who, presumably, are still dancing "like foreigners." See Klein and Haller (2009) and Petridou (2009) for good discussions of how authenticity among tango dancers becomes intertwined with the desire for distinction.

27. The activity of stereotyping dance partners according to their nationality is by no means limited to *porteños*. One of my Dutch informants had an elaborated typology for describing dancers: Chileans were "softer" and "more mellow" compared with the Argentineans with their "machismo"; Turks were "proud" and, especially the women, "super sensual"; and the Germans, "well, just scratch the surface and you will discover all this natural sensitivity."

28. See Hess (2004) for a sociological study of the emergence of the waltz in Europe and its association with the romantic ideals of the bourgeoisie.

29. This is not only because "European-ness" has historically been associated with a desirable elite. The longstanding antagonisms between the Americas as well as the United States' problematic interventions in support of military regimes throughout South America, including Argentina, have made Americans generally less popular than Europeans in Argentina. See McPherson (2006) for an interesting discussion of the history and current manifestations of anti-Americanism in Latin America.

30. In addition to not wanting to risk a dance with someone when one doesn't know whether he or she can dance, some local women have the additional concern that their regular partners will refuse to dance with them if they dance with foreigners. This form of punishment is not uncommon in the salons, although it has become less effective, at least among the locals. Ironically, many tourists are beguiled into waiting for hours until a particular *milonguero* asks them to dance because, according to tango mythology, this is the path toward the "real dancing experience." However, as one of my local informants laughingly noted, "These woman are crazy. They like suffering more than pleasure."

31. Here Nava draws upon the work of the psychoanalyst Adam Phillips (2000), who argues that sameness offers security, but at the price of unconsciously killing desire. Desire is predicated on difference and the willingness to take risks with the unfamiliar.

32. Nava calls this fascination with difference "visceral cosmopolitanism." She sets it apart from the much-criticized Western colonial gaze, which is treated as inevitably voyeuristic and exploitative, suggesting instead that transnational popular culture has made exoticization much more ambiguous, contradictory, and, in some cases, even emancipatory (Nava, 2002:38; see also Nava, 2007).

33. Anzaldi (2012a:137–39) provides a convincing analysis of how these two understandings of national identity have been mobilized differently by Peronists and anti-Peronists. The former drew upon tango as symbolic representation of the Peronist nation, using it critically against interventions from the "imperialist West." With the cultural globalization of tango, the urban middle-class tango dancers in anti-Peronist Buenos Aires are, therefore, more likely to draw upon representations of the cosmopolitan tango of the Golden Age, when tango took the world by storm.

34. While the acceptance of tango on the UNESCO list of cultural legacies (along with other religious and cultural practices like the Procession of the Holy Blood in Bruges, lace making in Croatia, and the flying men fertility dance in Mexico) has certainly been important for the touristic exploitation of tango in Buenos Aires, it implies that globalization has been problematic for tango's survival and that tango ultimately belongs to Argentina. However, tango is clearly a far cry from other world cultural legacies that, while important locally, have hardly traveled in the same way. See 'Tango takes its turn on UN cultural body's list of

intangible heritage,' *UN News Center*, 30 September 2009, and "Tango gets UN approval," *BBC News*, 30 September 2009.

35. A well-known joke I have heard from both locals and visitors is: "How does a *porteño* commit suicide? Answer: He jumps off his ego." While locals laugh when telling this, it is, nevertheless, accepted as a pretty accurate expression of the national character. See also Kaminsky (2008) for a historically informed discussion of the intricacies of pride and national identity in Argentina.

36. Cited in "Tangomarathons voor een rondreizende gemeenschap van tangodans-verslaafden," *La Cadena* no. 19, Summer 2013, p. 13.

37. See Pollock et al. (2002) for a programmatic statement.

38. See Guillén (2001) for a nice overview of these debates in the social sciences

39. See, for example, Robertson (1992), Held et al. (1999), and Giddens (2000), to name just a few of the more well-known sociologists to concern themselves with the "ins" and "outs" of globalization.

40. This debate includes the voices of Rabinow (1986), who argues that cosmopolitanism should be extended to include particular as well as universal experiences; Appadurai (1991), who criticizes the assumption that cosmopolitanism is a Western experience only; Cohen (1992), who prefers to describe cosmopolitanism as "rooted," or Bhabha (1996), who qualifies it as "vernacular"; and Robbins (1998a), who argues for thinking about "actually existing cosmopolitanism" as a fluid and changing reality of "attachment, multiple attachment, or attachment at a distance" (p. 3). What they have in common is a dissatisfaction with treating cosmopolitanism as an abstract ideal (rather than as a grounded practice), as a binary that stands in opposition to nationalism, or as something that is invariably negative.

Abu-Lughod, Lila. 1990. "Can There Be a Feminist Ethnography?" *Women and Performance* 5, no. 1:7–27.

Ahmed, Sara. 2004. *The Cultural Politics of Emotion*. Edinburgh: Edinburgh University Press.

Anderson, Leon. 2006. "Analytic Autoethnography." *Journal of Contemporary Ethnography* 35, no. 4:373–95.

Anzaldi, Franco Barrionuevo. 2012a. *Politischer Tango: Intellektuelle Kämpfe um Tanzkultur im Zeichen des Peronismus*. Bielefeld: transcript.

———. 2012b. "The new tango era in Buenos Aires: the transformation of a popular culture into a touristic 'experience economy.'" Paper presented at the II ISA Forum of Sociology, Buenos Aires, 1–4 August.

Appadurai, Arjun. 1991. "Global Ethnoscapes: Notes and Queries for a Transnational Anthropology." In *Recapturing Anthropology: Working in the Present*, ed. Richard G. Fox, 191–210. Santa Fe, N.M.: School of American Research Press.

Archetti, Eduardo P. 1999. *Masculinities: Football, Polo, and the Tango in Argentina*. Oxford: Berg.

Arrizon, Alicia. 2006. *Queering Mestizaje: Transculturation and Performance*. Ann Arbor: University of Michigan Press.

Baim, Jo. 2007. *Tango: Creation of a Cultural Icon*. Bloomington and Indianapolis: Indiana University Press.

Balderson, Daniel, and Donna Guy, eds. 1997. *Sex and Sexuality in Latin America*. New York: New York University Press.

Barzalai, Shuli. 1990. "Reading 'Snow White': The Mother's Story." *Signs* 15, no. 3:515–34.

Bauman, Zygmunt. 2000. *Liquid Modernity*. Cambridge: Polity Press.

———. 2003. *Liquid Love*. Cambridge: Polity Press.

Beck, Ulrich. 1992. *Risk Society: Towards a New Modernity*. London: Sage.

Beck, Ulrich, and Elisabeth Beck-Gernsheim. 2002. *Individualization: Institutionalized Individualism and Its Social and Political Consequences*. London: Sage.

Benzecry, Claudio E. 2011. *The Opera Fanatic: Ethnography of an Obsession*. Chicago: University of Chicago Press.

Bergero, Adriana J. 2008. *Intersecting Tango: Cultural Geographies of Buenos Aires, 1900–1930*. Pittsburgh: University of Pittsburgh Press.

Bhabha, Homi. 1996. "Unsatisfied Notes on Vernacular Cosmopolitanism." In *Text and Narration*, ed. Peter C. Pfeiffer and Laura García-Moreno, 191–207. Columbia, S.C.: Camden House.

Billig, Michael. 1987. *Arguing and Thinking: A Rhetorical Approach to Social Psychology*. Cambridge: Cambridge University Press.

———. 1991. *Ideology and Opinions*. London: Sage.

Billig, Michael, Susan Condor, Derek Edwards, Mike Gane, David Middleton, and Alan Radley. 1988. *Ideological Dilemmas: A Social Psychology of Everyday Thinking*. London: Sage.

Blackman, Lisa. 2011. "Affect, Performance and Queer Subjectivities." *Cultural Studies* 25, no. 2:183–99.

Bourdieu, Pierre. 1996. *The Rules of Art*, trans. Susan Emanuel. Stanford, Calif.: Stanford University Press.

Boutellier, Hans. 2002. *De veiligheidsutopie: Hedendaags onbehagen en verlangen rond misdaad en straf*. Den Haag: Boom.

Bowman, Paul. 2010. "Editor's Introduction." In *The Rey Chow Reader*, ed. Paul Bowman, ix–xxiii. New York: Columbia University Press.

Burawoy, Michael, Joseph A. Blum, Sheba George, Zsuzsa Gille, Teresa Gowan, Lynne Hanley, Maren Klawiter, Steven H. Lopez, Seán Ó Riain, and Millie Thayer. 2000. *Global Ethnography: Forces, Connections, and Imaginations in a Postmodern World*. Berkeley: University of California Press.

Butler, Judith. 1989. *Gender Trouble: Feminism and the Subversion of Identity*. New York: Routledge.

———. 1993. *Bodies That Matter*. New York: Routledge.

———. 1995. "Melancholy Gender/Refused Identification." In *Constructing Masculinity*, ed. Maurice Berger, Brian Wallis, and Simon Watson, 21–37. New York: Routledge.

Cara, Ana C. 2009. "Entangled Tangos: Passionate Displays, Intimate Dialogues." *Journal of American Folklore* 122:438–65.

Carozzi, María Julia. 2013. "Light women dancing tango: Gender images as allegories of heterosexual relationships." *Current Sociology* 61, no. 1:22–39.

Castro, Donald. 1998. "Carlos Gardel and the Argentine Tango: The Lyric of Social Irresponsibility and Male Inadequacy." In *The Passion of Music and Dance: Body, Gender and Sexuality*, ed. William Washabaugh, 63–78. Oxford: Berg.

Cecconi, Sofia. 2012. "Tango Queer: territorio y performance de una apropiación divergente." *Trans. Revista Transcultural de Música* (http://www.sibetrans.com/trans/articulo/54/tango-queer-territorio-y-performance-de-una-apropiaci-oacuten-divergente).

Cheah, Pheng, and Bruce Robbins, eds. 1998. *Cosmopolitics: Thinking and Feeling Beyond the Nation*. Minneapolis: University of Minnesota Press.

Chen, Patrizia. 2009. *It Takes Two*. New York: Scribner.

Clifford, James. 1998. "Mixed Feelings." In *Cosmopolitics: Thinking and Feeling Beyond the Nation*, ed. Pheng Cheah and Bruce Robbins, 362–70. Minneapolis: University of Minnesota Press.

Cohen, Mitchell. 1992. "Rooted Cosmopolitanism." *Dissent* 39, no. 4.

Collier, Simon. 1993. *¡Tango! The Dance, the Song, the Story.* London: Thames and Hudson.

Connell, John. 2006. "Medical tourism: Sea, sun, sand and . . . surgery." *Tourism Management* 27, no. 6:1093–100.

Cook, Susan C. 1998. "Passionless Dancing and Passionate Reform: Respectability, Modernism, and the Social Dancing of Irene and Vernon Castle." In *The Passion of Music and Dance: Body, Gender and Sexuality*, ed. William Washabaugh, 133–50. Oxford: Berg.

Cozarkinsky, Edgardo. 2007. *Milongas.* Buenos Aires: Edhasa.

Creef, Elena Tajima. 2000. "Discovering My Mother as the Other in the *Saturday Evening Post*." *Qualitative Inquiry* 6, no. 4:443–55.

Cressey, Paul G. 1932. *The Taxi-Dance Hall.* New York: Greenwood Press.

Crossley, Nick. 1995. "Merleau-Ponty, the Elusive Body and Carnal Sociology." *Body & Society* 1, no. 1:43–63.

Cusumano, Camille. 2008. *Tango: An Argentine Love Story.* Berkeley, Calif.: Seal Press.

Darke, Shane. 2011. *The Life of the Heroin User: Typical Beginning, Trajectories and Outcomes.* New York: Cambridge University Press.

Delaney, Jean H. 2002. "Imagining 'El Ser Argentino': Cultural Nationalism and Romantic Concepts of Nationhood in Early Twentieth-Century Argentina." *Journal of Latin American Studies* 34, no. 3:625–58.

De Lauretis, Theresa. 1991. "Queer Theory: Lesbian and Gay Sexualities, An Introduction." *differences* 3, no. 2:iii–xviii.

Deleuze, Gilles, and Félix Guattari. 1972/2004. *Anti-Œdipus*, trans. Robert Hurley, Mark Seem, and Helen R. Lane. London: Continuum.

Desmond, Jane C. 1997. "Embodying Difference: Issues in Dance and Cultural Studies." In *Everynight Life: Culture and Dance in Latin/o America*, ed. Celeste Fraser Delgado and José Esteban Muñoz, 33–64. Durham, N.C.: Duke University Press.

De Vries, Marleen. 2009. *De Wetten van de Tango.* Amsterdam: Prometheus.

Dreher, Jochen, and Silvana K. Figueroa-Deher. 2009. "*Soñando todos el mismo sueño.* Zur rituellen Überschreitung kultureller Grenzen im Tango." In *Tango in Translation: Tanz zwischen Medien, Kulturen, Kunst und Politik*, ed. Gabriele Klein, 39–56. Bielefeld: transcript.

Elias, Norbert. 2000 [1939]. *The Civilizing Process*, rev. ed. Oxford: Blackwell.

Eliasoph, Nina. 2005. "Theorizing from the Neck Down: Why Social Research Must Understand Bodies Acting in Real Space and Time (and Why It's So Hard to Spell Out What We Learn from This)." *Qualitative Sociology* 28, no. 2:159–69.

Ericksen, Julia A. 2011. *Dance with Me: Ballroom Dancing and the Promise of Instant Intimacy.* New York: New York University Press.

Ferrer, Horacio, and Wouter Brave. 1989. *El Arte del Tango: Muziek, Dans, Lyriek.* Amsterdam: Tango Palace Dansstudio.

Fischer, Lucy. 2004. "'Dancing through the Minefield': Passion, Pedagogy, Politics, and Production in *The Tango Lesson*." *Cinema Journal* 43, no. 3:42–58.

Foster, Susan Leigh. 1998. "Choreographies of Gender." *Signs* 24, no. 1:1–34.

Garfinkel, Harold. 1967. *Studies in Ethnomethodology.* Englewood Cliffs, N.J.: Prentice-Hall.

Geertz, Clifford. 1973. *The Interpretation of Cultures: Selected Essays.* New York: Basic Books.

Giddens, Anthony. 1991. *Modernity and Self-Identity.* Cambridge: Polity Press.

———. 1992. *The Transformation of Intimacy.* Cambridge: Polity Press.

———. 2000. *Runaway World: How Globalization Is Reshaping Our Lives.* New York: Routledge.

Gill, Rosalind. 2007. *Gender and the Media.* Cambridge: Polity Press.

Glaser, Barney C., and Anselm Strauss. 1967. *The Discovery of Grounded Theory.* Chicago: Aldine.

Goldstein-Gidoni, Ofra, and Michal Daliot-Bul. 2002. "'Shall We *Dansu*?': Dancing with the 'West' in Contemporary Japan." *Japan Forum* 14, no. 1:63–75.

Groeneboer, Joost. 2003. "Van getemde passie tot verslindende levensstijl." In *Cultuur en migratie in Nederland: Kunsten in beweging 1900–1980*, ed. Maaike Meijer and Rosemarie Buikema, 39–56. The Hague: Sdu Uitgevers.

Guano, Emanuela. 2004. "She Looks at Him with the Eyes of a Camera: Female Visual Pleasures and the Polemic with Fetishism in Sally Potter's *Tango Lesson*." *Third Text* 18, no. 5:461–74.

Guillén, Mauro F. 2001. "Is Globalization Civilizing, Destructive or Feeble? A Critique of Five Key Debates in the Social Science Literature." *Annual Review of Sociology* 27:235–60.

Guy, Donna J. 1990. *Sex and Danger in Buenos Aires.* Lincoln: University of Nebraska Press.

Hearn, Jeff. 1999. "A Crisis in Masculinity, or New Agendas for Me." In *New Agendas for Women*, ed. Sylvia Walby, 148–68. London: Macmillan.

Held, David, Anthony McGrew, David Goldblatt, and Jonathan Perraton. 1999. *Global Transformations.* Stanford, Calif.: Stanford University Press.

Hennessy, Rosemary. 1993. "Queer Theory: A Review of the *differences* Special Issue and Wittig's *The Straight Mind*." *Signs* 18, no. 4:964–73.

Hess, Remi. 2004. *El vals: Un romanticismo revolucionario.* Buenos Aires: Paidós Diagonales.

Hille, Michaela, and Ute Walter. 2006. "Queer tango, de 'nuevos milongueros.'" *Cadena* no. 119:27–28.

Hollway, Wendy, and Tony Jefferson. 2000. *Doing Qualitative Research Differently: Free Association, Narrative, and the Interview Method.* London: Sage.

Hopkins, Lori. 2002. "The Transatlantic Tango: Sally Potter's *The Tango Lesson*." *Studies in Latin American Popular Culture* 21:119–30.

Hopkins, Patrick D. 1994. "Rethinking Sadomasochism: Feminism, Interpretation, and Simulation." *Hypatia* 9, no. 1:116–41.

Horowitz, Katie R. 2013. "The Trouble with 'Queerness': Drag and the Making of Two Cultures." *Signs* 38, no. 2:303–26.

Illousz, Eva. 1997. *Consuming the Romantic Utopia: Love and the Cultural Contradictions of Capitalism.* Berkeley: University of California Press.

———. 1998. "The Lost Innocence of Love: Romance as a Postmodern Condition." *Theory, Culture & Society* 15, no. 3–4:161–86.

———. 2012. *Why Love Hurts: A Sociological Explanation.* Cambridge: Polity Press.

Jakubs, Deborah L. 1984. "From Bawdyhouse to Cabaret: The Evolution of the Tango as an Expression of Argentine Popular Culture." *Journal of Popular Culture* 18, no. 1:133–45.

Kaminsky, Amy K. 2008. *Argentina: Stories for a Nation.* Minneapolis: University of Minnesota Press.

Kešić, Josip. 2012. "More Pure than Pure: Registers of Authenticity in Dutch Flamenco." Unpublished MA thesis, Social Sciences, University of Amsterdam, Amsterdam, The Netherlands, July 2012.

Kessler, Susanne J., and Wendy McKenna. 1978/1985. *Gender: An Ethnomethodological Approach.* Chicago: University of Chicago Press.

Klein, Gabriele. 2009. "Bodies in Translation: Tango als kulturelle Übersetzung." In *Tango in Translation: Tanz zwischen Medien, Kulturen, Kunst und Politik,* ed. Gabriele Klein, 15–38. Bielefeld: transcript.

Klein, Gabriele, and Melanie Haller. 2008. "*Café Buenos Aires* und *Galeria del Latino:* Zur Translokalität und Hybridität städtischer Tanzkulturen." In *Bewegungsraum und Stadtkultur: Sozial- und kulturwissenschaftliche Perspektiven,* ed. Jürgen Funke-Wieneke and Gabriele Klein, 51–74. Bielefeld: transcript.

———. 2009. "Körpererfahrung und Naturglaube: Subjektivierungsstrategien in der Tangokultur." In *Tango in Translation: Tanz zwischen Medien, Kulturen, Kunst und Politik,* ed. Gabriele Klein, 123–36. Bielefeld: transcript.

Kowalksa, Marta. 2010. "Between local and global: Biographical adjustment scenarios and narrative ethnography." Paper presented at XVII Congress of International Sociological Association Congress, Goteborg, Sweden, 11–17 July.

Kraicer, Shelly. 1997. "Happy Together." *Chinese Cinema Page,* 17 October 1997, http://www.chinesecinemas.org/happy.html.

Liska, Maria Mercedes. 2009. "El cuerpo en la música: La propuesta del tango *queer* y su vinculación con el tango electrónico." *Boletin Onteaiken,* no. 8:45–52.

Littig, Beate. 2013. "On High Heels: A Praxiography of Doing Argentine Tango." *The European Journal of Women's Studies* 20, no. 4:455–67.

Lund, Joshua. 2001. "Barbarian Theorizing and the Limits of Latin American Exceptionalism." *Cultural Critique* 47:54–90.

Manning, Erin. 2007. *Politics of Touch: Sense, Movement, Sovereignty.* Minneapolis: University of Minnesota Press.

Marcus, George E. 1995. "Ethnography in/of the World System: The Emergence of Multi-Sited Ethnography." *Annual Review of Anthropology* 24:95–117.

Martin, Biddy. 1994. "Sexualities without Genders and Other Queer Utopias." *diacritics* 24, no. 2–3:104–21.

McClintock, Anne, Aamir Mufti, and Ella Shohat, eds. 1997. *Dangerous Liaisons*. Minneapolis: University of Minnesota Press.

McPherson, Alan. 2006. *Anti-Americanism in Latin America and the Caribbean*. Oxford, N.Y.: Berghahn Books.

Meisch, Lynn A. 1995. "Gringas and Otavaleños: Changing Tourist Relations." *Annals of Tourism Research* 22, no. 2:441–62.

Melul, Sara. 2007. *El chamuyo en las milongas*. Buenos Aires: Ediciones El Chamuyo.

Modleski, Tania. 1982. *Loving with a Vengeance: Mass-produced Fantasies for Women*. New York: Routledge.

Mora, Richard. 2012. "'Do It for All Your Pubic Hairs!' Latino Boys, Masculinity, and Puberty." *Gender & Society* 26, no. 3:433–60.

Naipaul, V. S. 1980/1974. *The Return of Eva Perón and the Killings in Trinidad*. Middlesex: Penguin.

Nava, Mica. 2002. "Cosmopolitan Modernity: Everyday Imaginaries and the Register of Difference." *Theory, Culture & Society* 19, no. 1–2:81–99.

———. 2007. *Visceral Cosmopolitanism: Gender, Culture and the Normalisation of Difference*. Oxford: Berg.

Niemel, Babette. 1997. *Een hartstikke vrij mens: Interviews met negen vluchtelingen in Nederland*. Utrecht: VON.

Nouzeilles, Gabriela, and Graciela Montalda, eds. 2002. *The Argentina Reader: History, Culture, Politics*. Durham, N.C.: Duke University Press.

Olszewski, Brandon. 2008. "*El Cuerpo del Baile*: The Kinetic and Social Fundaments of Tango." *Body & Society* 14, no. 2:63–81.

Osumare, Halifu. 2002. "Global Breakdancing and the Intercultural Body." *Dance Research Journal* 34, no. 2:30–45.

Palmer, Marina. 2006. *Kiss & Tango: Diary of a Dancehall Seductress*. New York: HarperCollins.

Pelinski, Ramón Aldolfo. 2000. *El tango nómade: ensayos sobre la diáspora del tango*. Buenos Aires: Corregidor.

Pellarolo, Sirena. 2008. "Queering Tango: Glitches in the Hetero-National Matrix of a Liminal Cultural Production." *Theater Journal* 60:409–31.

Petridou, Elia. 2009. "Experiencing Tango as It Goes Global: Passion, Ritual and Play." In *Tango in Translation: Tanz zwischen Medien, Kulturen, Kunst und Politik*, ed. Gabriele Klein, 57–74. Bielefeld: transcript.

Philippe, Frederick L., Robert J. Vallerand, and Geneviève L. Lavigne. 2009. "Passion Does Make a Difference in People's Lives: A Look at Well-Being in Passionate and Non-Passionate Individuals." *Applied Psychology: Health and Well-Being* 1, no. 1:3–22.

Phillips, Adam. 2000. *Promises, Promises*. London: Faber and Faber.

Podalsky, Laura. 2002. "'Tango, Like Scotch, Is Best Taken Straight': Cosmopolitan Tastes and Bodies Out of Place." *Studies in Latin American Popular Culture* 21:131–54.

Pollock, Sheldon, Homi K. Bhabha, Carol A. Breckenridge, and Dipesh Chakrabarty. 2002. "Cosmopolitanisms." In *Cosmopolitanism*, ed. Carol A. Breckenridge, Sheldon Pollock, Homi K. Bhabha, and Dipesh Chakrabarty, 1–14. Durham, N.C.: Duke University Press.

Potter, Sally. 1997. *The Tango Lesson*. London: Faber and Faber.

Pritchard, Annette, Nigel Morgen, Irena Ateljevic, and Candice Harris, eds. 2007. *Tourism and Gender: Embodiment, Sensuality and Experience*. Wallingford and Cambridge: CABI International.

Rabinow, Paul. 1998. "Representations Are Social Facts: Modernity and Post-Modernity in Anthropology." In *Writing Culture: The Poetics and Politics of Ethnography*, ed. James Clifford and George Marcus, 234–61. Berkeley: University of California Press.

Radway, Janice. 1984. *Reading the Romance: Women, Patriarchy, and Popular Literature*. New York: Verso.

Riemann, Gerhard, and Fritz Schütze. 1991. "'Trajectory' as a Basic Theoretical Concept for Analyzing Suffering and Disorderly Social Processes." In *Social Organization and Social Process: Essays in Honor of Anselm Strauss*, ed. David R. Maines, 333–57. New York: Aldine de Gruyter.

Robben, A.C.G.M. 2005. *Political Violence and Trauma in Argentina*. Philadelphia: University of Pennsylvania Press.

Robbins, Bruce. 1998a. "Actually Existing Cosmopolitanism." In *Cosmopolitics: Thinking and Feeling Beyond the Nation*, ed. Pheng Cheah and Bruce Robbins, 1–19. Minneapolis: University of Minnesota Press.

———. 1998b. "Comparative Cosmopolitanisms." In *Cosmopolitics: Thinking and Feeling Beyond the Nation*, ed. Pheng Cheah and Bruce Robbins, 246–64. Minneapolis: University of Minnesota Press.

Robertson, Roland. 1992. *Globalization: Social Theory and Global Culture*. London: Sage.

Sabini, John, and Maury Silver. 1996. "On the possible non-existence of emotions: the passions." *Journal for the Theory of Social Behavior* 26:375–98.

Saikin, Magali. 2004. *Tango y Género*. Stuttgart: Abrazos Books.

Salessi, Jorge. 1997. "Medics, Crooks, and Tango Queens: The National Appropriation of a Gay Tango." In *Everynight Life: Culture and Dance in Latin/o America*, ed. Celeste Fraser Delgado and José Esteban Muñoz, 141–74. Durham, N.C.: Duke University Press.

———. 2000. *Médicos, maleantes y maricas: Higiene, criminología y homosexualidad en la construcción de la nación argentina (Buenos Aires 1871–1914)*. Rosario: Beatriz Viterbo Editora.

Saraza, Dyv. 2008. *Aleph Bravo Tango*. Venice, Calif.: Pull Don't Press.

Savigliano, Marta E. 1992. "Tango in Japan and the world economy of passion." In *Re-Made in Japan: Everyday Life and Consumer Taste in a Changing Society*, ed. Joseph J. Tobin, 235–54. New Haven, Conn.: Yale University Press.

———. 1995. *Tango and the Political Economy of Passion*. Boulder, Colo.: Westview Press.

———. 1998. "From Wallflowers to Femmes Fatales: Tango and the Performance of Passionate Femininity." In *The Passion of Music and Dance: Body, Gender and Sexuality*, ed. William Washabaugh, 103–10. Oxford: Berg.

———. 2003. *Angora Matta: Fatal Acts of North–South Translation*. Middletown, Conn.: Wesleyan University Press.

———. 2010. "Notes on Tango (as) Queer (Commodity)." *Anthropological Notebooks* 16, no. 3:135–43.

Sedgwick, Eve Kosofsky. 1990. *Epistemology of the Closet*. Berkeley: University of California Press.

Sennett, Richard, and Jonathan Cobb. 1972/1977. *The Hidden Injuries of Class*. Cambridge: Cambridge University Press.

Simmel, Georg. 1958. "The Adventure." In *Simmel on Culture*, ed. David Frisby and Mike Featherstone, 221–32. London: Sage.

Sivori, Horacio Federico. 2005. *Locas, chongos y gays: sociabilidad homosexual masculine durante la 1990*. Buenos Aires: Antropofagia.

Soriano, Osvaldo. 1987. *Rebeldes, soñadores y fugitivos*. Buenos Aires: De Editorial.

Stacey, Judith. 1988. "Can There Be a Feminist Ethnography?" *Women's Studies International Forum* 11, no. 1:21–27.

Stear, Nils-Hennes. 2009. "Sadomasochism as *Make-Believe*." *Hypatia* 24, no. 2:21–38.

Stoler, Ann Laura. 2002. *Carnal Knowledge and Imperial Power: Race and the Intimate in Colonial Rule*. Berkeley: University of California Press.

Strathern, Marilyn. 1987. "The Limits of Auto-anthropology." In *Anthropology at Home*, ed. Anthony Jackson, 16–37. London: Tavistock Publications.

Strauss, Anselm, and Barney Glaser. 1970. *Anguish: The Case Study of a Dying Trajectory*. Mill Valley, Calif.: Sociology Press.

Subsecretaría de Industrías Culturales. 2007. *El Tango en la Economía de la Ciudad de Buenos Aires*. Santiago, Chile: Eure.

Taylor, Julie. 1976. "Tango: Theme of Class and Nation." *Ethnomusicology* 20, no. 2:273–92.

———. 1987. "Tango." *Cultural Anthropology* 2, no. 4:481–93.

———. 1998. *Paper Tangos*. Durham, N.C.: Duke University Press.

Thompson, Robert Farris. 2005. *Tango: The Art History of Love*. New York: Vintage Books.

Tobin, Jeffrey. 1998. "Tango and the Scandal of Homosocial Desire." In *The Passion of Music and Dance: Body, Gender and Sexuality*, ed. William Washabaugh, 79–102. Oxford: Berg.

———. 2009. "Models of Machismo: The Troublesome Masculinity of Argentine Male Tango Dancers." In *Tango in Translation: Tanz zwischen Medien, Kulturen, Kunst und Politik*, ed. Gabriele Klein, 139–69. Bielefeld: transcript.

Torgovnick, Marianna. 1990. *Gone Primitive*. Chicago: University of Chicago Press.

Törnqvist, Maria. 2011. "Love Impossible: Troubling Tales of Eroticized Difference in Buenos Aires." In *Sexuality, Gender and Power: Intersectional and Transnational*

Perspectives, ed. Anna G. Jónasdóttir, Valerie Bryson, and Kathleen B. Jones, 92–105. New York: Routledge.

———. 2012. "Troubling Romance Tourism: Sex, Gender and Class Inside the Argentinean Tango Clubs." *Feminist Review* 102:21–40.

———. 2013. *Tourism and the Globalization of Emotions: The Intimate Economy of Tango*. New York: Routledge.

Törnqvist, Maria, and Kate Hardy. 2010. "Taxi Dancers: Tango Labour and Commercialized Intimacy in Buenos Aires." In *New Sociologies of Sex Work*, ed. Kate Hardy, Sarah Kingston, and Teela Sanders, 137–48. Farnham: Ashgate.

Turner, Victor. 1987/1964. "Betwixt and Between: The Liminal Period in *Rites de Passage*." In *Betwixt and Between: Patterns of Masculine and Feminine Initiation*, ed. Louise Carus Madhi, Steven Foster, and Meredith Little, 3–19. Peru, Ill.: Open Court Publishing Company.

Ulla, Noemí. 1982. *Tango, rebelión y nostalgia*. Buenos Aires: Centro Editor de América Latina.

Unger, Roberto Mangabeira. 1984. *Passion: An Essay on Personality*. New York: Free Press.

Urquía, Norman. 2005. "The Re-Branding of Salsa in London's Dance Clubs: How an Ethnicized Form of Cultural Capital Was Institutionalised." *Leisure Studies* 24, no. 4:385–97.

Urry, John. 2005. *The Tourist Gaze*. London: Sage.

Viladrich, Anahí. 2006. "Neither Virgins nor Whores: Tango Lyrics and Gender Representations in the Tango World." *The Journal of Popular Culture* 39, no. 2:272–93.

———. 2013. *More Than Two to Tango: Argentine Tango Immigrants in New York City*. Tuscon: University of Arizona Press.

Villa, Paula-Irene. 2001. *Sexy Bodies: Eine soziologische Reise durch den Geschlechtskörper*. Opladen: Leske & Budrich.

———. 2009. "'Das fühlt so anders an . . .' Zum produktiven 'Scheitern' des Transfers zwischen ästhetischen Diskursen und tänzerischen Praxen im Tango." In *Tango in Translation: Tanz zwischen Medien, Kulturen, Kunst und Politik*, ed. Gabriele Klein, 105–22. Bielefeld: transcript.

———. 2010. "Bewegte Diskurse, die bewegen: Warum der Tango die (Geschlechter-) Verhältnisse zum Tanzen bringen kann." In *Körper Wissen Geschlecht*, ed. Angelika Wetterer, 141–64. Sulzbach/Taunus:Ulrike Helmer Verlag.

Visweswaran, Kamala. 1994. *Fictions of Feminist Ethnography*. Minneapolis: University of Minnesota Press.

Wacquant, Loïc. 2004. *Body & Soul: Notebooks of an Apprentice Boxer*. Oxford: Oxford University Press.

———. 2005. "Carnal Connections: On Embodiment, Apprenticeship, and Membership." *Qualitative Sociology* 28, no. 4:445–74.

Wade, Lisa. 2011. "The emancipator promise of the habitus: Lindy hop, the body, and social change." *Ethnography* 12, no. 2:224–46.

Walters, Suzanna Danuta. 1996. "From Here to Queer: Radical Feminism, Postmodernism, and the Lesbian Menace (Or, Why Can't a Woman Be More Like a Fag?)." *Signs* 21, no. 4:830–69.

Ward, Andrew. 1997. "Dancing around Meaning (and the Meaning around Dance)." In *Dance in the City*, ed. Helen Thomas, 3–20. Houndmills: Macmillan.

Warner, Michael, ed. 1993. *Fear of a Queer Planet: Queer Politics and Social Theory.* Minneapolis: University of Minnesota Press.

Washabaugh, William. 1998. "Introduction: Music, Dance, and the Politics of Passion." In *The Passion of Music and Dance*, ed. William Washabaugh, 1–26. Oxford: Berg.

West, Candace, and Don H. Zimmerman. 1987. "Doing Gender." *Gender & Society* 1:125–51.

Winter, Brian. 2007. *Long After Midnight at the Niño Bien.* New York: Public Affairs.

Young, Richard A. 1996. "Films, Tangos and Cultural Practices." *Cinémas: Journal of Film Studies* 7, no. 1–2:187–203.

Young, Robert. 1990. *White Mythologies: Writing History and the West.* London: Routledge.

———. 1995. *Colonial Desire: Hybridity in Theory, Culture and Race.* London: Routledge.

Zhao, Ning. 2008. "Analyzing the Meaning in Interaction in Politeness Strategies in *Scent of a Woman*." *The Journal of International Social Research* 1, no. 4:629–47.

ABOUT THE AUTHOR

Kathy Davis is Senior Research Fellow in the Sociology Department of the VU University in Amsterdam in the Netherlands. She is the author of numerous books and articles, including *Reshaping the Female Body* (1995), *Dubious Equalities and Embodied Differences* (2003), and *The Making of 'Our Bodies, Ourselves': How Feminism Travels across Borders* (2007).